# Military Alliances in the Twenty-First Century

*Pour Maximilien, la source de ma joie*

# Military Alliances in the Twenty-First Century

Alexander Lanoszka

polity

The right of Alexander Lanoszka to be identified as Author of this Work has been asserted in accordance with the UK Copyright, Designs and Patents Act 1988.

First published in 2022 by Polity Press

Polity Press
65 Bridge Street
Cambridge CB2 1UR, UK

Polity Press
101 Station Landing
Suite 300
Medford, MA 02155, USA

ISBN-13: 978-1-5095-4556-8
ISBN-13: 978-1-5095-4557-5 (pb)

A catalogue record for this book is available from the British Library.

Library of Congress Control Number: 2021939862

Typeset in 10.5 on 12pt Sabon
by Fakenham Prepress Solutions, Fakenham, Norfolk NR21 8NL
Printed and bound in Great Britain by CPI Group (UK) Ltd, Croydon

The publisher has used its best endeavours to ensure that the URLs for external websites referred to in this book are correct and active at the time of going to press. However, the publisher has no responsibility for the websites and can make no guarantee that a site will remain live or that the content is or will remain appropriate.

Every effort has been made to trace all copyright holders, but if any have been overlooked the publisher will be pleased to include any necessary credits in any subsequent reprint or edition.

For further information on Polity, visit our website:
politybooks.com

# Contents

# Tables and Figure

# Acknowledgments

In writing this book, I am most certainly standing on the shoulders of giants. I have never met Paul Schroeder, Glenn Snyder, or Patricia Weitsman, and, unfortunately, I will never be able to do so. However, their influence is everywhere in this book even if I am not referencing them directly. Their foundational scholarship has, collectively, been a rich source of inspiration and insight for me. Although this book synthesizes diverse areas of inquiry as regards alliance politics, it ultimately is but a small token of my own appreciation for their pioneering work.

I owe a big debt of gratitude to Louise Knight for proposing the idea for this book in the first place and for pushing me to think hard about which arguments I would like to make. If it were not for her, then this book would surely not exist. I have had much help along the way while writing it. Inès Boxman shepherded the book through the review and publication process. Jordan Cohen offered excellent commentaries on drafts of each chapter. Bradley Sylvestre provided terrific research assistance. Because I wrote this book during the SARS-CoV-2 pandemic, I organized a virtual workshop on its first complete draft. Jordan Cohen, Katherine Elgin, Matthew Fay, and Michael Hunzeker gave incisive and excellent commentary that forced me to clarify and strengthen my arguments. I must also thank Hugo Meijer and Luis Simón for their comments on different parts of the manuscript. Very helpfully, two anonymous readers noted key weaknesses and made useful suggestions for remedying them. Over the years, too, I have absorbed much wisdom and knowledge from various teachers, mentors, friends, and colleagues at Princeton University, the Massachusetts Institute of Technology, Dartmouth College, City, University of London, and the University of Waterloo. They have opened up a diverse set of competing views and ideas relevant to the issues explored in this book. With all that said, I bear full responsibility for any infelicities and errors that sneaked into the finished product.

Lastly, I would like to thank my wife, Emmanuelle Richez, for her extensive support and enthusiasm for the project, even if it meant enduring some of my long discourses over meals (what she would call "rants"). The writing of this book also overlapped with the arrival, and the first year in this crazy world, of our son Maximilien. This book is dedicated to him. His coming into our lives, the pandemic, and the writing of the book almost perfectly coincided in their timing. It was strange to be effectively in lockdown for such a long stretch of time, but he made the experience so much better for us.

Windsor, Ontario

# Introduction

It seems hard to pin down exactly when it was that alliance politics became once again the basis of so many news headlines, as is now the case in the third decade of the twenty-first century. Intuitively, some readers might point to 2016, when British voters chose to withdraw their country from the European Union (EU) and voters in the United States elected Donald J. Trump to be their next president. These twin events signaled a deep disenchantment with multilateral cooperation in two countries that have historically underpinned what many call the liberal rules-based international order. Trump's broadsides against longstanding treaty partners, whether as regards their economic policies or their military spending, alarmed governments around the world that are friendly to the United States. Still, one can just as well point to the twelve months spanning March 14, 2013 and March 18, 2014. The first date is when Xi Jinping became President of the People's Republic of China for life, prompting fresh concerns among US partners in East Asia over China's foreign policy direction under his authoritarian leadership. The second date marks the signing of the Treaty on Accession of the Republic of Crimea to Russia, thus formalizing the first territorial annexation in Europe since 1945. Unsurprisingly, many of Russia's Western neighbors reacted with alarm. They feared that they themselves would soon become objects of military aggression and so looked to the United States for protection. At least with respect to those alliances led by the United States, the events bookmarking those twelve months helped produce the insecurity that the fateful votes cast in 2016 simply aggravated.

Few may have realized it at the time, but 2008 was arguably the watershed year for how the United States managed its military alliances around the world. The first major event to be considered here took place in the Romanian capital of Bucharest, where leaders of all twenty-six North Atlantic Treaty Organization (NATO) member states gathered to discuss the future of the alliance. One key item on the agenda was whether to extend Membership Action Plans (MAPs) to Georgia and Ukraine, a move that, if approved, would set those countries on the path toward full membership. Under George W. Bush's leadership, the United States advocated strongly for their inclusion. Getting endorsement from Washington was a big deal for Georgia and Ukraine. After all, thanks largely to the United States, other East Central European countries like Poland and Latvia had been able to become NATO members in the previous decade. Yet, despite Washington's record of consistently getting what it wanted with NATO enlargement, this time was different. At the summit in Bucharest, France and Germany pushed back against the US initiative, in part because they did not wish to antagonize Russia, which was opposed to those countries' prospective membership in NATO. As NATO makes decisions based on full consensus, Georgia and Ukraine ended up being denied those MAPs that they had coveted so much. Several months later, in August, Georgia fought a brief war with Russia. The pro-Western coalition government ruling Ukraine at the time collapsed one month later.

The second major event in 2008 was the financial crash. To be sure, the declared bankruptcy of major investment bank Lehman Brothers in mid-September that year was the culminating point of a smoldering crisis that had already been roiling the subprime mortgage market since early 2007. Nevertheless, the bankruptcy of that particular bank precipitated major stock market losses and the failure of several other important financial institutions located in the United States. The US unemployment rate increased to its highest level in decades, while the output of goods and services plummeted dramatically. The crisis was wide-reaching, impacting European and Asian markets as well and becoming the most serious crash since the Great Depression. Joseph Nye (2011) even opined that the financial crisis plaguing the United States gave China an opportunity to assert its foreign policy interests more actively, now that the hobbled super-power appeared to be on the decline. With so much wealth wiped out, and so much debt incurred to reinvigorate the US economy, many questioned whether Washington could afford to maintain its international commitments. In the aftermath of this crisis, some security analysts advocated that the United States must retrench by withdrawing military support to allies in order to focus on domestic problems. Those allies, they argued, were strong enough to provide for their own defense (see MacDonald and Parent 2018; Posen 2014).

The third event was the election of Democratic nominee Barack Obama to the US presidency in November 2008. As candidate, he pledged to repair the United States' standing in the world, arguing that Bush had squandered much of the international goodwill his administration received following the September 11, 2001 attacks by waging an unpopular war in Iraq. Obama spoke in favor of re-engaging with countries like Russia, while calling for US military alliances and partnerships to be rebuilt so that they could deal with threats ranging from nuclear proliferation to terrorism. He also promised to reinvigorate the NATO-led campaign in Afghanistan. But despite meeting with European leaders and giving a major foreign policy address to a large crowd in Berlin over the course of his campaign, Obama's presidential agenda was to be primarily domestic. He advocated expanding healthcare coverage and, once the financial crisis was in full swing, focused his rhetoric on stabilizing markets, job creation, and tax reforms. Although much optimism greeted his electoral victory, the economic damage wrought by the financial crisis suggested that the United States would turn inward during his presidency. With global capitalism in severe distress, Obama voiced skepticism toward global free trade, pledging to renegotiate trade treaties while embracing protectionist measures that called on companies to "Buy American."

All the basic themes in alliance politics that this book explores figured in the events of that one year, 2008. Those events have reverberations that carry through to the present day. The United States sought to *form* new official alliance partnerships by way of enlarging NATO further, only to be rejected by some of its longstanding partners out of fear of being *entrapped* in disputes with Russia they did not wish to have. Amid the fallout of a terrible economic crisis, allies began to worry that the United States might loosen its commitments to them, thereby stoking fears of *abandonment*. Some Obama administration officials – most notably, Secretary of Defense Robert Gates – would indeed later chastise US allies for free-riding and call for more equitable *burden-sharing*. Part of the frustration that Gates articulated emerged from the US experience in Afghanistan, where the NATO-led mission saw not only greater US troop numbers, but European partners placing caveats that inhibited the military effectiveness of their own national forces. The wars in both Iraq and Afghanistan were examples of coalition *warfare* that saw the participation of some US allies and partners, but not others. Still, the geopolitical shifts produced by the 2008 financial crisis suggested that some alliances could eventually come to an end, if the United States was no longer able or willing to support them. Of course, no alliance was ever truly at risk of being revoked during the Obama administration, but how sustainable such commitments could be and whether some should be *terminated* became increasingly a matter of debate.

What these observations also suggest is that these issues were very much alive before Trump became president in 2016 or even 2013–14 when fears of Chinese assertiveness and Russian aggression gained salience. During Trump's first presidential election campaign, he labeled NATO as "obsolete" and suggested that the United States would not come to the aid of those allies that had not fulfilled their defense spending commitments. He intimated that he might acquiesce to efforts by South Korea and Japan to acquire their own nuclear weapons, thereby contradicting decades-old US nuclear nonproliferation policy toward treaty allies. As president, his approach to alliance management softened little. He pointedly refused to endorse Article V of the Washington Treaty (also known as the North Atlantic Treaty) – which provides that an attack on one NATO member is an attack against all – when given the opportunity to do so. He launched trade wars with European allies and Japan, and threatened major economic sanctions while renegotiating free trade agreements with Canada and South Korea – all of which were longstanding US allies. He repeatedly lambasted NATO members for not paying their fair share. His administration had demanded extortionary amounts of money from South Korea in talks over the status and financing of US bases in that country. His desire to strike deals with Russia and North Korea unsettled allies located on their frontiers, fueling concern that a grand bargain would be made at their expense.

It would thus be tempting to conclude that, given Trump's presidency, the end of US military alliances had seemed imminent. Perhaps that really would have been the case had he won re-election in 2020. We will never know. And yet the record of the previous decade suggests an alternative assessment: many of the seemingly intractable problems that abound in alliance management today have appeared before. It is safe to say that they will persist into the future, even if Trumpism is – possibly – in the rearview mirror. As this book will show, sometimes these problems were far more severe in the past, as in the Cold War or in previous historical epochs like the interwar period in Europe. Friction is inevitable in alliance politics, especially when adversaries pose new threats and challenges. Just as in the past decision-makers were able to confront those challenges with some success, so they look poised to do so again. Contrary to appearances, the end of most US alliance commitments is not upon us. For all the vitriolic rhetoric about free-riding allies, the United States in fact stepped up its military commitments to Europe during Trump's presidency, with an increased presence in both Germany and Poland. Trump did not withdraw major numbers of military forces from any treaty ally, despite a late effort to rearrange US force posture in Europe (Lanoszka and Simón 2021). Under his administration, the United States acquired new treaty allies when Montenegro and North Macedonia joined NATO in 2017 and 2020, respectively.

That said, as the events in 2008 demonstrated, changes are afoot in world politics that portend important adjustments in US security guarantees in Europe and East Asia, on the one hand, and, on the other, military partnerships that involve China, Russia, or both. These changes are not reducible to the personal character or rhetoric of any one leader, including someone like Trump, Putin, or even Xi. Rather, these changes reflect a transforming international environment characterized by the rise of China, the roguishness of Russia, and the maturation and proliferation of once cutting-edge technologies like precision strike as well as the malicious use of cyber operations and disinformation campaigns. In fact, these changes had already begun years before Trump declared his candidacy for the US presidency, and will continue to unfold into the future. After all, alliance politics is usually marked by divergent geopolitical interests, worries about the consequences of commitment-making, and, in today's technological context, burden-sharing controversies. These issues will shape alliance politics going forward even if Trump's successor, Joseph Biden, has consistently spoken favorably of US military alliances. The SARS-CoV-2 pandemic could accelerate these trends as countries grapple with its economic and political fallout.

## The Arguments of this Book

Alliance politics will remain a persistent feature of international affairs, but, as this book argues, that is because military alliances operate in ways that are often surprising, counterintuitive, and difficult to understand. To see why, consider the following standard claims that scholars and practitioners often make regarding how alliances function, or should function, from when these arrangements are first negotiated to when they meet their eventual demise. In outlining, in the discussion below, what those pieces of conventional wisdom are and why they are problematic, I offer a preview of the argument that each chapter in this book advances.

## Conventional wisdom #1: States form alliances to balance power and/or to gain influence over other states

Many observers agree that states form military alliances in order to aggregate power in the face of a security challenge or to gain influence over another. Sometimes both motives are operative. There is much to be said for this canonical understanding of alliance formation: it is intuitive and easy to grasp.

Still, as shown in Chapter 1, although balancing power and influence-seeking can drive particular instances of alliance formation, these explanations are at best insufficient and may not even identify conditions necessary for states to agree to a military alliance. They indeed tend to overpredict how many alliances actually form. Most importantly, it is unclear why having a written alliance by way of a treaty is at all necessary for balancing power against adversaries or for projecting influence over would-be allies.

Writing down an alliance commitment accomplishes two strategic but seemingly contradictory tasks. One is that it allows signatories to communicate to international and domestic audiences that they have a serious stake in addressing a particular security challenge. Another is that it permits the signatories to leave purposely vague the conditions under which a treaty obligation would become operational, keeping both allies and adversaries in the dark as to what exactly would trigger a major defensive response. This vagueness is important in part because treaty allies have similar but not identical interests. Differences, just as much as commonalities, drive the need for written commitments. Treaties enable states to thread the needle more effectively between certifying a commitment for augmenting deterrence and allowing for enough ambiguity to keep allies and adversaries alike off balance. This in turn can lead the way for even more military cooperation because states become more comfortable about investing in their security relationship. Nevertheless, some alignments between states never rise to the level of a written commitment because their differences outweigh those commonalities too much.

### Conventional wisdom #2: The alliance dilemma is a fundamental problem shared by all military alliances

Scholars and observers frequently allude to something called the alliance dilemma to highlight the steep trade-offs that come with commitment-making in the face of possible war. When providing an ally with a broad military commitment, a state may worry that the benefiting ally would be emboldened to have a more aggressive foreign policy than it would otherwise have, thereby upping the risk of some undesirable war. However, weakening a military commitment to offset those so-called entrapment risks could leave the receiving state fearful that its allies will abandon it to the depredations of an adversary. Entrapment and abandonment are thus two sides of the same coin, with severe trade-offs confronting decision-makers when they are designing and managing alliances.

How severe is the alliance dilemma? Chapters 2 and 3 explore the issues of entrapment and abandonment, respectively, to build up an argument that this dilemma is not really a dilemma. The problems highlighted here are instead tractable; certainly, they are not endemic to all alliances. Chapter 2 notes the different sources of entrapment risks that exist and what strategies allies can adopt to mitigate them. These sources can be the alliance treaty itself, systemic factors like polarity and the offense–defense balance, obsession with reputation, and transnational ideological networks. Sometimes these risk factors can be mutually reinforcing; sometimes they can cancel each other out. Nevertheless, although entrapment is empirically rare, the historical record reveals that decision-makers do genuinely worry about it. But precisely because they take it seriously, entrapment becomes a self-denying prophecy. As for abandonment fears, no state should ever be rationally confident that it would receive support from a defender against a militarily capable adversary. Chapter 3 explains that, although abandonment fears are normal in the face of an external threat, such fears seldom reach a level of intensity that leads states to consider neutralism or nuclear proliferation. This chapter probes the factors that can affect the intensity of abandonment concerns and discusses how states practice reassurance to convince allies that their security concerns are being addressed.

Taken together, the punchline of Chapters 2 and 3 is that the alliance dilemma is not as pronounced as often asserted because tools are available for addressing it. The trade-offs implied by the dilemma do not always exist. Sometimes states are so aligned in their political interests with one another vis-à-vis their adversaries that they simply do not face such conundrums in their alliance decision-making. Still, certain measures that some observers advocate for addressing contemporary forms of subversion may not be necessary and may even be counterproductive with respect to reassuring worried allies.

*Conventional wisdom #3: Members of US alliances must do more to bear their fair share of the common defense burden*

President Trump frequently chided allies in Europe and East Asia for not spending enough on their militaries and thus not bearing their share of the collective defense burden. He menacingly threatened abandonment in pushing NATO members to spend 2 percent of their gross domestic product (GDP) on defense so as to fulfill the pledges made in 2014. Yet, among US presidents, Trump was unique mostly only in tone. Many of his predecessors had complained that US allies could do more to bear the burden more equitably. During the Cold War, US presidents were exasperated by the perceived inadequacy of their allies. Though these alliance criticisms have been around for a long time, such complaints have gathered force in more recent times because the United States is not as powerful as it used to be.

The premise of most contemporary burden-sharing controversies, financially grounded as they often are, is a faulty one, however. The presumption is that allies could contribute to the common defense burden in a more equitable manner. That sounds reasonable enough, but what does it really mean in practice? Chapter 4 notes that part of the reason why burden-sharing controversies arose in the first place is because of how military alliances have come to last longer, a result of how war itself has become so costly in light of nuclear weapons. Crucially, advances in military technology create contradictory incentives when it comes to defense spending. On the one hand, the growing sophistication and complexity of weapons platforms require sustained long-term investment on the part of states to ensure that their militaries do not lag behind their competitors or even allies. On the other hand,  nuclear deterrence may make militarized conflict less likely, which in turn drives down the willingness of states to spend on defense. Some states might even believe that spending on conventional military power could make nuclear war more probable. The relationship between defense spending and the collective good of deterrence is, to say the least, hardly linear. Common thresholds for evaluating defense contributions – as in the 2 percent guideline used by NATO – make little sense.

*Conventional wisdom #4: Military alliances aggregate capabilities and thus allow their members to confront security challenges more effectively*

Recall the earlier standard claim that one motivation for forming alliances is to balance against a shared threat. One implication of this claim is that states can see off their security challenges more effectively in unison with their allies, provided that they have some, than they would without them.

This view is plausible, but Chapter 5 argues that it is at best incomplete. Most, if not all, present-day alliances exist to prevent war, but no US-led (or even Soviet/Russian) alliance since the end of the Second World War has fought directly against its primary adversary. In fact, alliances generally do not fight wars – ad hoc arrangements like coalitions do. And when wars are fought or multinational military campaigns are undertaken, treaty allies often work alongside nontreaty partners in those coalitions to advance common, but usually not identical, goals. Their motivations for participating in those operations may vary, especially when their own alliance obligations may not be directly relevant to the campaign at hand. Moreover, capability aggregation hardly guarantees military effectiveness. One might think that alliances serve to aggregate capabilities, implying that the more military power and the more members there are, the more effective and successful these alliances would be against adversaries. However, strategic, organizational, and technical factors can create a range of problems that hamper the ability of coalitions in going about multilateral military operations as successfully as they would like. That said, military alliances may still be more effective fighting organizations thanks to the joint military exercising and standardization that can occur under their auspices, but that would not be because they simply aggregate capabilities.

*Conventional wisdom #5: Military alliances are only useful for as long as the strategic circumstances that led to their emergence hold*

Proponents of one school of thought – realism – contend that a military alliance exists, or at least should exist, in proportion to the strategic need that gave rise to it. To consider again the first standard claim described earlier, if states no longer have to balance against a particular threat or to have influence over another state for whatever reason, then the military alliance founded for advancing such interests should cease to exist.

Military alliances can end for different reasons, though. In discussing how alliance treaties have historically defined the terms of their expiry, Chapter 6 outlines how alliances have historically come to an end: fulfillment of their original functions, military defeat, downgrading, unilateral abrogation, and transformation. A key observation made in Chapter 6 is that the factors that push states to establish alliances are seldom the factors that explain why those alliances meet their demise. Sometimes the strategic need that spurs the creation of the alliance outlasts that alliance. The view that alliances should only exist as a function of specific needs and strategic circumstances is rather a normative one. It is not descriptive of what happens empirically.

* * *

Put together, in scrutinizing these standard claims and making these critical arguments, this book seeks to impress upon the reader one main point about military alliances: that these organizations defy easy explanations and are often so puzzling that it should be small wonder that US military alliances – or any alliance for that matter – can at times seem very dysfunctional. States write down their political and military commitments in treaties so as both to clarify their intentions and to create ambiguity over the circumstances in which they would act. Leaders fear that their country will be dragged into disputes they do not wish to have due to the reckless behavior of allied states, but precisely because they have such apprehensions, those fears rarely – if ever – become reality. Worrying about abandonment by an ally is natural and rational, but seldom do these concerns intensify to a level that dramatically reshapes a state's foreign and defense policy. This may just as well be due to skillful alliance management. Though burden-sharing controversies have dominated many intra-alliance debates since the beginning of the Cold War, they are partly the result of those alliances lasting much longer than ever before, thanks, arguably, to nuclear deterrence, which can create disincentives for states to spend on their militaries. Of course, states do ultimately, though unevenly, build up their military capabilities in order to deter in peacetime and to prevail in wartime, but many, if not most, multinational military campaigns do not involve the full membership of an alliance. They oftentimes include non-allies, which may lead some to ask why it is worth even bothering to have a formal alliance at all. The factor that illuminates why states agree to form a military alliance in the first place often sheds little, if any, light on why that alliance comes to an end. Contradictions are pervasive.

## Defining Military Alliances

Before fleshing out these arguments in greater detail, a crucial question remains: what exactly is a military alliance? This question is deceptively simple, not least because news media often invoke the term to describe a wide variety of security arrangements like NATO, bilateral partnerships that involve the United States and countries such as Israel, Saudi Arabia, and Pakistan, as well as the burgeoning cooperation between China and Russia. And indeed, some scholars would agree that such relationships constitute alliances. Michael Barnett and Jack Levy (1991: 370) define an alliance "in its broadest sense to refer to a formal or informal relationship of security cooperation between two or more states and involving mutual expectations of some degree of policy coordination on security issues under certain conditions in the future." In his seminal study on alliances, Stephen Walt (1987: 12) similarly defines them as "a formal or informal arrangement for security cooperation between two or more sovereign states." As such, scholars have counted alliances in all sorts of ways, creating confusion as to the true count, and running the risk of comparing apples to oranges. Mira Rapp-Hooper (2020: 17) writes, for example, that the United States had thirty-seven allies as of 2020, but she includes in her count Israel and Pakistan (which do not have a formal defense agreement with the United States) and omits countries that make up the Inter-American Treaty of Reciprocal Assistance, popularly known as the Rio Pact (which notionally does contain one).

For its purposes, this book adopts a more restrictive definition. Specifically, I define military alliances as arrangements made between two or more sovereign states on the basis of a written treaty that serves to coordinate military policy toward at least one common goal. This definition has several components that need unpacking.

First, only sovereign states have military alliances. Sovereignty is, of course, a fraught concept. Few states, if any, are fully sovereign in terms of their own domestic and foreign policies, whether because they delegate some juridical authority to international organizations, subordinate some decision-making to a stronger state, or both (Krasner 1999). In the modern context, though, a country is at least nominally sovereign if it has its own representation at international bodies and, most importantly, is recognized as a state by other states. Of course, violent nonstate actors can align themselves with states or even other nonstate actors so as to have an alliance in the common sense of the term (Tamm 2016; see also Grynaviski 2015). The most famous formal example is the 1778 Treaty of Alliance signed by the Kingdom of France and the Thirteen United States of America during the American Revolutionary War. This example notwithstanding, such relationships are often ad hoc and, as we will see, lack the other key ingredients that make up a military alliance. That said, sovereign states can forge, and have forged, military alliances in order to counter threats emanating from transnational movements.

Second, military alliances are based on some written treaty. This feature is crucial to the definition I use in this book. Treaties outline, with varying degrees of clarity (or, one might say, ambiguity), the rules of the game that constrain their relationship: they spell out the promises and obligations, sometimes even listing the conditions under which their provisions would or would not be activated. Not all written commitments are alike. A mutual defense treaty with reciprocal obligations could constitute the alliance, as in the case of NATO, but a security treaty could simply entail one-sided obligations, as in the case of the US–Japan alliance. The United States is an ally of Thailand even though the founding treaty – the Southeast Asia Collective Defense Treaty (popularly known as the Manila Pact) – produced a multilateral organization that was eventually dissolved in 1977. In addition to the Manila Pact, the 1962 Thanat-Rusk communiqué and the 2012 Joint Vision Statement for the Thai–US Defense Alliance form the basis of their ongoing security partnership.

By stressing the importance of having a written treaty, I exclude informal partnerships or alignments that other scholars like Barnett, Levy, and Walt include in their studies. I also do not cover so-called "alliances of convenience" – that is, instances where adversaries cooperate informally to tackle urgent security challenges (Resnick 2010/11). I believe excluding them is defensible on several grounds. Incorporating both informal (i.e., nontreaty) and formal (i.e., treaty) arrangements in a definition of alliance blurs the distinction between friendly diplomacy and active military partnership. We distinguish between dating and marriage when we discuss romantic relations because they entail different expectations and obligations. We should make similar distinctions with respect to international security cooperation. Treating alignment and alliance as interchangeable introduces unnecessary difficulties in measuring the concept: in the absence of a treaty, how much alignment must we see for it to qualify as a military alliance? The answer to this question is not self-evident. In emphasizing the formal signing of military alliances, I avoid these difficulties. Nevertheless, I am aware that other problems could arise with my decision. The United States is a treaty ally of North Macedonia via NATO, but not of Israel or Saudi Arabia. China and Russia arguably engage in more military cooperation now than some treaty allies have had historically. The reinvigorated Quadrilateral Security Dialogue (the Quad) – comprising Australia, India, Japan, and the United States – does not qualify as an alliance because it is not based on documented security guarantees. Why, then, leave out these more strategically significant relationships from the analysis? Suffice it to say for now, not extending a treaty to such states, however closely aligned they appear to be, is a deliberate choice to avoid the very problems that can come with alliances.

Third, military alliances are focused primarily on coordinating military policy. This point seems redundant, but it is worth highlighting because states cooperate with one another on a wide range of issues. In the economic sphere, they can form free or preferential trade areas, common markets, as well as customs, monetary, or other types of economic unions. They can also participate in other international organizations that center on human rights promotion, environmental protection, or social development. Yet none of these international organizations would qualify as a military alliance because they are not geared toward coordinating military policy – specifically, plans and decisions relating to the kinetic and lethal use of force against third parties. Hence, the United States is not, formally speaking, a military ally of the EU, even though many EU members are also part of NATO. Of course, military alliances do sometimes feature nonmilitary provisions in their charters. Article II of NATO's founding document – the Washington Treaty – provides that its members "will contribute toward the further development of peaceful and friendly international relations by strengthening their free institutions" as well as "encourage economic collaboration between any or all of them" (NATO 2019). That said, nonmilitary goals are often aspirational and usually handled through alternative modes of cooperation such as, in the case of many NATO members, the European Community (now the EU), the General Agreement on Trade and Tariffs (now the World Trade Organization), and the International Monetary Fund (IMF). Many of NATO's internal debates turned on defense planning and war preparations in case the Soviet Union were to carry out a strike against Western Europe, North America, or the Eastern Mediterranean. One scholar even described Article II as "a dead letter during the cold war" (Haglund 1997: 469). Nevertheless, the business of a military alliance need not focus exclusively on high-intensity threats. NATO, for its part, also does counterterrorism, defense sector reforms, counterproliferation, counterpiracy, intelligence cooperation, and civil emergency planning.

Fourth, and finally, alliances are a means by which their members strive to achieve some common security goal. The purposes of an alliance could be defensive or offensive. A defensive alliance serves to prevent a war and to maintain the territorial integrity and political autonomy of its members vis-à-vis adversaries; defensive alliances uphold the status quo. In contrast, offensive alliances function as a way for states to coordinate their war-making in the pursuit of gaining territory and direct influence over other sovereign states. Offensive alliances are historically very rare and so receive far less coverage in this book than defensive ones. Note that military alliances do not require members to agree on everything. In fact, precisely because states have different interests and often disagree, the alliance management issues of the sort discussed in this book exist. The more that is at stake for any one member, the greater the discord. Yes, states form alliances because they broadly agree on issues of core military concern, but, as we will see, they form alliances in order to manage their disagreements as well.

Military alliances are, therefore, distinct from other types of security cooperation. Unfortunately, many datasets that aim to collect information on alliances for quantitative study often pool military alliances together with coalitions, nonaggression pacts, and ententes (Wilkins 2012: 57). These arrangements should not be conflated. Coalitions are ad hoc and usually built around a specific military campaign or mission set in wartime, even though states sometimes draw on their military alliances to build those coalitions. Nonaggression pacts involve states pledging not to attack one other; they do not contain promises to render assistance if a party to the agreement comes under attack by a third party. An entente – from the French for "understanding" – is, by dint of lacking a treaty basis, "a far less conspicuous form of association than alliance" and can be construed as an amiable form of geopolitical alignment (Kann 1976: 616). Nor are military alliances "concerts," which stress "the preservation of peace and order through the negotiated adjustment of conflict" (Snyder 1997: 368). Concerts can involve the provision of mutual protection, but, as the archetypal example of the nineteenth-century Concert of Europe indicates, they often serve to regulate

Table 0.1: Military alliances that are active as of 2021

| *Involving the United States* | |
| --- | --- |
| Australia, New Zealand, United States Security (ANZUS) Treaty | NATO (29 other countries) |
| Inter-American Treaty of Reciprocal Assistance (16 other countries) | Treaty of Mutual Cooperation and Security Between the United States and Japan |
| Mutual Defense Treaty Between the United States of America and the Republic of Korea | Thai–US Defense Alliance |
| Mutual Defense Treaty Between the Republic of Philippines and the United States of America | |

| *Involving China* | *Involving Russia* |
| --- | --- |
| Sino-North Korean Mutual Aid and Cooperation Friendship Treaty | Collective Security Treaty Organization (5 other countries) |

interstate relations among states that do not necessarily see each other as friends, let alone as allies (Slantchev 2005: 579).

## Plan of the Book

This book is about contemporary military alliance politics. Combining theoretical rigor with a historical sensibility, it will cover the main practical problems and policy debates relating to alliance management. As indicated, Chapter 1 explores why states establish military alliances. Chapter 2 tackles the issue of entrapment, whereas Chapter 3 focuses on abandonment. Chapters 4 and 5 address alliance burden-sharing controversies and coalition war-fighting, respectively.

Chapter 6 discusses alliance termination. The Conclusion recapitulates the book's arguments and offers final thoughts on the value of military alliances and the difficulties of assuring partners moving forward. US-led alliances will dominate this book because, as Table 0.1 indicates, most military alliances as of 2021 involve the United States. It will consider non-US alliances such as China–North Korea and the Russian-led Collective Security Treaty Organization (CSTO), as well as the prospects for new alliances, including one between Russia and China. Many examples will be drawn from the historical record: Germany's late nineteenth- and early twentieth-century alliance with Austria-Hungary, France's interwar alliances with Central European states, the Cold War-era Warsaw Pact, North Korea's alliance with the Soviet Union, among others.

# 1

# Formation

Why do states establish military alliances? For a time, this question no longer appeared to have policy relevance and thus could only have inspired historical interest. The Bush administration may have overseen the incorporation of seven European countries into NATO, but it failed in its bid to put Georgia and Ukraine on a clear path toward eventual membership. Most importantly, under Bush's leadership the United States opted to build a "coalition of the willing" to wage a military campaign against Iraq. Even the NATO mission in Afghanistan saw some countries place caveats over the use of their military forces there, much to the dismay and resentment of some of their partners. With Obama taking over the White House amid profound global economic crisis in 2009, military alliances seemed to have become too rigid and impractical as a tool.

Looser security arrangements were destined to be commonplace. Thomas Wilkins (2012: 54) averred that "formal military alliances [based] on the pre-WWI/Cold War paradigm have now ceased to represent the standard for allied security cooperation." Bruno Tertrais (2004: 139) noted unequivocally that "permanent multinational alliances appear increasingly to belong to the past." As he saw it, many US allies had grown wary of US leadership, while the

United States itself came to view alliances as much more burdensome than before. Rajan Menon (2003: 16) went further and declared "the end of alliances," be they bilateral or multilateral. He argued: "America will revert to a pattern it has followed for most of its history, operating in the world without fixed, long-term alliances and pursuing its cooperation with a range of partners." Echoing this sentiment, Stephen Walt (2009: 137–8) wrote that, because of its global dominance, Washington "is likely to rely more heavily on ad hoc coalitions, flexible deployments, and bilateral arrangements that maximize its own leverage and freedom of action." Similarly, Parag Khanna (2008: 324) observed that states now operate "in a world of alignments, not alliances."

And yet barely a decade after these pronouncements were made, military alliances began to experience a revival. Seth Cropsey (2020) of the Hudson Institute has argued in favour of "[s]trengthening the US–Taiwan Alliance [*sic*]" in order to improve regional defense against an increasingly powerful China. At least one scholar argues that China is "on the verge of an alliance" with Russia (Korolev 2019). In the spring of 2020, India and Australia signed a mutual logistic support agreement that would allow each country to access the other's military balance, signaling that they may be involved in more military exchanges and exercises in the future. Already across the Indo-Pacific region a patchwork of different security relationships has taken shape between countries that have previously avoided military cooperation, suggesting that new defense pacts may yet form with the goal of managing the rise of China and its attendant challenges (Simón et al. 2021). Though admittedly more of a case of alliance enlargement than of alliance formation, the United States added two new treaty allies to its roster, with Montenegro and North Macedonia joining NATO in 2017 and 2020, respectively. Indeed, the security challenge posed by Russia following its annexation of Crimea from Ukraine reanimated NATO. Some alliance scholars have spoken of how NATO could contribute to balancing efforts against China (Moller and Rynning 2021: 185). Whereas London and Washington may have had a "special relationship" in the twentieth century to confront threats in Europe and elsewhere, Tokyo and Washington may yet have one in the twenty-first century on the basis of their Security Treaty as the center of gravity in international affairs shifts toward the Indo-Pacific.

The standard view is that states establish military alliances for at least two, non-mutually exclusive, reasons. The first is that states wish to balance against a threat that they commonly face. The second motive is that strong states use the alliance relationship as a vehicle for expanding their influence over others. This is supposed to be especially true of asymmetric alliances, in which at least one member is significantly greater in military and economic capabilities than another. In these arrangements, the stronger state is able to extract key concessions from its weaker counterpart.

As this chapter illustrates, however, the problem with these standard arguments about alliance formation is threefold. First, although threat-based arguments provide a powerful explanation for why states form alliances, they remain insufficient in accounting for the patterns that we see, for the simple reason that shared threat perceptions do not always lead to formal alliances. No one set of factors will ever systematically lead states to sign an alliance, in part because alliances are costly. States sometimes might not wish to get exposed to the disputes of potential allies. Second, existing understandings overstate the concessions that even great powers can extract from weaker states by way of a treaty. And third, the foregoing explanations of alliance formation do not explain why a written alliance treaty is actually a necessary condition for achieving such ends as balancing and concession-extracting. This chapter argues that a signed alliance treaty is desirable not just for defining the terms of a commitment, but also, ironically, for injecting a certain amount of vagueness into the language of the agreement itself. Alliance treaties thread the needle between certainty and ambiguity, permitting states to be more comfortable about deepening their military cooperation, if they choose to do so.

## Uncertainty, Violence, and Political Difference

Any discussion of why states establish alliances must begin with at least three observations about international politics. The first is that states form and sustain their military alliances in an anarchic international environment. No higher governmental authority exists above the state – none that can make and enforce rules that states would feel, for whatever reason, they have little choice but to obey. Accordingly, states are uncertain about the intentions of others, be they allies or adversaries, because the absence of a higher authority compounds the difficulties of getting reliable information about what others are planning to do. There is lively scholarly debate about the nature of uncertainty in world politics (see Rathbun 2007) or the meaning of anarchy (see Nedal and Nexon 2019), but the point is that some degree of uncertainty ultimately exists in international relations.

The second observation is that violence not only is possible under anarchy, but can, in the extreme, lead to the elimination of a state or its governing political system (Fazal 2007). This potential for violence raises the stakes for international cooperation. Some states may be able to wield sufficient capabilities that they can defend against most threats without needing the support of others. Most states are not so fortunate and thus may have to seek outside assistance in order to get a handle on the challenges that they face. Precisely because of the high stakes that are involved, alliance decisions can be emotional, sometimes turning on fear, distrust, and even anger. That alliance politics can have a strong emotional dimension does not automatically imply irrational behavior. A park visitor would be right to be afraid of a hungry grizzly bear in his or her path, but some responses to mitigate that danger are more sensible than others.

The third observation is that states have different interests that they wish to advance in their foreign policymaking. Of course, many states want the same things: territorial integrity, freedom to determine their foreign and domestic policies, economic prosperity, higher welfare for their citizens, and safety from harm. Nevertheless, that interests often overlap does not imply that states are all favorably predisposed to the status quo or that they interpret the status quo in the same way. Their leaders might have conflicting beliefs on how to obtain those goods – some might even be hostile to the status quo, valuing expansion over security (Schweller 1996: 106–7). Alternatively, states might value the same things but have different priorities, creating disagreement over which matters most. Because we live in a world of scarcity, whether in terms of material resources, time, or attention, states must make choices about which capabilities to develop and how they should use them to achieve their desired ends. Compounding these issues is the problem of modernity, which John Ikenberry (2020: 14) describes "as the set of deep, worldwide transformations in domestic and international society unleashed by the forces of science, technology, and industrialism" that began in the eighteenth century. Modernity means that different societies, and the states that govern them, can exhibit varying levels of development and so have contrasting preferences or ideas on how to achieve wealth and prosperity. Such discord can exist despite how, or perhaps because, societies around the world have become increasingly connected with one another. How to organize relations in such a complex global system itself can be an object of contention. International politics, in a nutshell, is about states often having conflicting interests and values in an environment where violence is possible, where no overarching supreme authority is available to act as a referee.

These three basic observations about international politics do not imply a single theory for what drives alliance formation. After all, military alliances can be either offensive or defensive. Offensive alliances, which help states coordinate an attack against others, are relatively simple to grasp. Jack Levy (1981: 590) finds that military alliances were often offensive prior to 1815, with their founding treaties calling for the use of force even in the absence of an external military attack. Following the Napoleonic Wars (1803–15), the offensive alliance became a very rare form of international political organization, at least as far as the public record is concerned. Still, according to Randall Schweller (1994: 79, 87), states sometimes bandwagon for profit, forming offensive alliances with a more powerful state to "share in the spoils of victory" as well as "to improve their position." For example, the leaders of Austria, France, and Spain came together in 1508 as the League of Cambrai in a bid to divide Venetian territory amongst themselves. Fascist Italian leader Benito Mussolini overcame his initial reservations about Adolf Hitler and signed his country to the Pact of Steel with Nazi Germany in March 1939. Though blindsided by the German invasion of Poland later that year, Mussolini participated in the Battle of France after some delay in June 1940. In each case, leaders held a shared belief that the status quo was undesirable and that their partnership would allow them to revise it in a mutually satisfactory manner.

The vast majority of military alliances are defensive in character, however. Yet the notion of a defensive alliance is a misnomer, for defensive military alliances do not serve to fight defensively as much as they serve to deter war. Indeed, defensive military alliances practice extended deterrence. Deterrence refers here to how military alliances strive to prevent war by communicating to an adversary that the costs of aggression are too high for it to be worthwhile. Extended deterrence is a form of deterrence put into practice by a defender that wishes to prevent external aggression against another state – typically, a treaty ally. A defensive military alliance need not have to demonstrate that it would win a potential war for (extended) deterrence to work, but it must somehow convey that it has the political will, military capability, and resolve to inflict unacceptable pain on an adversary that it believes to be against the status quo (Jervis 1979). Deterrence is admittedly a deceptively simple concept. Just because an adversary has not acted aggressively does not necessarily mean that deterrence has worked. The adversary may never have had a desire to attack, making successful deterrence an illusion and thus a false positive (Lebow and Stein 1995). Divining adversarial intentions can be tricky, and with the stakes being sometimes existential, countries feel that they must err on the side of caution to undertake measures, like forming military alliances, to augment deterrence. And finally, deterrence does not imply having a militarily defensive strategy. Sometimes going on the offence is the best way to impose costs if deterrence fails.

## Balancing Threat as a Classic Explanation of Alliance Formation

But what exactly is the danger that drives alliance formation? A classic explanation for why states establish defensive military alliances is that they are seeking to balance power. According to balance of power theory, states tend to band together so as to prevent a potential hegemon – that is, a state forecast to wield a preponderance of military and economic capabilities – from rising up and dominating the system (Levy 2004: 37). A military alliance can help reinforce the status quo and thus provide an invaluable tool for preserving it.

At first blush, this argument is intuitive and plausible. The emergence of Napoleonic France and Nazi Germany pushed states to unite in common cause and to aggregate their capabilities to defeat such bids for supremacy. On closer inspection, however, balance of power theory explains very little. Empirically, too many states across world history have been able to dominate regional systems by defeating rival coalitions (Wohlforth et al. 2007). Even in the foregoing cases, countries did not forge strong alliances (or, more accurately, military coalitions) against Napoleonic France and Nazi Germany until after those aspiring hegemons pursued conquest through war. Seven coalitions were attempted before Napoleonic France was defeated for good. Critically, the most powerful state in international politics in 2022 – the United States – has far more alliances than its potential rival China, which only has North Korea as a formal treaty ally. Balance of power theory, in its simplest incarnation, cannot explain the international environment in the early twenty-first century (Brooks and Wohlforth 2008). If anything, since the Cold War ended, there have been many more instances of bandwagoning (or joining the stronger side) with the United States than there have been attempts to balance against it.

Scholars have thus tried to refine balance of power theory to explain alliance formation better. Most notably, Stephen Walt (1987: 5) argues that states appraise others on the basis of perceived threat, which can be a composite of factors that include geography, perceived hostile intent, and offensive capabilities. In a twist on this argument, Paul Poast (2019) contends that compatibility in war plans and availability of outside options (buck-passing, unilateral action, or another alliance) drive alliance formation. Thomas Christensen and Jack Snyder postulate that if prevailing military technology favors the offence over the defense, then, all things being equal, states will be more likely to ally with one another against a common threat. The reasoning is simple. When defense is relatively easy, states might believe that others can do the fighting themselves against a perceived threat. Alliances do not happen – or at least will remain very weak – because of such "buck-passing" and "free riding." However, if attacking is easier than defending, then the balance could be more easily overthrown. And so, "to uphold the balance and to have an effect on the outcome of the fighting, policymakers [believe] that they [have] to conclude binding alliances in advance and throw their full weight into the battle at the outset" (1990: 148). To be sure, according to Christensen and Snyder, such imperatives are most acute when more than two great powers among the states are present in a regional or international context – that is, under multipolarity. Otherwise, under bipolarity, whereby there are only two great powers of roughly equal standing, alliances should be much less consequential for actual war-fighting because no one ally or group thereof can tip the balance.

These refined arguments regarding the influence of the military balance have themselves come under criticism. The problem with Poast's argument is that alliances often do not agree on actual war plans until sometime after they are established and after even more negotiation, if ever at all. How, then, can compatibility in war plans predict alliance formation but not actual alliance war plans? Moving on, some scholars take issue with whether we can neatly categorize weapons systems in an offence–defense binary – a point we will revisit later when we discuss theories of entrapment. In arguing against Snyder and Christensen, James Morrow asserts that states face a trade-off in choosing between establishing an alliance (i.e., external balancing) and developing one's armaments (i.e., internal balancing). An alliance can enhance a state's sense of security relatively quickly, but at the cost of sacrificing certain interests and flexibility to gain the cooperation of a prospective ally that may or may not come to its aid in an actual crisis. Building armaments gives the state a more reliable source of military power – its own – but at the political expense of allocating resources away from other uses. States manage this trade-off by selecting some mixture of arms and alliances, trying to optimize between them such that the costs of procuring either do not exceed their benefits. What determines these costs is usually domestic politics (Morrow 1993: 216). Acquiring armaments often hinges on how much the state is able to extract from society in order to meet its pressing security needs. Typically, great powers can mobilize enough manpower and military capabilities – hence their greatness – so they have a lesser need for alliances. For smaller states, there might exist domestic impediments to forming a military alliance. Though only small relative to the United States, Saudi Arabia is an illustrative example: anti-Americanism is sufficiently strong among members of its society that its leaders may be disinclined to negotiate an alliance treaty with the United States (Pollack 2003: 37). Whether such a trade-off exists between alliances and arms remains debatable: Morrow (1993: 214) acknowledges that allied states are not toothless, and an ally without arms would not be very desirable from a strictly security perspective (see also Horowitz et al. 2017). The proposition that states rationally allocate resources between arms and alliances would surprise those familiar with how dysfunctional military procurement efforts can be (Alic 2007: 107).

The notion that states face such a trade-off does highlight the importance of domestic politics for military alliances.

It is perhaps no accident that the Cold War saw two competing superpowers – the Soviet Union and the United States – form rival military alliances on the basis of ideology, with communist countries grouped in one camp and anti-communist countries grouped in another. One study finds that, since 1945, states with similar regime types – whether they are both democratic or both autocratic – are more likely to ally with one another (Lai and Reiter 2000). Other statistical analyses have had trouble uncovering a correlation between alliance formation and regime type, with NATO and the Warsaw Pact being anomalies in the historical record (Simon and Gartzke 1996). NATO itself was mostly democratic but it did contain nondemocracies (Greece between 1967 and 1974 and Turkey at odd junctures) during the Cold War. Nevertheless, even if countries with different political systems form alliances, domestic politics, and, for that matter, ideology, can still matter. Some countries allied with the United States during the Cold War may not have been democratic, but their leaders still shared the same fears regarding communist expansion and subversion. Syngman Rhee was one such leader: although autocratic in method and disposition, he expressed anti-communist ideals long before becoming South Korean President (Kraus 2017: 261–2).

All the foregoing arguments suggest that states form defensive military alliances as a way to manage a security challenge posed by some external threat. In that sense, Walt's original theory, at its core, prevails. However, states have sometimes established alliances so as to mitigate conflict with each other. Paul Schroeder (2004: 196) observes "that alliances in practice do not always serve to increase a nation's power and security, and that allies often clash with each other more than they unite in common cause." Patricia Weitsman (1997: 162–5) invokes the term "tethering" to describe how states form alliances in order to manage each other's potential hostility, with which they may hope to build friendlier relations over time. The League of the Three Emperors had this purpose. Lasting from 1873 to 1880, the German, Russian, and Austro-Hungarian Empires used this alliance in part to coordinate their activities in the Balkans

– a region where Vienna and Moscow had been jockeying for control. Indeed, expectations of more generalized conflict might drive alliance formation. Take, for example, NATO enlargement. In the early 1990s, many observers predicted that much instability would come to Europe because the US and Soviet troops stationed on the continent during the Cold War kept a lid on states' nuclear ambitions and ethnic grievances (see Mearsheimer 1990; Lanoszka 2020b: 453–5). By incorporating former communist countries like Poland into NATO, some US decision-makers and their Central European counterparts believed that they would enhance the European continent's prospects for peace. Civil–military relations would proceed along democratic lines, whereas norms of territorial integrity would persevere with nationalist conflict managed and risky defense policies discouraged (Epstein 2005).

Threat-based arguments allow for the possibility that states form military alliances to deal with internal or transnational threats. Steven David (1991) introduced the term "omni-balancing" to describe situations where states balance against both external and internal threats. By internal threats, David meant potential coup plotters or insurgent groups, which may or may not have outside support (1991: 240–1). Accordingly, leaders might align themselves with a strong state that might threaten their own state's interests but nevertheless can offer assistance against internal threats. David largely focuses his analysis on the developing countries in the Global South, but his argument can throw a light on alliance patterns in Europe. Apart from managing great power competition in the Balkan region, one reason for the League of the Three Emperors was that it offered a vehicle for coordinating imperial power against the troublesome Polish minority whose country the alliance members had conspired to eliminate in the late eighteenth century. A motivation for creating NATO was to protect anti-communist states from internal subversion and fickle publics (Sayle 2019: 2–7).

## Concession-Extraction as Another Standard Explanation of Alliance Formation

A second common explanation of alliance formation looks less at threat perceptions and focuses more on the differences in military power that potential allies can bring to the table. To be sure, the arms versus alliances trade-off mentioned earlier suggests that stronger states should be more reluctant to forge alliances than their weaker counterparts. After all, a strong state presumably can generate enough military power to withstand threats on its own – at minimum, it should be less reliant on others. If weaker states form alliances, then the aim should be to use those alliances to balance against the strongest states.

And yet, as already noted, the most powerful state today – the United States – has the most allies, many of which lack sufficient military power to deter adversaries on their own. In fact, most existing alliances today are asymmetric – that is, alliances in which military power is largely concentrated in one member. The Mutual Defense Treaty between the Philippines and the United States is one example of an asymmetric alliance. North Korea's alliance with China is another. Yet these arrangements are puzzling. Should these weaker allies not fear domination by their stronger patron as well? Why would a strong state form a pact with a much weaker state – one that might even be a liability in a war if it is unable to defend itself from another great power? Are such partnerships not superfluous if the great power can rely on its nuclear weapons arsenal as the ultimate source for its security?

One simple answer to all these questions is that asymmetric alliances often reflect mutually beneficial bargains, whereby the strong state and the weak state have overlapping interests but derive different benefits. Consider how the strong state has more security than that of the weak state. The latter may have autonomy, but it does not have security against a particular threat due to its lack of relative military power. Scholars like James Morrow thus argue that the strong state trades away some of its security to the weaker state in return for policy concessions that reduce the latter's autonomy (1991: 914). These concessions can include hosting military bases and giving access to strategic locations useful for projecting power. The strong state may even win rights to shape the domestic and foreign policy of the weaker state. Alternatively, the strong state could have greater input in shaping the language and content of the alliance treaty – a point to which we will return when we discuss entrapment (Johnson 2015). What the weak state gets in return is a security guarantee against another state that it fears much more, whether for ideological or military reasons. Shared threat perceptions provide the basis for the partnership, but a loss of autonomy on the part of the weaker state seals the deal.

To what extent is this view correct? It seemingly has much going for it. The United States had military bases or forward deployed military assets in all of its most important treaty partners – Canada, France, Germany, Italy, Japan, South Korea, and the United Kingdom – at one point or another during the Cold War. In many allied countries, it still retains a major military presence, although in some cases allies have tried to expel US military forces, or, at least, alter the terms of basing agreements, amid major domestic political change (Cooley 2008). Moreover, Washington and Moscow did occasionally intervene in the affairs of their allies during the Cold War, with the most spectacular episodes being those within the Soviet bloc. The Soviet intervention in the Hungarian Revolution in 1956 and the Warsaw Pact suppression of the Prague Spring in 1968 come to mind. Still, in the 1950s and the 1960s, the US intelligence community quietly contributed funds to Japan's Liberal Democratic Party (LDP), the conservative political party that would go on to dominate Japanese politics, and has done so ever since (Williams 2020). After the Cold War ended, those states that aspired to join NATO agreed to make a number of changes in their military organizations in order to qualify. Some scholars argue that the more troops that a major power has stationed on a weaker ally's territory, the more that weaker ally is subordinate to the authority of that major power (Lake 2011).

Nevertheless, the notion that reciprocal bargains exist of the sort postulated here has its problems. To begin with, although a weak state may provide military basing rights to a stronger state, it may not necessarily be a policy concession. In fact, the opposite may be true: forward military basing could be a concession that the great power makes to the weaker state. One reason why the United States stationed as many as a quarter of a million military personnel in West Germany in the Cold War was to strengthen the alliance, rendering Washington's promises to fight – using nuclear weapons, no less – on its European ally's behalf more believable by making any major Soviet invasion of its territory less likely to succeed without incurring massive cost. Indeed, the historical record features many allied leaders worrying that the United States might withdraw forces, thereby leaving them vulnerable to external aggression (Lanoszka 2018b). Moreover, it is unclear whether an alliance per se can grant major powers the right to interfere in the domestic and foreign policy-making of their weaker partner. The United States may have intervened in Italy's general elections in 1948, but this was one year before NATO was founded. The Soviet Union established the Warsaw Pact in 1955, partly in response to West Germany's incorporation in NATO. But by this time, it had already shaped the domestic and foreign policies of many of the alliance's members. If anything, Warsaw Pact members were able to assert their status as independent countries by using the formal alliance to demand concessions from the Soviet Union, making the organization less hierarchical over time. Documentary evidence shows Warsaw Pact leaders in Poland and East Germany pushing the Soviet leadership in the Kremlin to intervene in neighboring Czechoslovakia in order to put a stop to the Prague Spring and its liberalizing tendencies (Crump 2015). Amid public criticism that the alliance was too one-sided and domineering, US decision-makers agreed to renegotiate the 1951 Security Treaty with Japan, thus making the alliance ultimately much less intrusive within Japanese domestic politics (Swenson-Wright 2005).

The LDP also benefited from the covert support that it may have received from the United States. North Korea arguably conceded little in the two separate alliances that it forged with China and the Soviet Union in 1961.

If asymmetrical alliances are not entirely the result of concessions made by their weaker members, then what explains them? Why, to reiterate the puzzle, is the United States able to accumulate so many allies? Geography is one possible explanation. Specifically, the United States is separated from most of its allies by oceans. Thanks to physical distance, allies have less reason to fear it and so they are much more concerned with threats closer to home. They can leverage support from Washington to help deter nearby adversaries. The problem with this explanation – intuitive though it may be – is that geography is a double-edged sword. The United States may be less threatening because it is far away, but it may also be less militarily useful – and perhaps even unreliable – because it has to make up a lot of distance if it wishes to fight an adversary alongside a far-flung ally. Moreover, geographically contiguous states can be allies, and very good ones at that. Canada may fear the domination of US cultural products in its own domestic marketplace; it can even be anxious about preserving its own autonomy. Nevertheless, it does not fear a land invasion given that it engages in defense cooperation with the United States (Bow 2009). Joseph Jockel and Joel Sokolsky (2009: 323–4) even argue that Ottawa enjoys an "involuntary guarantee" from Washington because so many Canadians live close to the US border. In Central Asia, states such as Kazakhstan partic- ipate in the CSTO, of which Russia is the most powerful country. They too worry about their autonomy vis-à-vis the Kremlin, but they still willingly engage in some joint military exercises and other forms of military-to-military cooper- ation (Costa Buranelli 2018: 389). Of course, geographically contiguous allies may sometimes lack agency and be subject to domination because the powerful state projects a prepon- derance of power over them. At the beginning, many Warsaw Pact countries took directives from Moscow in part because the local presence of commissars and the Red Army had an outsized impact on local domestic politics (see Rice 1984). Geography is not destiny.

There are, of course, benefits in allying with a weaker state. The example of the Soviet bloc suggests how political control over domestic and foreign policy can be one such benefit, but again such control is often incomplete and can dissipate over time (Cooley and Spruyt 2009). A second benefit is to acquire so-called defense-in-depth. In military parlance, defense-in-depth refers to a strategy where an attacker must confront successively robust layers of defensive points designed to absorb the first blow, delay the attacker's forces, and buy time for the defender to respond. A third, cruder benefit is that allies can be buffer states if they provide a battleground away from the territory of the great power where fighting with the adversary will first take place. The Soviet presence in East Germany and Poland offered Moscow this defense-in-depth against Western Europe, which it did not really have prior to the Second World War. Still, a defense-in-depth strategy or a buffer zone is no good if allies wrangle with each other. In cases where allies have a history of acrimonious relations with one another, extending security guarantees to each of them can help diffuse tensions by reassuring them both that their interests are heeded. The US military presence in Europe has, arguably, had this stabilizing effect. By becoming a European power in its own right during the Cold War, the United States inserted itself between France and West Germany, allaying concerns that the historical antagonisms they had for each other could resurface and would lead each to take up their disputes with military force again.

A fourth possible benefit to military alliances is that they facilitate such military cooperation as joint military exercises, interoperability, and personnel exchanges. Military alliances are not entirely necessary in order to create this particular benefit, but they can provide an institutional foundation for their continuous and regular operation. True interoperability requires reducing uncertainty and so can benefit from technological transfers, unified command systems, intelligence sharing, and other cooperative endeavors that allies would not consider doing for those that they fear would almost certainly renege on their pledges. Of course, these institutional foundations may or may not be of service if the great power needs to cobble together a coalition of states to undertake a military campaign. As Chapter 5 highlights, major problems of interoperability can persist and hamper those military operations that even longstanding allies undertake. Finally, having an ally on one side may in some cases be better than having it in the enemy's camp. For example, the ally might be positioned near key waterways or other sites of strategic interest that could be useful for projecting power in a wartime situation. Turkey has been consistently valuable to NATO precisely because of its location vis-à-vis the Dardanelles and the Bosporus. Put together, it is unclear whether great powers really do give up their security to weaker states if such arrangements can augment their sense of security as well.

A version of the concession-extraction argument holds that alliance formation can result from an expansionist foreign policy that is pursued for its own sake. This sort of argument has gained currency in recent years among those critics of US foreign policy who allege that Washington has taken on too many alliance commitments as part of a global liberal crusade or hegemonic project (Posen 2014; Mearsheimer 2018). Allies might not necessarily have made concessions, to be sure, but alliances still serve to project influence in the pursuit of a grand ideological initiative. As an explanation for alliance formation, this thesis overlooks how the United States has been uneven in advancing liberalism abroad (Jervis 2020: 18–19). After all, Taiwan is a successful liberal democracy but receives no such treaty commitment from the United States despite Taipei's eagerness to have one. Nevertheless, it is possible that the United States emerged from the Cold War victorious and with so much power that it sought to exploit the situation by trying to widen its authority even more (Mearsheimer 2018). Again, if Washington aimed at achieving global hegemony, then the willingness of small states to jump on that bandwagon rather than oppose it still requires explanation. Part of the answer may be that, for democratic states especially, the United States is an attractive partner because its democratic constitution and willingness to use international institutions, however selective this may occasionally be, make it less likely to dominate other states (Ikenberry 2001). But even this explanation is incomplete. Not only should the United States be nonthreatening to potential allies, but, as the previous discussion suggests, those potential allies should likely perceive to some degree the same threats that the United States perceives.

## But Why Have an Alliance Treaty?

A major weakness of both sets of arguments discussed above – that alliances are formed to face threats and help states to extract small power concessions (and thus to gain influence) – is that they leave unexplained the existence of a treaty. States can collaborate in face of a threat without having to sign a treaty. Alarmed by Iran, the countries of Israel and Saudi Arabia have improved their ties despite the historical animosity that they felt for one another. Their security personnel and their defense officials have met on multiple occasions. Saudi Arabia has apparently signaled its "willingness to provide Israel an air corridor and air bases for rescue helicopters, tanker aircraft and drones in case Israel decided to bomb the Iranian nuclear facility" (Abadi 2019: 444). No alliance seems probable between them, however. Similarly, uneasy about the rise of China, Vietnam has signed memoranda of understanding and enhanced defense cooperation with Australia and Japan, but has so far not signed an alliance treaty with either (Liff 2016: 450). In the book in which he advances the theory that states forge alliances to balance threats, Walt (1987) considers both formal treaty alliances and informal alignments. As I highlight in Chapter 5, many coalitions of states have been formed in wartime and fought effectively against their adversaries, despite not having an alliance treaty beforehand. Leaders of states should just as easily be able to communicate their intention to stand firm against an adversary through public statements. In this vein, US President Franklin Delano Roosevelt pledged to defend

Canada in a thinly veiled reference to Nazi Germany when he accepted an honorary doctorate at Queen's University in Kingston, Ontario, in 1938 (Granatstein 2020: 145).

Strong states should not have to sign treaties if they wish to extract concessions from smaller states. They should be able to do so by dint of their strength alone, in keeping with the oft-repeated notion that "the strong do what they can and the weak suffer as they must." Strong states presumably have options other than alliance commitment if they wish to safeguard another state from external attack. As the United States did with Saudi Arabia between the 1990–1 Gulf War and 2003, a great power can station its forces on the partner's territory in the absence of an alliance treaty. Another option is to provide security assistance. This can involve the transfer of weapons, especially those that are largely defensive in character so as to lower the risk of the recipient starting an unwanted war of its own. The United States decided against extending a treaty commitment to Israel in the 1960s and the 1970s, but stepped up its arms transfers in part to ensure that Israel would not be outmatched by its Arab rivals. Not long after abrogating a treaty alliance with Taiwan in 1979, the United States supplied it with weapons as a means of deterring China from launching an assault across the strait (see Yarhi-Milo et al. 2016). As former Assistant Secretary of State for Political-Military Affairs Andrew Shapiro once remarked, "[w]hen a country acquires an advanced US defense system, they are not simply buying a product to enhance their security, they are also seeking a relationship with the United States" (2012: 20).

International relations scholar James Morrow (2000) argues that states write down their alliances because doing so serves to signal commitment. Recall how "defensive alliances" really aim to deter war rather than to fight a war on the defensive. But to deter a war, a state, or a group thereof, must communicate to its adversary which actions are unacceptable, what consequences would follow if those actions are undertaken, and, significantly, how resolved it is to follow through on imposing those consequences, provided that it has the will and capacity to do so. One prerequisite to deterrence is assurance: the notion that promises will be kept and good behavior will not be exploited. Assurance is key to defensive alliances just as much as deterrence, with respect to both allies and adversaries. States need to determine whether an ally will truly come to their aid in the event of an attack. They will look for, and oftentimes ask for, statements or gestures that indicate that the ally has every intention of adhering to its pledges.

Unfortunately, communication in international politics is not straightforward precisely because the anarchic environment creates uncertainty: states can say one thing but do another, without worrying too much about being held to account by a higher authority. There is no one thing that all states can say or do to achieve deterrence or assurance. Otherwise, every state would then be doing that one thing. Statements of interests can thus be muddy.

The solution to this problem is to take actions that are costly enough that not every state would perform them. Costs come in two forms: *ex ante* and *ex post*. *Ex ante* costs refer to sunk costs that states must pay before performing an action; they can include buying armaments and deploying military personnel abroad. *Ex post* costs reflect measures that may not be felt immediately but nevertheless can constrain future decision-making options (Fearon 1997: 70). According to this rationalist perspective, only in rare cases when interests are completely and obviously aligned – that is to say, identical and harmonious – would states not have to pay costs to demonstrate their support for one another. As may be possibly true of Israel and the United States, "the shared interest carries the entire relationship, and therefore that relationship need not be negotiated formally" (Morrow 2000: 64).

According to Morrow (2000), treaty alliances help to signal interests and, as an *ex post* cost, to make binding commitments. Indeed, "alliances are institutions" that help to define "the rules of the game" by creating greater predictability in what states are trying to achieve in their foreign relations (Keohane 1988: 184; North 1991: 3). To begin with, states usually have to ratify their international agreements through

their domestic legislatures. Treaty ratification can be particularly difficult and time-consuming in multiparty democracies
where opposition groups may have reasons for opposing
the foreign policy initiatives of the executive. A country's
leadership cannot embark on a treaty alliance capriciously
lest it loses domestic support over the issue (Morrow 2000:
72). In order to enhance its international reputation, the state
leadership will presumably only endure the pains of treaty-
making if it believes that it has enough shared interests with
another state to do so. Simply put, an alliance treaty – once
signed and ratified – indicates to others that the signatory
states have common interests.

An alliance treaty also generates *ex post* costs by way of
tying hands and, therefore, creating commitments. Signing a
treaty might only be worth the cost of the paper on which it
was written at the outset, but it conveys the state's intent to
come militarily to the aid of another under certain conditions.
The public nature of such a treaty creates reputation costs
that the signatory state would incur if it decides to renege on
promises made to its ally. That signatory state might come
to be seen as duplicitous and an unreliable partner for others
that confront similar challenges. Faced with greater distrust,
the unreliable state would be forced to make more concessions in order to assure potential allies in the future. The *ex
post* costs can also be domestic, especially in a democracy. If
domestic legislators ratify a treaty, then they may not wish
to see the executive violate the agreement when its obligations are operative, because the national interest, in their
view, would be harmed as a result. No such constraints
purportedly exist in the absence of a treaty. As such, leaders
may feel that they have to fulfill their alliance commitments
(Gaubatz 1996; Leeds and Savun 2007; Leeds et al. 2009).

Morrow's view has become standard in international
relations theory, but it has certain conceptual weaknesses.
The first weakness touches on whether shepherding an
alliance treaty through domestic legislative processes allows
the state to signal its interests more clearly to others. States
are certainly selective concerning the treaties they sign and
ratify, suggesting that, if they have done so, then they were

interested enough in striking those agreements. That said, foreign policy interests are not static. If such a signal is sent with the formation of a military alliance, then its strength can easily dissipate over time as new political leaders take power, resources become more or less available, and geopolitical events have the effect of changing citizens' attitudes and policy priorities (see, e.g., Gartzke and Gleditsch 2004). Even the example of the United States and Israel highlights that interests are not at all harmonious despite what leading theories of alliance formation might imply. President Obama and Israeli Prime Minister Benjamin Netanyahu clashed over issues like Jewish settlements in the West Bank and Iran's nuclear program (Gilboa 2013: 20–1). Such disagreements should presumably create more pressure for a treaty. Further, whether legislators, and their voters, care about foreign policy, much less military alliances, is an empirical question with no clear answer. In the United States, for example, Congress has historically deferred to the president on foreign policy issues, at least before the Vietnam War. Even afterwards, the White House still "matters more than Congress," although that is not to say that Congress has no influence on foreign policy, given that it controls the purse strings (Lindsay 1992/3: 608). Finally, there is a question about how reputation costs are generated. Suppose that legislators do care about foreign policy issues and have the capacity to punish the executive when it undertakes actions that are contrary to the national interest. Setting aside the implicit assumption that national interests transcend partisanship and other parochial interests (Trubowitz 1998), legislators and voting publics might still forgive the violation of an alliance treaty if they believe that the risks and costs of compliance outweigh its benefits. After all, fulfilling a treaty commitment could mean a devastating, unwelcome war. As discussed in Chapter 2, reputation concerns are but one of many inputs that figure into a decision to fight, if they matter at all.

So why, then, have written alliances? It may seem that "[a]lliances require specification because the allies need to clarify their degree of shared interests, both to each other and to others outside the alliance" (Morrow 2000: 64). Confirming this view, as discussed in the next chapter, is that states do use treaties to attach escape clauses or specify key conditions about the scope of their commitment, thereby preventing their ally from abusing their military support. However, this view is incomplete. There is not much that is specific in the Washington Treaty, for example. Article V, so often seen as the gold standard of alliance commitments, provides that NATO countries:

> agree that an armed attack against one or more of them in Europe or North America shall be considered an attack against them all and consequently they agree that, if such an armed attack occurs, each of them ... will assist the Party or Parties so attacked by taking forthwith, individually and in concert with the other Parties, such action as it deems necessary, including the use of armed force, to restore and maintain the security of the North Atlantic area. (NATO 1949 [2019])

Most of the specificity contained in the most important article of the Washington Treaty concerns geography – a major issue of contention, to be sure, in light of how several European countries still had colonies in adjacent regions and even further afield when the treaty was signed (see Coker 1982). Indeed, Article VI further delineates the territorial scope of Article 5 and notes that the attack could be "on the forces, vessels, or aircraft" of members in Europe, on the Mediterranean Sea, or in the North Atlantic area north of the Tropic of Cancer. But there is no automatic obligation to do anything even when an attack occurs. No details are given on what assistance is necessary. Mira Rapp-Hooper (2015: 16) finds that alliance treaties have become much vaguer since the Second World War relative to their pre-war antecedents. Still, alliances require at once specification and ambiguity. Written treaties ironically allow for both.

The reason why anyone would want to have a signed agreement is to avoid a future misunderstanding by managing expectations regarding how the signatories are to behave across a range of possible scenarios. Such expectations can be managed not only by defining the conditions under which the main provisions of an alliance treaty become operative, but also by leaving vague as to what might constitute an attack. Clarity can convey to allies and adversaries an intent to advance certain interests internationally and to highlight a willingness to defend militarily a common set of values. Nevertheless, enough ambiguity can allow states sufficient wiggle room to extricate themselves from an alliance obligation if so desired. Adversaries know well enough that a direct attack of some sort would precipitate an alliance reaction, but the vagueness keeps them in the dark as to which scenarios would produce a particular kind of reaction and which would not. The downside, of course, is that adversaries might still exploit this ambiguity in order to see what they can get away with. Not having a public treaty creates too much ambiguity over interests, but no alliance treaty can be completely unambiguous too. Excessive clarity is impossible because an alliance treaty cannot cover every single contingency, especially when looking further into the future. But even if a high level of clarity is possible, it would be impractical and even useless because states will simply adapt or exploit new opportunities as technology evolves, political priorities are adjusted, and threat perceptions change. With too much precision, adversaries would know how to work around a treaty to their own advantage – for example, whether to attack in ways that stop short of clear red lines. When we explore entrapment risks in the next chapter, we will see that states often design their treaty commitments to mitigate such concerns.

Another reason to have a written agreement is that it indicates who is in and who is out. Put another way, the choice is not only whether to sign a treaty with one state, but whether to sign the same treaty with multiple states. Military alliances can be either bilateral or multilateral, with contrasting benefits and shortcomings for each. John Ikenberry (2005: 146–7) argues that the United States opted for bilateral alliances in East Asia because it saw less need to give up policy autonomy to partners that were much more differentiated in size than in Europe. Bilateral alliances are thus easier to manage and so can provide a strong state with more flexibility and greater control over its weaker counterpart (see also Cha 2016). In contrast, the United States preferred multilateralism in Europe because it had a much more ambitious agenda that went beyond simply deterring the Soviet Union – one that required the partnership of "roughly equal-sized states" in order to consolidate centrist democratic governance. A multilateral arrangement like NATO would allay concerns over domination because it provided those partners with more opportunities to articulate their policy demands and to restrain the United States (Ikenberry 2005: 146–7). More cynically, some argue that racial prejudices have shaped alliance decisions – as Christopher Hemmer and Peter Katzenstein (2002), for example, allege in their explanation for why no NATO equivalent exists in East Asia. In their reading, US decision-makers saw East Asian leaders as culturally alien and lacking the racial fitness necessary for multilateral cooperation. This argument may be taking it too far. In Europe, geography and the ground threat posed by the Red Army encouraged a common front, whereas the maritime environment and the difficulties of projecting power over water lessened such a need. Moreover, countries have a say in whether they prefer bilateralism or multilateralism. The United States was, and has been, in fact keen on connecting its bilateral allies in East Asia (Izumiwaka 2020). Unfortunately for Washington, many of them were too suspicious of Japan, so formal multilateral defense pacts were invariably stillborn (Robb and Gill 2019: 161–3). For their part, Japanese leaders themselves were reluctant to build regional security institutions (Izumiwaka 2020: 26–9) Deciding against multilateralism does not imply a total aversion to fostering wider defense ties, but it can indicate a wish to avoid being exposed in the disputes of others. As such, bilateralism lends clarity to the limits of alignment within a wider bloc of states, although states are increasingly opting for multilateral arrangements over bilateral ones (Kuo 2021).

Regardless of the format, a treaty alliance allows for greater efficiency in security cooperation. Of course, greater efficiency does not necessarily imply actual efficiency. At a minimum, uncertainty over intentions and differences in capabilities will put bounds on how credible their alliance will be. That said, a written alliance gives signatories enough confidence that, if they so choose, they can pursue further military coordination, including the drawing up of war plans. This in turn can foster a degree of institutionalization that enables the alliance to weather variable conditions. Arguably, decision-makers sign alliances in part because they anticipate that threat perceptions will shift. Alliances help "lock-in" cooperation so as to mitigate any adverse consequences those changing threat perceptions might have. Interests between prospective allies are already divergent enough at the time of signature for the treaty to be able to manage those differences. Whether by attaching escape clauses or by injecting some ambiguity in the treaty language, states can discourage undesirable behavior on the part of their ally. By treading the fine line between uncertainty and clarity, states can take their security relationship to the next level. Perhaps that is one reason why arms transfers are not a perfect substitute for treaty alliances: arms transfers complement alliances more often than they substitute for them. At least since 2001, according to one study, "the United States sells over twice as much to allies as to nonallies" (Thrall et al. 2020: 113).

## Predicting Future Military Alliances

Some readers may be frustrated by the lack of resolution here. Yet that is the point: military alliances are finicky creatures in international politics. Common explanations of why alliances form tend to overpredict them or to overstate their benefits. Many states face common threats but still refrain from signing an alliance. Unequal alliances may not involve the degree of concession-making often ascribed to them. In either case, the purported goal of the alliance does not seem to require having an actual written treaty. The argument that states need a signed alliance in order to specify their commitments is not sustainable. Alliance treaties can be deeply ambiguous, sometimes on the most important points, and yet that very ambiguity is paradoxically worth conveying on paper. States can leverage equivocal treaty language to disclaim any responsibility if they decide against saving a beleaguered ally, but they can still use this language to keep the adversary off balance or to induce it to back down in a crisis. It can be hard to specify the conditions under which they form because threats are what states decide them to be, and the anarchic condition in global affairs makes clear communication difficult and sometimes even undesirable. The ambivalent character of military alliances can thus be infuriating: the treaties underpinning the alliances allow for anything to happen even when the highest of stakes are at play.

That theories of alliance formation are not, and cannot be, deterministic makes it hard to consider the prospect of new alliances. And indeed, if alliance treaties offer states enough ambiguity to sidestep their responsibilities, then why do not more military alliances exist? More specifically, why have Taiwan and the United States not yet rekindled a treaty alliance? Why have China and Russia so far stopped short of signing an alliance treaty? If alliance treaties are sufficiently vague by design, then why not sign as many of them as possible to hedge one's bets?

The problem is that states need to consider the balance between their shared interests and the differences they have, in addition to the uncertainties and risks of partnership. These assessments are necessarily subjective. Consider how China and Russia have so much in common that a military alliance between them is now imaginable. They are both authoritarian and share a deep suspicion of liberal democracy. US policy documents like the 2018 National Defense Strategy have identified both as strategic competitors that serve to undermine US and allied interests around the world (Mattis 2018: 2). More importantly, China and Russia have stepped up military cooperation by way of more regular consultations, personnel exchanges, joint military exercises, and inter-military trust-building (Korolev 2019: 247). All these indicators point to the potential formation of a treaty-based military alliance, but those countries may not yet have signed a mutual defense treaty. To date, the key bilateral agreement that frames their relationship is the 2001 Treaty of Good-Neighborliness and Friendly Cooperation (often called "the Big Treaty"), which largely emphasizes non-aggression and consultation. The absence of a proper defense pact may be because such an agreement would be liable to be activated as soon as it is signed. Russia is engaged in a war in eastern Ukraine and China might fear that a new alliance would precipitate its involvement in that conflict. Likewise, China has maritime disputes with neighbors in the East and South China Seas as well as land disputes with India. Russia might worry that a new treaty could quickly obligate it to take China's side in those conflicts. Drafting a meaningful treaty that can work around these concerns would be difficult because too many caveats and conditions would undermine the alliance at its own inception. Other states could exploit those treaty features to stoke tensions between Beijing and Moscow. Not having a treaty sidesteps these thorny issues. However, there could be other reasons for not having a treaty. After all, states have in the past established formal military alliances when territorial disputes were in train. US alliances with South Korea and Japan come to mind, as does China's and the Soviet Union's alliances with North Korea. Perhaps, then, the leaders of these two countries have personal idiosyncrasies such that they do not believe in the worth of a treaty (see Han and Papa 2020; Silaev 2021). Perhaps they fear each other by dint of their large size, population mass, and nuclear arsenals. Perhaps it is just a matter of time.

The case of Taiwan and its current relationship with the United States is also illustrative. The island's international status as a sovereign country has deteriorated in recent years as more and more countries have withdrawn diplomatic recognition. By 2020, only fifteen countries had retained diplomatic relations with Taipei. Although its geopolitical challenge is almost exclusively mainland China, Taipei has sometimes adopted a conciliatory approach, with the political party Kuomintang emphasizing economic links across the strait when in power in Taiwan's democratic era. For its part, the United States has, until recently, favored a strategy of political and economic engagement with China. Washington may have supplied Taipei with military weapons, but, in order to minimize protest from Beijing, it restricted those arms transfers to include only those that serve defensive purposes – a policy established in 1979 in anticipation of the United States ending its formal alliance with Taiwan at the time. More recently, however, both Taiwan and the United States have worked more closely together in face of a perceived threat from China. Since Xi Jinping became Paramount Leader in China in 2012, concerns have grown among leaders in Taiwan – especially those from the Democratic Progressive Party – that China might act on unifying the island with the mainland using military force. China's military build-up and steady abrogation of the "one country, two systems" policy in Hong Kong have only fueled these anxieties. Under the Trump administration, the United States adopted a confrontational posture toward China in light of the latter's economic policies and military assertiveness in the East and South China Seas. Early indications suggest that the Biden administration will keep some pressure on China, too. An alliance with Taiwan was long unthinkable because the United States wished neither to antagonize China nor to rekindle a smoldering sovereignty dispute in the Taiwan Strait. Now, such inhibitions may be weakening amid greater wariness with China. Although this alliance would be asymmetric, it need not involve Taiwan making major concessions. A formal military alliance would instead reflect converging threat perceptions and help advance the United States' interests in keeping China mostly hemmed in within the First Island Chain.

Still, an alliance may not yet happen, if ever at all, despite the overlapping threat perceptions. Perhaps leaders in the United States believe that the price of an alliance with Taiwan is too high. Needless to say, it would inflame tensions with China. More uncertain is what would happen if Washington and Taipei were to decide to reformalize ties: would war break out or would the confrontation with

China escalate into a new phase of hostilities? Or perhaps, again, it could be just a matter of time before the two former allies start to salami-slice their way toward a rejuvenated alliance precisely to avoid giving China a clear pretext for aggression.

# 2

# Entrapment

A year after Montenegro joined NATO, in June 2017, President Trump gave an interview to Fox News host Tucker Carlson. When Carlson asked why his own son should "go to Montenegro to defend it from attack," Trump responded that he himself had pondered over this question, before making the observation that "[t]hey're very aggressive people. They may get aggressive, and congratulations you're in World War Three" (Martin 2018). Unsurprisingly, Trump's remarks precipitated a storm of criticism, with many commentators declaring that he had undermined alliance solidarity and thrown into question US security guarantees to NATO. Notwithstanding the crudeness of his answer to Carlson, Trump's words reflected a longstanding anxiety that exists among states with respect to military alliances: that of being dragged into a war that they do not wish to fight because of the unilateral actions of an ally.

Such is what scholars of alliance politics call entrapment. It is a worry that dates back many centuries, even millennia. Ancient Greek historian and general, Thucydides, recorded that, during the epic debate as to whether Sparta should wage war against Athens, one of the Spartan kings – Archidamus – advised that his fellow Spartans should first husband their resources and not get "carried away by the talk of our allies," particularly because Sparta's allies will not bear the "largest share of responsibility" in the conflict (Thucydides 2008: 46–7). The first US president, George Washington, famously warned in his 1796 Farewell Address that, with respect to European great powers, it would be "unwise in us to implicate ourselves, by artificial ties, in the ordinary vicissitudes of her politics, or the ordinary combinations and collisions of her friendships or enmities" (1892: 316). In his First Inaugural Address as president five years later, Thomas Jefferson promised to have "peace, commerce, and honest friendship with all nations – entangling alliances with none" (Yale Law School 2008d). In the time between the First and the Second World War, the United Kingdom worried that extending a "continental commitment" to European land powers would lead to fighting the wars of others.

Chapter 1 ended by conjecturing that several alliances may not (yet) have been formed because potential partners may be anxious about becoming embroiled in certain disputes. This chapter argues that entrapment is a self-denying prophecy. Precisely because leaders worry about becoming entrapped, they take steps that minimize the risk of it happening in the first place. Sometimes entrapment seems to have occurred, insofar as a state fights alongside an ally for dubious strategic reasons, but such an assessment is often a misdiagnosis of what had really taken place. States might go to war, even when the rationale is not sensible, out of the belief that the use of military force is inevitable or even desirable. The reason why Archidamus' plea for caution fell flat on its face was that the war party in Sparta was too anxious to fight their imperial rival due to their sense of besmirched honor. Yet fears of entrapment can have different – sometimes contradictory – sources and thus different solutions.

This chapter explains what those sources are and what measures are available to defenders for mitigating them. In so doing, it shows that, although entrapment is empirically rare, the historical record reveals that decision-makers from various countries facing diverse circumstances do genuinely worry about it. Powerful states are not the only ones that fear entrapment. Some allies have worried about becoming entrapped by the *great* powers, including the United States. These concerns could even intensify if great power competition were to heat up regardless of who occupies the White House, and conflict then becomes more likely.

## What Is Entrapment?

All alliances entangle their members in each other's security affairs, but entrapment is less common. In fact, entanglement is inherent in military alliances. Just as government would not be necessary if everyone were an angel, so alliances would not be necessary if everyone were certain that they would be supported by another in the event of a crisis. As international security scholar Tongfi Kim (2011: 355) explains, entanglement occurs when a "state is compelled to aid an ally in a costly and unprofitable enterprise *because of the* alliance." By contrast, "entrapment is a form of *undesirable* entanglement in which the entangling state adopts a *risky or offensive* policy not specified in the alliance agreement" (emphases in original). In other words, there is no alliance that does not involve entanglement. When states sign a treaty establishing a military alliance, they are therefore implicating themselves in a conflict with a third party. Consider the US alliance with South Korea, which was established after the 1950–3 Korean War. If North Korea were to launch another major assault on South Korea without warning, for example, then the United States might feel compelled to participate in defense of its ally, as per the terms of their Mutual Defense Treaty (Yale Law School 2008b). Such a contingency was expected when the agreement was first negotiated. However, according to Kim's definition, South Korea could be attempting to entrap the United States if it decides to undertake offensive operations against the North. Such actions would be outside the bounds of the alliance treaty. In this scenario, US leaders might feel under pressure to respond if the ensuing conflagration endangers US soldiers or if South Korea begins to lose and needs to be saved. By joining the fray, the United States experiences entrapment.

Scholars have identified several conditions under which entrapment is likely to occur. These arguments can be classified in four categories: treaty, systemic, reputational, and transnational ideological (see also Lanoszka 2018d: 236). Each argument brings to bear its own perspective for when or how an ally might become liable to entrap a defender. Each category also indicates which potential measures can address those risks. These categories are not always mutually exclusive, but they do sometimes contradict one another, suggesting that the effects on the likelihood of entrapment can wash out. To preview the following discussion, some of these perspectives problematically do not even require that a formal treaty exists, which, as we will see, raises important questions about whether they are conceptually sound. Not being beholden to a treaty should give leaders an escape from possible entrapment – they should not be constrained by any apparently binding document, after all. In going about these arguments, three distinct types of actors need to be considered: the defender, the ally, and the adversary. Of these three actors, the ally is the one that might try to entrap the defender into engaging in a war against an adversary that the defender does not want to fight.

## Treaty risks

The first source of risk is the alliance treaty itself – that is, the language of the alliance treaty, or even its very existence, could increase the likelihood of entrapment. The danger compensation principle, or the Peltzman Effect, allegedly kicks in when safety improvements give rise to greater risk-taking, thereby offsetting any security that would be gained. Not long after the wearing of seat belts started to become mandatory in parts of North America, a worry abounded that, as much as they may prevent death and injury in car accidents, they could also embolden drivers to drive faster and thus have more crashes (Evans et al. 1982: 41–2). Just enjoying a security guarantee by way of a formal treaty could lead to similar pathologies. Similarly, entrapment is a case of moral hazard: by providing a form of insurance to an ally, the defender risks creating perverse incentives for bad behavior. Others argue that the scope of the alliance treaty itself provides opportunities for the ally to entrap its defender. The broader the institutional commitment, this argument goes, the greater the entrapment risk (Snyder 1997: 44). A broad institutional commitment involves treaty language that places few, if any, conditions on the provision of military support. Such conditions could relate to geographic scope, war initiation, or threshold of military force. Absent such conditions, the defender exposes itself to a moral hazard problem. If the ally knows it can rely on the support of its defender no matter what it does, then the ally might believe that it will be shielded from the costs of its own actions (Benson 2012: 43–70). As such, the ally could adopt much more aggressive foreign policies than it otherwise would.

The historical example that seems best to capture these worries is the Dual Alliance struck between Germany and Austria-Hungary in 1879. Its founding treaty provided that, if either of the two were to "be attacked by Russia, the High Contracting Parties are bound to come to the assistance one of the other with the whole war strength of their Empires." In other words, if Russia were somehow deemed, by another state, to be an accessory to an attack on either Germany or Austria-Hungary, then the treaty would be activated (Yale Law School 2008a). Compounding the vagueness of the language of this treaty was what was communicated, and perhaps more importantly not communicated, between the two allies in their diplomatic exchanges. Foreshadowing the July Crisis in 1914, in 1909 the German Chief of the General Staff Helmuth von Moltke the Younger reiterated Germany's unconditional support for Austria in a closed meeting of high-ranking officials (Jones 2016: 303). Despite such close alignment between the two Central European powers, their war plans remained uncoordinated and strategic planning followed imperial lines rather than a shared alliance track. Such was the context when Germany decided to give a "blank check" to Austria-Hungary during the latter's dispute with Serbia on the eve of the First World War. German Chancellor Theobald von Bethmann-Hollweg informed the

Austrian ambassador in Berlin that the Austrian Emperor Franz Josef could "rest assured" that the German Kaiser would "faithfully stand by Austria-Hungary, as is required by the obligations of his alliance and of his ancient friendship" (Brigham Young University Library 2020). Shortly thereafter, Vienna presented Sarajevo with a list of onerous demands that made war all but inevitable. When Serbia refused to comply with one single demand, the end result was a local conflict that would go on to escalate into a continental war that involved Germany fighting other European great powers on multiple fronts. After four years of brutal fighting, Germany would go on to lose that war.

Focusing on the treaty offers solutions that can mitigate the risk of entrapment. One could be to deprive an ally of a written commitment. The United States eschewed extending a defense pact with Israel in the 1960s so as to avoid getting embroiled in the disputes with members of the Arab world (Yarhi-Milo et al. 2016). Another solution is not to provide unconditional pledges of support. A defender could make it clear – secretly, if necessary – that it will not come to the aid of an ally in certain circumstances; it could also introduce legal loopholes or outline the precise nature of its obligations (Kim 2011: 358–9). That is what the Eisenhower administration did in the 1950s when it affixed a secret clause to its mutual defense treaty with Taiwan that specified that the United States would not assist the island country if it engaged in offensive operations against mainland China (Christensen 2011: 239). Similarly, the alliance treaty between the United States and South Korea included an understanding on the part of the United States whereby

> neither party is obligated ... to come to the aid of the other except in case of an external armed attack against such party; nor shall anything in the present Treaty be construed as requiring the United States to give assistance to Korea except in the event of an armed attack against territory which has been recognized by the United States as lawfully brought under the administrative control of the Republic of Korea. (Yale Law School 2008b)

This understanding thereby excludes scenarios in which South Korea was an aggressor, as well as instances in which North Korea engages in political subversion that falls below the threshold for war. Even the Washington Treaty included conditions intended to narrow the commitment. By restricting its geographical ambit to "Europe or North America," NATO excluded attacks on the colonies that certain members still possessed at the time. In fact, French President Charles de Gaulle would later inquire as to how that alliance might cover parts of North Africa (Sayle 2019: 47). Finally, some argue that the alliance itself can be a source of restraint. Victor Cha (2016) claims that the United States opted for multiple individualized bilateral alliances with East Asian partners rather than one multilateral alliance in order to exert greater control on each of them individually.

Notwithstanding these potential solutions, does an alliance treaty, or features thereof, really create entrapment risks? If this were the case, then one wonders why critics of allies that engage in "reckless driving" – that is, they become more aggressive in their foreign policies – tend to single out those that do not even have an alliance treaty with the United States, like Israel or post-occupation Iraq (Posen 2014: 44–50). Such criticisms suggest that the institutional features of an alliance have little to do with the problem of entrapment, and may even, ironically, provide a source of restraint. To recall Kim's definition, if entrapment results from a feature of the alliance agreement, then it is likely not actually entrapment but, rather, a form of entanglement.

Conceptually, strengthening a commitment – in lieu of weakening it – might decrease the risk of entrapment. To quote Glenn Snyder (1997: 185): "If the ally is deemed unrestrainable, taking a firm position behind it may yet avoid war by causing the opponent to back down; entrapment is avoided through deterrence. Or supporting the ally might improve its sense of security enough that it could feel safer in conciliating its opponent." In the first instance, because war is an interaction between two fighting forces, an adversary may decide not to do battle against the defender's ally upon assessing that the costs of doing so are too high. No entrapment ends up taking place. Instead, the adversary might make concessions to the ally and its defender. In the second instance, an ally might try to entrap its defender because it feels insecure. Perhaps because it feels that the defender provides inadequate support and that the adversary is accumulating military power, the ally decides to go on the attack when the odds of winning still favor it. Moreover, a tight alliance should, by virtue of its very tightness, give opportunities for the defender to monitor and to restrain the ally so that the latter does not engage in unwanted aggressive behavior (Tierney 2011: 289–91).

The German "blank check" example is alas a problematic illustration of entrapment because it implies that Austro-Hungarian overconfidence forced Germany to go to war. Yet historians have uncovered evidence that German leaders understood what they were doing and even accepted the possibility of war. The German leadership may have viewed 1914 as a desirable time to fight in light of worsening trends in the military balance (Copeland 2001: 56–78). Some historians have gone as far as to argue that German leaders sought to dominate Europe and had already agreed in previous years to wage a major war (Fischer 1974). Others are dubious about the notion that Germany had such ambitions, but nevertheless maintain that its leaders accepted the risk of war and, in fact, may have used Austria as a pretext to fight against Russia (Strachan 2004: 73–4; Clark 2012: 418–19). German leaders may have believed, rightly or wrongly, that a strong alliance with Vienna was essential to German security, since Austria-Hungary helped to safeguard German interests in the Balkans, to prevent complete encirclement, and to manage local Slavic populations (Vermeiren 2016: 84). The "blank check" may have been ill-advised given the costly defeat that would eventually come – former German chancellor Bernhard von Bulöw later called the day of its delivery "a black day for Germany" – but at the time it was a conscious choice that fit Germany's political ambitions and war calculus (quoted in Vermeiren 2016: 56).

In sum, entrapment risks might spring from treaty sources, but treaty solutions are available. If a defender were to worry about entrapment, it would find a way – treaty avoidance, conditionality, precise language, and commitment strengthening – appropriate to the problem at hand. Failure to incorporate restrictions may be a deliberate decision, rather than a fit of short-sightedness and lapsed judgment. To be sure, some might argue that the restraining effects of a treaty's design should attenuate with time. Commitments could even grow beyond what the original signatories intended. Mira Rapp-Hooper (2020: 19) astutely introduces the term "dilation" to describe this phenomenon. She is careful to note that, though such dilation may bear costs, what causes it is nevertheless very difficult – "impossible," in her words – to pinpoint. The longer that the alliance endures, after all, the more likely it is that the foreign policy interests driving each commitment-making ally will change. This transformation need not be fatal to the alliance. On the contrary, the alliance could be flexible enough to adapt and to accommodate such changes.

## Systemic risks

Scholars have identified two sources of systemic risks that, though different, often interact with one another in affecting the likelihood of entrapment. The first is polarity within the international system – that is, how many great powers or different poles of political and military power exist at the regional or global levels. The second is a military-technological factor that scholars call the offense–defense balance, a shorthand term to describe the difficulty or ease of attacking relative to defending. These risks are systemic because they characterize the international system and so are beyond the manipulation of any one state.

Polarity purportedly matters because it affects the relative importance of a great power's ally. In a bipolar context like the Cold War, in which there were only two great powers, an ally did not tip the balance and thus did not have much significance for the security of either great power. In a unipolar context like the post-Cold War period, a single great power – the United States – is so powerful that military alliances should no longer be relevant to its security. At least theoretically, the great power should prefer looser security arrangements (Walt 2009). In a multipolar context, in which there are more than two great powers, the balance of power is more uncertain. An ally could potentially tip the balance, thereby affecting whether a great power could prevail in war against another (Waltz 1979 [2010]: 167–70). Europe in the lead-up to the First World War was multipolar and appears to have exhibited these dynamics. Russia saw Serbia as a partner that could shift the balance against its geopolitical rival in Austria-Hungary, an ally that Germany could not go without. War broke out because chain-ganging – a term scholars use to refer to when states seek to preserve not alliances per se, but the balance of power at all costs – made alliances take on an exaggerated importance (Kim 2011: 358). States find themselves fighting wars they would rationally have preferred to avoid.

The second systemic factor that scholars say can matter is the offence–defense balance. If the defender believes that attacking is easier or cheaper to do than defending, then the ally becomes more valuable to it. The reasoning here is straightforward. A defender might prize an ally because the latter has access to much coveted resources or occupies a geographic position of strategic importance. If defense is relatively easy, then the ally may be expected to resist aggression and protect those assets without much assistance. The defender can accordingly pass the buck to the ally. If attacking is easier, however, then the ally might fall prey to the adversary and assisting it may therefore become a matter of necessity. Accordingly, the defender will be more protective of its ally and so will be much more likely to come to its aid (Christensen and Snyder 1990: 138). This situation creates perverse incentives for the ally, emboldening it to take more aggressive action against the adversary. Being able to distinguish between offensive and defensive capabilities also matters: if offense is dominant and weapons are not distinguishable, the possibility of entrapment intensifies. What made pre-1914 Europe especially volatile, from this perspective, was not just multipolarity, but the apparently widespread belief that attacking was relatively easy.

European armies were in thrall to a "cult of the offensive," imbibing militarist values and irrationally adopting military doctrines that envisioned going on the attack against adversaries (Van Evera 1984). Hence, alliance commitments impelled European countries to march to war following the assassination of the Austrian Archduke Franz Ferdinand on June 28, 1914.

Partly because they are systemic, the effects of these two factors are hard to pin down. Thomas Christensen and Jack Snyder observe (1990) that multipolarity characterized the international system ahead of both world wars, and yet entrapment and chain-ganging dynamics only unfolded in 1914. Getting an ally to bear the costs of war by way of buck-passing was more typical of the interwar period. More importantly, leaders seem to worry about entrapment however many great powers there are out there. As noted, Victor Cha (2016) finds evidence that entrapment concerns relating to East Asian partners like South Korea and Taiwan in the early part of the Cold War encouraged US decision-makers to forge bilateral treaties with them. The Peloponnesian War – a conflict linked to alliance entrapment – unfolded in an ancient bipolar context.

Polarity is an indeterminate factor, but the offense–defense balance is difficult to measure, especially before conflict breaks out. To repeat, the balance is offensive-dominant if the attack is relatively easy. This could be due to geographical reasons – conducting offensive military operations over mountainous terrain or major bodies of water is tricky – but it could also be a function of how mobile and how lethal the most important weapon systems of the day are. The greater the mobility and the firepower, the more offensive-dominant is the balance (Lieber 2005: 35–45). Nevertheless, scholars disagree over how to measure weapons in this manner. Sea-based nuclear-tipped missiles are mobile and have lots of firepower, but they are seen as instruments of deterrence rather than of offensive power. Defensive walls are obviously static and lack firepower, but they release soldiers from the duty of defending fixed points. To be sure, what may matter most are the perceptions of civilian and military leaders concerning the balance. Scholarly efforts to develop an objective measure of this variable may very well be futile. Still, defenders can in fact use weapons transfers to restrain potentially entrapping allies. The United States has historically refrained from providing Taiwan with offensive capabilities that could be used to launch a cross-strait attack against China. Indeed, the 1979 Taiwan Relations Act makes plain that the United States must only offer defensive weapons (Yarhi-Milo et al. 2016). The Soviet Union deliberately kept ammunition supplies of its Warsaw Pact allies low in order to reduce their scope for adventurism (Dawisha 1990: 106).

Yet military doctrinal choices may not have to depend on beliefs about military technology. Consider again the notion of the "cult of the offensive" and pre-1914 Europe. Scott Sagan (1986) argues that European countries adopted offensive military doctrines not because they were enamored with militarist values, but because their alliance commitments made them necessary. If France and Russia had adopted defensive military doctrines instead, then neither of them would find the other to be reliable, as both would be clearly trying to pass the buck on to the other. Having offensive military doctrines thus signaled that they were both willing to take the fight to Germany. The political and military leaders of France, Germany, and even the United Kingdom also thought they had no choice but to adopt offensive postures because they doubted that their states were robust enough to endure a prolonged war of attrition (Hunzeker 2021: 47). Entrapment thus did not occur in the First World War because differences in political interests – independent of alliances – generated the conflict.

In sum, entrapment risks might result from systemic sources, but the unwieldiness and indeterminacy of the relevant concepts make this set of arguments difficult to sustain and to measure.

### Reputational risks

Concern for its reputation might explain why a defender would wage an otherwise strategically undesirable war on behalf of an ally. Reputation here refers to the belief that others would have regarding the probability of the defender aiding an ally in a future crisis. This argument is significant given the propensity of leaders – and pundits – to invoke reputation as a reason for justifying a wide range of foreign policy decisions. Christopher Fettweis (2013: 95) declares: "While all states remain concerned to some degree with their reputation, no country today seems to take the imperative to remain credible as seriously as the United States." US President Lyndon B. Johnson privately believed that military escalation in Vietnam was justified because his own credibility, as well as that of the Democratic Party and the country, were at stake (Logevall 2001: 392–3). Another President – Bill Clinton – argued that the United States needed to remain engaged in Somalia because otherwise "[o]ur own credibility with friends and allies would be severely damaged" (quoted in Yarhi-Milo 2018: 237). Lending intellectual credence to these views, Nobel Prize-winning economist and strategist Thomas Schelling (1966 [2009]: 55–6) wrote that "face" – or a "reputation for action" – is "one of the few things worth fighting over." If a defender falls into disrepute, this thinking goes, then allies might seek other partners and adversaries might go on the offensive.

Entrapment may be due to reputational concerns through at least two different pathways. The first pathway is that members of the defender's chief executive believe they must fight on behalf of an ally out of fear for the reputational consequences that might follow if they do not. In failing to abide by a treaty commitment, these consequences could consist of greater policy concessions to soothe the concerns of distrustful partners or a painful sense of besmirched national honor (Miller 2003; Dafoe et al. 2014). Studies have found that adversaries are more likely to attack if they believe, on the basis of past behavior, the defender will back down (Weisiger and Yarhi-Milo 2015). Leaders might fear being punished by the political coalition that brought them to power if they are perceived to be undermining their country's prestige and status (Fearon 1994). Accordingly, the defender fights for its ally not because a compelling strategic rationale exists, but because the alliance commitment starts taking on intrinsic value. The alliance becomes an end unto itself regardless of what the ally is actually doing. The second pathway is that an ally believes correctly that the defender cares about its own reputation enough for it to fight on the ally's behalf. Sensing opportunity, the ally becomes more aggressive toward the adversary, thinking that its reputation-obsessed defender will bail it out (Layne 2006: 163–72; Posen 2014: 33–50).

Despite leaders' own statements about the importance of credibility, the first pathway has two problems. One is that what allies want is often not a given and could in fact be contrary to what the defender's leaders believe them to be. An ally might wish for the defender to fight for its own interests, but not necessarily for the interests of the other allies that the defender might have, especially if it means diverting resources and attention elsewhere (Henry 2020). Take the example of the Vietnam War: many US allies in Europe and East Asia were unenthusiastic, even ambivalent, about the United States fighting in Vietnam. Some skeptics within the Johnson administration – for example, Under Secretary of State George Ball – advocated that allies would prefer a political settlement to war (Logevall 2001: 244). In fact, the ally may even fear being entrapped by the United States if the conflict is at risk of widening or implicating them by way of their alliance association. Alternatively, as many US treaty partners had believed during the Vietnam War, the ally might think that a military intervention under-taken elsewhere could mean that it would receive insufficient support from the defender in a crisis that directly involves it (Beckley 2015: 33–8, 46–7; Krebs and Spindel 2018). Refraining from supporting a reckless ally might be what truly enhances the defender's reputation instead.

The second, and related, problem is that other national security concerns are likely at play in a defender's decision to back an ally. Reputation is but one factor among many; it may not even be the most important, if it matters at all. To begin with, the loss of an ally could entail giving up strategic territory or other resources to an adversary. If conquest of territory is economically profitable, as some scholars argue, then the adversary could become stronger relative to the defender (Liberman 1998). The defender might calculate that it needs to fight now rather than at a later date when it will find itself at a greater disadvantage. As discussed, such was what drove German decision-making toward Austria before the First World War. The Cold War strategy of the United States was ultimately hinged on the belief that, if Europe were allowed to fall to communism, then the Soviet Union could dominate the continent and use it to project power abroad. The domino theory was popular in US strategic thinking early in the Cold War precisely because it articulated the belief that the loss of one anti-communist state would lead to more losses. The domino theory was as much about keeping a reputation for resolve as it was about relative gains in the overall balance of power, which should not have mattered under bipolarity, if some international relations scholars are to be believed (Waltz 1979 [2010]). Of course, allies would always try to convince the defender of their own indispensability. Yet consider again why states forge alliances in the first place: they do so because they agree that they face a common threat and that a written treaty is useful for conveying their commitment to one another. The mere existence of an alliance reveals that they have some stake in each other's welfare for reasons that are independent of the actual commitment.

What are we, then, to make of statements made by leaders about how national credibility is implicated in one foreign policy crisis or another? Keren Yarhi-Milo (2018) shows that certain political leaders – like Lyndon Johnson, Ronald Reagan, and Bill Clinton – are what she calls "high self-monitoring" and thus adjust their behaviors in accordance with the audiences that they face. Because these leaders genuinely care about the beliefs of others, they tend to articulate sincere concerns about reputation and are more willing to use military force to demonstrate their toughness. If Yarhi-Milo is correct, then what creates the reputation concern is not the alliance per se but individual leaders' own predispositions. Some leaders might believe in such a thing as national honor and so may be more likely to use military force to avenge it if they feel personally impugned (Butt 2019; Dafoe and Caughey 2016). Blaming the alliance for an apparent entrapment may be a misdiagnosis of the problem. Some leaders – like US President Jimmy Carter – have been low self-monitoring and therefore much more critical of the notion that they had to act aggressively to signal their resolve to allies and adversaries.

For the second pathway to operate, three things must be true. The first is that the ally needs to be very confident that the defender will come to its aid in a militarized crisis. As we will see in the next chapter on abandonment, however, confidence in allies is rarely high because war is costly and could lead to unintended consequences. Defenders may decide, in the end, not to support an ally in wartime or even a major crisis. Their support often cannot be taken for granted. For an ally to feel confident about its received commitment, it should at least perceive that their interests and attitudes toward an adversary are already highly congruent (Tierney 2011). A very favorable military balance should further cement that confidence. The second is that the defender comes to its aid only because of reputational concerns. Unfortunately, this axiom might violate the first one: if states share compatible interests, then values other than reputation are at play, making it less clear as to why reputation should be the more significant causal factor. The third is that other allies would support the defender in this venture. After all, if the defender is fighting to preserve its standing with its allies, then those very allies must greet the action approvingly. Nevertheless, if the entrapping ally is fighting a war on dubious grounds that are out of synch with the defender's own interests, then this incompatibility ought to be apparent to the other allies. As such, they should be less likely to support the defender and even voice their displeasure. The defender would thus lose standing – that is, the very thing for which it is supposedly fighting – among them. The only way for these contradictions not to exist is if the majority of the defender's allies think alike and want the same war. Still, because the treaty commitments reflect shared interests and common threat perceptions, acting on the wishes of the majority may be justified on non-reputational grounds as well.

In sum, although many leaders invoke reputation and credibility to justify their foreign policy decisions, sufficient doubt exists as to whether these intangibles create entrapment risks. States may help their reputation by not fighting frivolous or reckless wars, and if they do fight such wars, then they might be acting according to their own definition of national interest rather than the alliance commitment per se.

### Transnational ideological risks

A common argument made about NATO early in the twenty-first century has been that this alliance became less concerned with hard security and more concerned with the transmission of liberal democratic norms and values, as well as the safeguarding of a unique Atlantic identity (Fierke and Wiener 1999; Kitchen 2009: 109). To some extent, this argument became popular because of the justifications that leaders gave for enlarging the Alliance in the post-Cold War period. No longer focused on collective defense against a shared threat thanks to the collapse of the Soviet Union, NATO supposedly took on new commitments that no longer represented the vital security interests of its core members. This "issue slippage," as some scholars call this situation, is problematic because leaders can shrewdly appeal to the alliance's dominant ideology so as to gain membership and eventually to ensnare others in their own conflicts (Driscoll and Maliniak 2016: 594). Elite networks are usually the means by which these leaders are able to manipulate would-be defenders. Such leaders can develop embassy connections, pay lobbyists with privileged access to decision-makers, procure the services of foreign policy experts willing to champion their cause via think-tank publications and popular media, and make rhetorical appeals to ideology (Cooley and Nexon 2016: 88–94). They can even change the make-up of their own state's institutions or play on ethnic affinities to ingratiate themselves with potential defenders (Driscoll and Maliniak 2016). In whatever manner it is done, the potential ally is trying to co-opt a defender by using transnational linkages and ideological arguments. Its goal is to make that defender believe, erroneously, that they share the same vital interests. The archetypal example is Georgia in the years between the 2003 Rose Revolution and its 2008 war with Russia. Its leader Mikheil Saakashvili asserted his liberal democratic leanings so as to appeal to US Congressmen and decision-makers, hoping to gain membership of NATO for his country. If NATO had not entertained his ambitions, according to this line of reasoning, there would have been peace in the Caucasus in the 2000s, or at least a much greater chance thereof.

This argument is flawed. At the most fundamental level, it assumes that the defender's leaders are blinded by their own ideological commitments such that they have a deeply mistaken – if not dangerous – assessment of their own country's true vital interests. One can just as well argue that this claim itself can be ideological, for it presumes a particular view of what those vital interests are and prescribes what should be done instead. Leaders may very well be ideologically driven, but those studying them can be too. A state's interests are seldom given and are usually negotiated among different groups that have their own economic or political preferences (see Trubowitz 1998). Crucially, how leaders' preferences shape foreign policy is rarely direct. For every output of foreign policy, there could be many inputs; it does not mean that the defender has come under foreign influence if it takes a decision that matches the interests of an ally. To repeat what has already been said, a state can fight alongside an ally if multiple values – and not just the alliance commitment per se – are at stake. A state's lobbying efforts could be one cause among many; it may not even be the most important. Besides, lobbying is a competitive process. Others could just as well lobby for the defender to take a position that is contrary to the interests of the ally. Indeed, the more members that an alliance contains, the more challenging is it for a state outside that alliance to go about lobbying successfully. It would somehow have to convince a critical number of members – each with their own varied political institutions and interests – to embrace policies that they would not otherwise adopt. This sort of suasion may only work if sufficient common ground exists. However, if that were really the case, then, logically, allies are not acting contrary to their own interests.

Although the case of Georgia seems to be a cautionary tale regarding the risks of transnational ideological commitments, it in fact highlights empirically the problems that this argument has (Lanoszka 2018d). Upon becoming president in 2004, Saakashvili did make rhetorical appeals to liberal democracy and had sought for his country to receive a Membership Action Plan (MAP) from NATO, which would have put Georgia clearly on the path toward being a member of the alliance. In the meantime, he had gone about rebuilding Georgian state power, asserted that Tbilisi needed to regain control over the breakaway provinces of Abkhazia and South Ossetia, and clashed diplomatically with Russian President Vladimir Putin. However, his efforts to become a formal treaty ally failed at the 2008 NATO Summit in Bucharest. In part anxious not to antagonize Russia and also not to get embroiled in Georgia's longstanding territorial disputes, France and Germany rejected Georgia's MAP application. The Bucharest Summit declaration did say that its members "agreed today that these countries will become members of NATO," but deliberately refrained from suggesting a timeframe (NATO 2008 [2014]). Given German and French opposition, these prospects were dim, despite the use of the auxiliary verb in that declaration. Amid growing tensions between Moscow and Tbilisi, US and NATO decision-makers alike warned Saakashvili against taking steps that risked starting a war with Russia (Tsygankov and Tarver-Wahlquist 2009: 323). Saakashvili did not heed that advice and got ensnared in a trap set out for him when he approved of Georgian forces attacking South Ossetian positions near the city of Tskhinvali in early August 2008. A brief war subsequently ensued between Russia and Georgia, one that saw the United States refrain from providing military support until a month after hostilities had ended.

Several observations are worth making here. For one, Saakashvili anticipated conflict with Russia precisely because of ongoing territorial disputes in Abkhazia and South Ossetia and so sought NATO membership to bolster his position. For another, Saakashvili may have found support in Washington, but he did not find much in Berlin and Paris. The result was that he failed to achieve NATO membership for Georgia. Ironically, Saakashvili had come under criticism in the European Union for his authoritarian tactics at home – tactics that the Bush administration was willing to overlook, suggesting that it had other interests in mind with Georgia (Delcour and Wolczuk 2015: 464). The Bush administration perhaps wanted to compete with Russia on its borders or to support energy projects that would reduce European dependence on Russian natural gas. That said, the United States could have offered a bilateral defense pact to Georgia following its failure at the Bucharest Summit in the spring of 2008. That it chose not to do so, and has not done so since, suggests that Washington does have concerns regarding formalizing security ties with Georgia by way of an alliance. Put together, these observations suggest there were risk factors other than the specter of an alliance that made relations between Georgia and Russia deteriorate over the course of the 2000s. Most importantly, entrapment did not occur because NATO members supposed that armed conflict was at hand and kept themselves out of it. Of course, war might never have occurred in August 2008 had it not been for the preceding controversy over Georgia's status within NATO. Yet because of the personalities involved (Saakashvili and Putin), and because of how difficult and prone to violence territorial disputes can be (see Johnson and Toft 2013/14: 11–17), we cannot say with full confidence that war would not have happened in the 2000s had NATO been completely out of the picture.

In sum, transnational ideological networks allegedly cause states to believe that the vital interests of others are their own, leading them to assume dangerous commitments that carry the risk of entrapment. Nevertheless, the Georgian case suggests that this supposed "issue slippage" is exaggerated.

States remain aware of their own interests and recognize the risks that come with conflict-prone states. Just because they sometimes accept those risks does not imply that they do not know what they are doing.

## Entrapment Risks in the Contemporary Era

In his treatise *Being and Nothingness*, French philosopher Jean-Paul Sartre (1948 [1984]: 96–103) suggested that people deceive themselves by believing that they lack free will and by identifying too strongly with the roles assigned to them by others. To illustrate such "bad faith," as he calls it, in practice, he offers several examples. The first is that of a man employed as a waiter. In adopting the surly and routinized mannerisms often associated with waiters, or at least Parisian ones, the man exercises bad faith because he performs the role expected of him rather than being true to his own personality. The second is that of a woman on a date with a flirtatious man. Although she understands the implications of his advances and knows that she must decide how she will respond, she keeps postponing this decision even when he finally takes her hand. She has bad faith because she denies to herself the options that she has for dealing with her entreating companion.

Entrapment theories ultimately accuse states of practicing bad faith. Specifically, they tend to see states as putting aside their own interests and playing the role of defender in order to fulfill the expectations of others. Rather than ascribing to states the notion that they are making decisions true to themselves, they see such states succumb to the entreaties of others, in part because alliances become ends in themselves rather than means to address security challenges. The entrapping ally has somehow more agency than the entrapped defender despite the power asymmetry that may exist between them. And so arguments about alliance entrapment may be misplaced in their concerns. The historical record indicates that states do worry about it. However, precisely because they worry about it, they take measures to avoid it. Entrapment should be empirically rare. In point of fact, Michael Beckley (2015) finds that, of a possible 188 uses of forces by the United States, only five cases suggest that an alliance commitment might have been at root: the 1954–5 and 1995–6 Taiwan Strait crises, the Vietnam War, the Bosnian War, and the Kosovo War. Yet, in each of these cases, the United States had other motives and interests that led it to behave as it did. Significantly, over the course of the Cold War, US allies engaged in many high-profile military conflicts that did not see the United States directly intervene, including the Suez Crisis (France and the United Kingdom), the United Kingdom and the Malayan Emergency (Australia, New Zealand, and the United Kingdom), and the Falklands War (the United Kingdom). In one case – over Suez – the United States threatened to destabilize the pound sterling in order to force the United Kingdom to withdraw (Kunz 1991). Nor did Russia come rushing to the defense of Armenia – a member of the CSTO – in the latter's 2020 war with Azerbaijan over Nagorno-Karabakh (Popescu 2020). Entrapment is thus a self-denying prophecy. If entrapment risks flow from institutional sources, then institutional solutions are available for managing them. Although scholars contend that entrapment concerns can emerge from systemic factors, reputational concerns, and transnational ideologies, states retain enough room for maneuver to make their own choices. And when they do decide on pursuing courses of action that serve the interests of an ally, they may do so for reasons other than the commitment per se. They might still have freedom of action, as Beckley puts it.

But if entrapment concerns – rather than entrapment per se – remain a feature in alliance politics, how are they manifest in the contemporary era? Already mentioned was Trump's stated concerns about Montenegro. Taken seriously, the fear may be that Montenegro would be emboldened to stoke hostilities with Serbia. Yet this prospect is unlikely considering how relatively peaceful their union and separation had been. Critically, the rest of NATO would not stand idly by even if a conflict between the two did appear imminent. The alliance could very well be a source of restraint. If some states do get involved on Montenegro's side, then it would likely be because they want the fight with Serbia.

More important is the notion that change is afoot in international politics – a change recognized by the 2018 US National Defense Strategy. It avers that "inter-state strategic competition … is now the primary concern in US national security" (Mattis 2018: 1), singling out China, Russia, North Korea, and Iran as competitors in order of priority. This declared focus of the National Defense Strategy may reflect how the global distribution of power has shifted. Although the United States remains by far the strongest country, unipolarity is not as robust as before (Brooks and Wohlforth 2016). China and Russia have been building up their military capabilities and engaging in behaviors that have deeply unsettled the United States and its treaty allies in East Asia and Europe, respectively. Strategic competition may shape entrapment risks if those US allies believe that statements like the National Defense Strategy give them license to behave more aggressively against their adversaries. To be sure, the United States may tolerate – perhaps want – its allies to ratchet up pressure on China, Russia, and other potential adversaries; Washington could even accept a greater risk of military escalation if its allies were to become more hawkish. Conversely, it might chide those allies it deems as being too dovish, as exemplified by Trump's rough treatment of Germany (Helwig 2020). Accordingly, if war were somehow to erupt, entrapment may not necessarily be the root cause because the United States would be the ultimate instigator.

For some of its allies at least, the United States may be the one posing entrapment risks. This situation is ironic because most theories of alliance entrapment cast the defender as the one anxious to avoid war, not weaker allies. Consider the case of South Korea. With a treaty commitment and more than 26,000 US military personnel stationed on its territory, South Korea benefits from a relatively robust security guarantee against North Korean aggression. However, in mid-2017, the Trump administration ratcheted up its rhetoric against North Korea, with the president declaring that he would rain "fire and fury" on North Korea if it continued to make threats on the United States (see Jackson 2018b: 89–108). Had the crisis with North Korea spiraled out of control, US forces in South Korea might have been mobilized to fight. Given the integration of the two allied militaries on the peninsulas, Seoul would have found staying neutral in such a conflict to be almost impossible, and so such strong guarantees can generate pressure for greater independence and perhaps even for an independent nuclear arsenal (see Sukin 2020). Similar anxieties attended the Trump administration's stated goal of exerting "maximum pressure" on Iran by leaving the Joint Comprehensive Plan of Action and assassinating Islamic Revolutionary Guard Corps commander Qasem Soleimani in January 2020. Some countries fear that they might be entrapped if their alliance ties expose them to retaliatory measures. Issues of institutional design, reputation and honor, and transnational ideology may not be generating these entrapment risks as much as guilt by association.

Entrapment concerns do appear to be manifest in non-US alliances. The conventional wisdom holds that Belarus is closely aligned with Russia such that the two allies would indubitably fight alongside one another in any armed conflict with NATO. Yet, upon closer inspection, the Belarusian political leadership has refrained from committing itself too strongly to Russia – at least that was the case before mass protests broke out across Belarus following the August 2020 presidential election. Belarusian President Alexander Lukashenko has not endorsed Russian military actions against Georgia and Ukraine, and has even stymied initiatives to deepen political and military integration with Russia (Vysotskaya Guedes Vieira 2014; Marin 2020: 9–10). Other members of the Russian-led CSTO have also tried to keep their distance from some of Russia's controversial actions. Kazakhstan has pursued a "multi-vector" foreign policy designed to maximize its autonomy vis-à-vis Russia, China, and other great powers (İpek 2007). Armenia is arguably Russia's most loyal ally, but its desire to stand up to Azerbaijan and Turkey best explains its enthusiasm (Vasilyan 2017). Russia's allies modulate their commitments and accept varying levels of risk in light of their own foreign policy interests.

North Korea seems very likely to entrap China given the former's aggressive international behavior. Pyongyang's nuclear weapons program, missile testing, cross-border provocations, and bellicose rhetoric have raised the risk of war on multiple occasions. Since North Korea is China's sole treaty ally and offers a "strategic buffer," a war on the Korean peninsula could implicate Beijing (Park and Park 2017: 376). Short of war, North Korea's behavior has caused various headaches for China, not least of which is greater instability in East Asia and added incentives for Japan to build up its military (Chung and Choi 2013: 250). North Korean leaders have even issued threats against China. The standard line is that China cannot do too much to coerce North Korea for the purposes of restraint in part because it fears the humanitarian and political consequences of regime collapse. Accordingly, if North Korea were to entrap China in a conflict, then it would not be because of systemic polarity, military technology, reputation, or some ideological affinity. It would, rather, be because of certain interests that China would have at stake, independent of the actual alliance. Nevertheless, a war on the Korean peninsula need not automatically involve China. After all, China only intervened in the Korean War when US-led forces failed to heed its signals and were approaching menacingly toward the North Korean–Chinese border. One partial explanation of Pyongyang's distrust of alliances is because it was left to its own devices in the early phases of the Korean War (Pollack 2011). Though it was not a treaty ally of either China or the Soviet Union at the time, this brief experience of fighting has been one driver of North Korean behavior. As the next chapter observes, scholars have often seen abandonment and entrapment as two sides of the same alliance coin.

# 3

# Abandonment

The most salient fear among US treaty allies in recent years is not that they could be entrapped in a war instigated by the United States, but that the United States would abandon them to their adversaries. After all, as President Trump sometimes intimated, in a crisis the United States might not support those allies that had not contributed their fair share to the collective defense burden. He coupled such statements with threats to withdraw troops from Europe and East Asia; indeed, he seemed poised to follow through on those threats by announcing a major pull-out of military forces from Germany in the summer of 2020. He also sometimes made a point of expressing ambiguity in terms of his country's commitment to Article V of the Washington Treaty, which holds that an attack against one member of NATO would be considered as an attack against all members. The stakes became all the higher when Trump at times embraced more bellicose rhetoric toward North Korea while accentuating abandonment fears in South Korea and Japan. As international relations scholars Alexandre Debs and Nuno Monteiro warned (2018: 104), "when combined with the Trump administration's questioning of US security commitments to these two core East Asian allies, Washington's perceived recklessness in dealing with Pyongyang has great

potential for starting a [nuclear] proliferation cascade that
would destabilize international security in East Asia and well
beyond."

Abandonment fears preceded Trump's candidacy for the
Republican nomination. Obama's "pivot to Asia" was partly
an effort to reassure local allies and partners that the United
States would strengthen its engagement in the Western
Pacific despite the 2008 financial crisis and ongoing counter-
insurgencies in Afghanistan and Iraq. Yet this initiative had
a mixed reception, in part because, from the perspective
of those allies and partners, Washington did not seem to
back up this "pivot" with substantial military forces and
policy attention. In Europe, already made uneasy by the
priority accorded to East Asia, allies like Poland and the
Baltic countries sought NATO assurances following Russia's
annexation of Crimea and aggression in eastern Ukraine in
2014. Accordingly, when Trump took office on January 20,
2017, those and other US treaty allies became even more
nervous about whether the security guarantees provided by
Washington were any longer as good – setting aside questions
as to whether they really were so good to begin with – as they
might have been before.

Abandonment concerns are endemic to alliance politics.
As this chapter contends, the nature of international politics
always gives states a rational reason to fear abandonment
by their allies. That said, abandonment concerns are not
constant in their intensity: they wax and wane in terms
of how closely aligned are allies' foreign policy interests,
how militarily powerful allies are vis-à-vis adversaries, and
whether an ally undertakes special efforts to lend credibility
to its security commitments. This chapter highlights how
these efforts can include the forward positioning of conventional military forces that, first, demonstrate how an ally has
"skin in the game" and, second, can favorably shape battle
outcomes vis-à-vis adversaries. Although abandonment
concerns may appear significant these days, they have in
fact been so intense in the past that worried allies have even
sought to acquire their own nuclear weapons. Such drastic
military efforts are not the only consequence of profound

abandonment concerns. If it fears abandonment enough, a worried ally can, alternatively, sign nonaggression pacts or pursue appeasement strategies intended to diffuse adversarial threats.

Reassurance may have its complications, however. Some scholars argue that allies would never be satisfied and adversaries could themselves become dangerously insecure if allied reassurance is overdone. They point to the existence of two dilemmas – the alliance dilemma and the alliance security dilemma – that can make reassurance costly. Scholars routinely invoke these dilemmas to explain alliance politics, but this chapter makes the case that the trade-offs suggested by them are not nearly as intractable or absolute as often asserted. The chapter concludes by considering the extent to which subversive activities that fall short of war can fuel abandonment concerns and what could be done to mitigate them. As unwelcome and unsettling as those activities may be, adversaries might engage in them out of weakness rather than out of strength, which suggests that subterfuge of this variety may not on its own ratchet up abandonment fears on the part of targeted allies.

## Abandonment: Natural, Rare, but Consequential

In alliance politics, abandonment concerns reflect the apprehension that a defender might decide not to support its ally in a militarized crisis. Milder forms of abandonment can entail the withdrawal of, or refusal to provide, diplomatic support to an ally in its transactions with an adversary in peacetime. Still, the alliance literature focuses specifically on the record that states have for keeping up their commitments when war breaks out. According to one oft-cited study, allies have honored their commitments 75 percent of the time (Leeds et al. 2000: 695). Other researchers have determined that the violation rate has varied across historical periods. Molly Berkemeier and Matthew Fuhrmann (2018: 2) find that allies kept their commitments 66 percent of the time prior to 1945, but only 22 percent since then. Of course, whether the fulfillment rate is 75 percent or even 95 percent, no state wants to be the unlucky one that is relinquished to its adversary in wartime. Unfortunately, few, if any, allied states have much way of knowing in advance whether the defender will come to its aid, even if the consequences of abandonment are catastrophic. The classic example is interwar Poland. Poland concluded an alliance with France in 1921, but when Germany invaded in September 1939, France was too hamstrung by lack of readiness and shortages of military supplies to be able to mount an offensive to relieve pressure on its hapless ally (Alexander 1992: 357–64). By the following month, Poland had ceased to be an independent state. In contrast, had London not deployed the British Expeditionary Force to the Western Front in August 1914, Paris could have fallen to the German army, which would have profoundly altered the course of world history.

The major reasons for why such uncertainty exists are international anarchy and the possibility of violence. No agreement struck in international relations is automatically binding because no world government exists to enforce the pledges that states make to one another. As discussed in Chapter 1, states sometimes formalize their security partnerships by way of a written treaty to signal their commitment to one another. Yet those treaties often contain ambiguities about the exact nature of the commitments made. Although attempting to cover every single contingency is neither feasible nor desirable, treaty ambiguity is oftentimes strategic. Vagueness can deter and keep adversaries off balance, but it can also – as later discussed with respect to the alliance dilemma – reduce the risk of entrapment by preventing allies from becoming overly confident about their received security guarantees. However, this very vagueness can come at the cost of creating doubt over whether the defender will really fight for its ally. Given the violence that is possible under international anarchy, such ambiguity can be a matter of life and death.

Some might argue that allies will always say that they fear abandonment for the sake of receiving more political or military support than what they already have. According to this perspective, expressing abandonment fears is a bargaining tactic and so should not be taken seriously. This argument seems plausible, but history is replete with examples of states taking costly actions that are rooted in abandonment concerns.

Two types of action demonstrate that states act out of genuine concern of being abandoned by their defenders in a future crisis. The first is that a worried ally could decide that it has to realign its foreign policy. Most dramatically, an ally might bandwagon with an adversary in order to be united against an erstwhile defender. Though it lacked a formal treaty alliance with either of the communist great powers, North Vietnam eventually sided with the Soviet Union against China given how the latter had failed to give adequate military support against US and South Vietnamese invading forces (Elleman 1996). Such flipping – absent internal regime change – is rare in international politics. More common is the way in which an ally acts on intense abandonment fears by adopting a neutralist foreign policy or making policy concessions designed to accommodate the adversary. Early in the Cold War, West Germany refused to recognize East Germany formally. The Hallstein Doctrine, as this policy was called, meant that West Germany could not have diplomatic relations with other members of the Soviet bloc – with the exception of the Soviet Union – or recognize East Germany's border with Poland. Although this policy grew impractical over time for reasons that had little to do with its status in NATO, West Germany repudiated it in favor of *Ostpolitik* – which would ultimately entail the recognition of East Germany and its eastern border with Poland – following a decade of nagging doubts about the military robustness of US commitments (Lanoszka 2018b: 74–6). If an ally wishes not to make major concessions, then it still might resort to nonaggression pacts with its adversary, thinking that the agreement could impose reputation costs if it is violated (Mattes and Vonnahme 2010). Dismayed by the quality of the security guarantees provided by France, Polish leaders felt compelled to sign nonaggression pacts with Nazi

Germany and, subsequently, the Soviet Union in the early 1930s (Young 1987: 53). That said, sometimes the defender might not be averse to its ally being more accommodating toward adversaries. The defender could welcome the détente as an opportunity to focus on other security challenges or to reallocate its strategic resources. However, an ally realigning its foreign policy by way of appeasement or nonaggression pacts could be undesirable if joint war planning and deterrence were to suffer as a consequence.

The second type of action that intense abandonment fears could generate is that an ally could build up its own military power. Once again, the defender might sometimes welcome such efforts from its ally, especially if it is concerned that the ally is free-riding or lacks an appropriate level of military capacity. Nevertheless, since 1945 at least, states might be tempted to seek their own nuclear weapons capability if they face a major existential threat and have significant doubts about their defender's reliability. Debs and Monteiro's (2018) expressed concern regarding Trump at the outset of this chapter speaks to this issue. The historical record features a number of countries that have acted this way. In the late 1950s, France decided to pursue the bomb following a series of disagreements and frustrations with the United States that revealed how different their foreign policy interests really were. Even West Germany entered into a trilateral initiative with France and Italy when Chancellor Konrad Adenauer received indications that the United States was loosening its military commitment to Europe. About halfway into the Cold War, South Korea and Taiwan all initiated nuclear weapons programs amid worries about whether the United States would continue to support them against North Korea and China, respectively (see Lanoszka 2018b).

Nuclear proliferation on the part of allies can create a number of challenges that a defender might wish to avoid. One is that, if an adversary learns of the nuclear weapons effort, then it might launch a preventive war against the ally (Debs and Monteiro 2014). A preventive war launched for this reason could create unwanted entrapment risks for the defender. Another is that the defender could lose significant control over the ally and how it conducts its foreign policy (Kroenig 2011: 3; Gavin 2015). The defender could also worry that one ally's nuclear proliferation effort would inspire others to go down a similar path. Another concern for the defender is that it could lose "escalation control" – that is, the ability to manage the threat and use of nuclear weapons in a militarized crisis so as to prevent accidents or to avoid provoking adversaries (Rabinowitz and Miller 2015: 84–5). Finally, stopping a nuclear weapons program on the part of an ally is not easy and may even be harder than preventing it in the first place. Sanctions might not work against an ally dedicated to the pursuit of nuclear weapons because such punishment might already have been incorporated in the original risk calculation (Lanoszka 2018b). Some argue that threatening complete abandonment could restrain a proliferating ally, but such a strategy should at best be counterproductive, especially if the ally already believes that its defender is unreliable (Gerzhoy 2015). The net result is for there to be potentially greater regional instability and loss of control, which the defender in most circumstances would prefer to circumvent if possible.

## What Shapes the Intensity of Abandonment Fears?

If abandonment fears can have such negative consequences, what can the defender do to mitigate them? What factors might attenuate the risk of abandonment in the first place? Abandonment fears can never be eliminated, but an alliance commitment can be strong enough that those fears can lose their power. Clearly, such fears vary in intensity because allies do not always seek to acquire nuclear weapons or try to realign their foreign policy, at least not dramatically. Several factors affect the strength of an alliance commitment: foreign policy interests, the military balance between the defender and the adversary, and forward military deployments. The discussion below considers each in turn before examining whether alliance reliability could be bought with economic exchanges and arms purchases.

### Foreign policy interests

The extent to which the ally shares foreign policy interests with its defender is one factor that affects the strength of the received commitment. Unfortunately, expressions of foreign policy interests can be very unclear and leave much room for interpretation.

All things being equal, the more aligned the foreign policy interests of the defender and its ally, the more credible the security guarantee. The ally will be more confident of its defender's support in a crisis if it knows that they both assess threats in the same way and if they have a common understanding of what is to be done about those threats. If intimidated by an adversary, the ally would be more confident that a like-minded defender will be more willing to back it. The ally could gauge the similarity of the defender's interests with its own by examining the defender's record of past behavior to understand its priorities. It can also study official policy documents that the defender's chief executive and bureaucracy make public, as well as declaratory statements issued by the defender's leaders. More generally, some scholars argue that democracies are simply better able to make contracts with one another because their political decision-making is relatively transparent, their leaders have electoral incentives to keep promises, and their constitutions make for durable commitments (Lipson 2005).

Yet relying on leaders' statements and official documents – even those that convey military doctrine – to make inferences about the strength of a received security guarantee is problematic. Because of anarchy, or just simply bureaucratic dysfunction, states can say things that are dishonest or appear contradictory, a problem that can exist even with democracies. Consider some of the official policy documents released by the Department of Defense during the Trump administration. The 2018 National Defense Strategy, for example, declared that "[a] more lethal, resilient, and rapidly innovating Joint Force, combined with a robust constellation of allies and partners, will sustain American influence and ensure favorable balances of power that safeguard the free and open international order" (Mattis 2018: 1). Notwithstanding such expressions of alliance concern, the Trump administration's commitment to allies was seriously questioned, to say nothing of its intent to uphold a liberal international order (Ikenberry 2017). Official policy documents may be reassuring, but they may not matter if the chief executive has markedly different views. There could be a gap between rhetoric and reality.

Another problem is that leaders often send conflicting messages to different audiences simultaneously, be they international or domestic. For example, Trump pushed for closer bilateral ties with Poland and Russia on separate occasions, yet Polish leaders have sought to deepen their country's relationship with Washington precisely to address the perceived threat from Moscow. Alternatively, leaders might genuinely pursue one interest or set of values before changing tack abruptly, whether because of new resource constraints, shifting balances of power, a change in attitudes, or leadership turnover. US President Richard Nixon built his political career on being staunchly anti-communist, but he found it strategically useful and expedient to pursue diplomatic relations with the People's Republic of China at the expense of anti-communist Taiwan in his desire to find some sort of settlement to the Vietnam War. Complicating matters is that unfavorable alliance rhetoric need not imply that the security guarantee has become weaker. A defender can issue statements critical of an ally and still provide it with reinforcements. Such was Germany's experience when the Trump administration added 1,500 military personnel for a multiyear deployment between 2018 and 2020, even though Trump himself was excoriating the European ally for being unfair on trade and indolent in its contributions to NATO (Lanoszka 2018a: 92).

Given these contradictions, allied leaders might be tempted to choose those signals that accord with what they want to see. Motivated reasoning is a decision-making pathology whereby individuals infer the conclusions that they hoped to gather from the evidence presented to them, either because those conclusions are self-serving or because they have some basis in past experiences (Kunda 1990). In his dealings with President Nixon, South Korean dictator Park Chung-hee offers one possible example of motivated reasoning. Six months into his presidency, Nixon remarked to a journalist at a Guam press conference that "as far as the problems of military defense [are concerned], except for the threat of a major power involving nuclear weapons, ... the United States is going to encourage and has a right to expect that this problem will be increasingly handled by, and the responsibility for it taken by, the Asian nations themselves" (Government Printing Office 1971: 549). His response articulated what came to be known as the Nixon (or Guam) Doctrine – the notion that the United States would continue to provide extended nuclear deterrence to treaty allies but would expect allies and partners alike to step up to handle internal and conventional military threats. This speech should have signaled to Park that Nixon was seeking to reduce the US military presence in East Asia while shifting the burden of fighting the Vietnam War to the South Vietnamese government. And indeed, thinking that Nixon would be grateful for South Korea's participation in the Vietnam War, Park searchingly asked for reassurances when the two of them met in San Francisco a month after the Guam speech. Although Nixon proved evasive in that meeting, Park left San Francisco believing South Korea would be immune from any changes signaled by the Nixon Doctrine, in likely part because that is what he wanted to believe. Hence his shock when Nixon abruptly announced troop withdrawals from South Korea in the spring of 1970 (Lanoszka 2018b: 114–15). That leaders are vulnerable to these pathologies should not be surprising given the high stakes of international security: they might delude themselves into believing that they are not really in the worst-case scenario that they fear.

To be sure, regular consultations can go a long way toward reducing harmful misperceptions; they can figure significantly in an alliance relationship. As Snyder (1997: 361) observes, "[w]hether or not it is written into the alliance contract, the very making of the agreement carries with it an implicit obligation to consult with, or at least inform, the ally before taking any major policy initiatives, especially those that impinge on the ally's interests." One issue that dogged NATO in the first two decades of its existence concerned nuclear deterrence: Western European political and military leaders simply did not have much idea about how many nuclear weapons the United States had, what targets they would and could reach, and how they might be used in a conflict situation. This ignorance was not accidental: the United States was deliberately withholding information about its nuclear capabilities and nuclear strategy, even from its closest allies. In the end, Washington realized that its interests would be better served by providing more information to allies. It began inviting allied officials to various military facilities so as to explain nuclear force planning before finally establishing the Nuclear Planning Group to discuss vexing alliance-related issues that involve nuclear strategy (Sayle 2020). In a similar vein, the United States established the Extended Deterrence Strategy and Consultation Group in 2016 to help improve South Korean understandings of the US extended deterrent. With respect to the US–Japan alliance, the Security Consultative Committee – established in 1960 – is the main consultative body wherein leading decision-makers from both countries can exchange views on issues of mutual concern.

### The military balance

Another metric that an ally could use to evaluate its received commitment is the military balance between the defender and the adversary. The more powerful the defender is vis-à-vis the adversary, the better the security guarantee. However, because war is costly for everyone most of the time, a chance still exists that the defender might simply prefer to remain on the sidelines rather than fight. For the ally, the prospects of being abandoned intensify.

To understand why the military balance matters, recall that the problem for the ally is its uncertainty over whether the defender will back it in a militarized crisis. What produces this uncertainty is the costliness of war. If the defender were to engage in war in order to rescue its ally, it would have to expend both blood and capital. Rationally, the defender should therefore prefer to conclude some sort of peaceful settlement with the adversary that would avoid incurring those costs, and it may judge that rejecting this bargain for the sake of the welfare of the ally may not be worthwhile. This aversion to war might be strongest if the defender expects to lose. And so deterrence of a revisionist adversary could very well depend on the defender and the ally being collectively strong enough that they can plausibly do no worse than fight the adversary until they reach a mutually hurting stalemate. If the adversary is confident that it can prevail against the defender and the ally at an acceptable price, then it might be willing to aggress against the ally, if not strike a harder bargain. From an ally's perspective, therefore, it wants to see the defender enjoy military superiority over the adversary.

How might nuclear weapons affect the military balance? There are two schools of thought that bear on this question. One view is that, under certain conditions, nuclear weapons can negate the importance of the military balance between the defender and the adversary altogether. This argument, called the theory of the "nuclear revolution," is as follows. Before nuclear weapons, inflicting harm on a country's population required defeating its army first. Coercive leverage therefore went to the side favored by the military balance since war was usually a contest of strength. However, nuclear weapons – deliverable mostly by way of bombers or missiles – could confer the ability to hurt a population without having to defeat an opponent militarily beforehand. If both sides have survivable second-strike capabilities, whereby they can each absorb a nuclear strike and retaliate in kind, then war is no longer a contest of strength. Amid mutually assured destruction, each side loses enormously. Still, precisely because of the immense destruction that nuclear war entails, the side most willing to push the envelope might be the side more likely to prevail in negotiations. A contest of risk-taking thus determines who has coercive leverage (Jervis 1989). Another view is that nuclear weapons shape the military balance but do not transcend it. War and coercion remain contests of strength, and so having a stronger nuclear arsenal vis-à-vis an adversary confers certain advantages, not the least of which is more effective deterrence (Kroenig 2018; Lieber and Press 2020).

Nuclear superiority is arguably better for alliance politics. Recall how defensive military alliances embody extended deterrence, which a defender practices to dissuade an adversary from attacking an ally. Specifically, for the purposes of extended deterrence, the defender needs to communicate its military ability, political willingness, and resolve to use force against the adversary if it attacks the defender's ally, even if using force could result in a war that is very costly, even suicidal, for the defender. The theory of the nuclear revolution suggests that military strength may be inconsequential when the defender and the adversary alike have credible second-strike nuclear capabilities. Moreover, the political willingness in protecting an ally may be lacking because allies no longer have the same tangible impact on the military balance as before, implying that they can only marginally enhance the nuclear-armed defender's security, if at all. That leaves resolve – an intangible factor that is simply impossible for allies to assess with full confidence in peacetime. If the defender and the ally accept the theory of the nuclear revolution, then extended nuclear deterrence may be unworkable in the face of an adversary willing to accept more risk. Some might also add that there is no good reason to keeping an alliance since a second-strike capability should already ensure territorial integrity and political sovereignty. As former French President Charles de Gaulle remarked, nuclear weapons made alliances "obsolete" (quoted in Waltz 1981: 3). The ally's only rational option is to seek its own nuclear weapons capabilities. International relations scholars have advocated for more nuclear proliferation in the belief that the spread of nuclear weapons would promote greater international stability (Waltz 1981). And yet, as described above, the defender has strategic reasons not to tolerate nuclear proliferation on the part of its allies.

How might nuclear superiority improve the credibility of a security guarantee? One possible logic is that accumulating greater numbers of nuclear weapons signals some sort of resolve, given the costliness and riskiness that such investments entail (Kroenig 2013). Yet this argument may not be entirely correct: numerical superiority need not imply nuclear superiority if weapons cannot be delivered or remain vulnerable to a first strike. More plausible is that what counts as a second-strike capability is hardly stable given technological change and great power competition. A survivable nuclear capability one year could be vulnerable the next, or so decision-makers might believe. Accordingly, a great power defender may choose to expand and to diversify its nuclear weapons arsenal by acquiring more weapons that can be delivered at different ranges, whether sea-based missiles, ground-based missiles, or air-launched missiles or bombs. Doing so can complicate the ability of the adversary to launch a disarming first strike against the defender. Of course, the benefits of nuclear superiority should not be oversold. In 1953, the Eisenhower administration put forward a military strategy known as the New Look, which called for the United States to lean more on its relatively superior nuclear weapons arsenal to deter both conventional and nuclear threats. This strategy came under criticism precisely over concerns that threats to use nuclear weapons against many forms of aggression did not seem very believable (Kaufmann 1954).

Significantly, for the purposes of extended nuclear deterrence, an expanded and diversified arsenal is more capable of damage limitation – that is, of reducing the destruction and death toll that a nuclear exchange would have on one's population by way of so-called counterforce weapons that hold at risk the adversary's own nuclear and military capabilities. Some analysts have argued that extended nuclear deterrence requires the defender's society to be relatively invulnerable to an adversary's weapons (Ravenal 1982: 32). Along these lines, Nixon's National Security Advisor Henry Kissinger noted in 1969 that "Europeans don't realize [the] American nuclear umbrella depended on first strike" (quoted in Green 2020: 100). The reasoning here is that a government that expects an intolerable level of destruction in a nuclear exchange would be much less likely to risk one in the defense of an ally. Whether damage limitation is technically feasible or dangerously aspirational has been the subject of immense debate. What is clear is that US decision-makers have believed that damage limitation is possible in light of their investments in missile defense and counterforce weapons (Lieber and Press 2020). Finally, a diverse nuclear weapons arsenal can also mitigate the effects of decoupling – a situation that occurs when an adversary isolates the ally from its defender through the use of nuclear weapons ranged differentially so that the defender would be less likely to retaliate, preferring instead to sit out the conflict (Ravenal 1988: 61; Green 2020).

Weighty moral questions about general nuclear war notwithstanding, a major problem with using nuclear weapons relates, unsurprisingly, to their devastating effects on the ally's territory. West German citizens were horrified to learn of the results of NATO's Carte Blanche military exercise in 1956, which stimulated the nuclear defense of their country against Soviet aggression. Although the United States still held nuclear superiority over the Soviet Union at that time, the military exercises revealed that West Germany would incur mass casualties and significant devastation (Moody 2017: 831). A paradoxical situation thus arises: to save the ally by way of extended nuclear deterrence, it has to run the risk of the ally being destroyed. And because nuclear war is so costly, and mutually assured destruction so difficult to escape (once the defender and the adversary obtain what would be considered as survivable second-strike capabilities), the defender may still decide that the loss of an ally is preferable to fighting. The defender could very well seek nuclear superiority over the adversary to acquire an advantage, but basic problems of credibility remain and the ally could stay motivated to develop its own nuclear capabilities. How can the defender thus assuage abandonment concerns and prevent nuclear proliferation?

### Forward military deployments

Statements of foreign policy interests can be noisy, and even a militarily superior defender may not wish to countenance the risks of warfare, especially if it is nuclear. To signal commitment under these conditions, the defender could forward deploy its own military forces on or near the territory of its ally. Doing so can achieve two separate but sometimes overlapping benefits for reassurance.

One benefit stems from how forward deployed military forces are deliberately put in harm's way: if an adversary attacks the ally, then the defender's own military forces might come under fire as well. Even if they survive, the fact that they are in mortal danger binds the defender's own decision-makers to do something on their behalf. These decision-makers may even come under pressure domestically to escalate the conflict by widening the use of military force against the adversary. These tactics are what are known as trip-wires. The defender shows that it has "skin in the game" such that it cannot easily back off from the fight. The US Army's Berlin Brigade during the Cold War is the archetypal example of a "trip-wire" force. Containing several thousand military personnel in its ranks, and surrounded completely by hostile territory, the Berlin Brigade could not possibly have withstood a determined Soviet military effort to seize West Berlin. What was comforting, at least theoretically, was that their deaths would have precipitated a devastating US response, thereby preventing their deaths in the first place (Schelling 1966 [2009]: 47–8). The logic of the trip-wire did not just emerge with nuclear weapons. Prior to the First World War, French general Ferdinand Foch remarked that he only needed one British private to help guarantee British support for France, adding that he would see to it that the private would die if hostilities with Germany were to break out (Macmillan 2014: 376)

Another benefit comes from raising the direct costs of war that the adversary has to incur if it does choose to attack. Oftentimes, when a great power forward deploys military forces on the territory of an ally, it posts large numbers of them with access to heavy weapons and ammunition. These "combat-credible" forces can fight alongside the ally's military against an invading army at least until they reach a mutually hurting stalemate. Accordingly, the forward deployed personnel are not stationed on an ally's territory to be killed but to kill (Hunzeker and Lanoszka 2016: 18). This distinction is important because many analysts tend to conflate any forward deployed force with a trip-wire. As of 2021, US Forces Korea comprised 28,500 military personnel, but this is not a "trip-wire" per se because, in all likelihood, these forces – together with the South Korean military that falls under its wartime command – possess the firepower to defeat a North Korean invasion. That is not to say that dead Americans in Korea would not generate pressure for a harsh response. They probably would, but dying is not the core wartime function of those soldiers.

To be sure, combat credible forces do perform a deterrence mission and so some explanation of their exact deterrence role is necessary. Note that deterrence aims at preventing an adversary from using force to revise the status quo unilaterally by communicating clearly how such actions are unacceptable. Crucially, deterrence involves having the political willingness and military ability to respond to the adversary if it does try to change the status quo. With nuclear weapons and mutually assured destruction, nuclear deterrence typically takes the form of deterrence-by-punishment, whereby a certain type of aggression elicits a devastating nuclear riposte in one fell swoop. Yet deterrence-by-punishment can lack credibility when the costs of implementing the threat are greater than the cost incurred by the adversary's provocation. Surrender, no matter how distasteful it may be, is rationally better than dying. However, trip-wire forces can make the promise of deterrence-by-punishment more believable, even under mutually assured destruction, because of how they represent "skin in the game." In contrast, combat-credible forces that are forward deployed enhance deterrence-by-denial. Thanks to the firepower that they can bring to bear, they make it harder for the adversary to win on the battlefield in any military operation launched against the ally. Deterrence-by-denial is not the same as defense since the latter would involve forward deployed forces protecting every point of the ally's territory (Schelling 1966 [2009]: 78).

The type of forward deployed forces that the defender might send depends on geography. Military power operates in multiple physical domains – ground, sea, and air – and can be deployed abroad permanently or rotationally. Strictly speaking, of course, nothing in international politics is permanent. In military parlance, however, a permanent presence means that certain units are stationed indefinitely on the territory of an ally, whereas a rotational presence means that units are deployed in a limited time frame before being cycled out. A permanent ground force presence is arguably the strongest military commitment that the defender can forward deploy. People live on the land, and wars are generally fought over territory. Ground forces are relatively unmovable, for "ships and aircraft can sail and fly away on short notice, but it takes considerable time and money to re-deploy thousands of ground troops" (Hunzeker and Lanoszka 2016: 21). That said, a major ground presence may not always make sense for the ally. Countries in a largely maritime environment will value – and so might receive – sea (and air) power more. Whereas the US Army is most represented in South Korea and continental Europe, the US Navy, the US Marine Corps, and the US Air Force constitute the bulk of the forces that the United States has in Japan.

Political constraints can push a defender to deploy rotational forces in lieu of forward basing permanent forces, however. Rotational forces have the allure of flexibility, something that a defender might desire if it wishes not to overcommit to the ally. On occasion, international agreements or understandings between rivals prevent anything but rotational deployments. For example, the 1997 NATO–Russia Founding Act provides that "the Alliance will carry out its collective defense and other missions by ensuring the necessary interoperability, integration, and capability for reinforcement rather than by additional permanent stationing of substantial combat forces" (NATO 1997 [2009]). Accordingly, the United States and other NATO member countries have been reluctant to establish a permanent presence in the Baltic littoral region so as to remain in good standing under the terms of the Founding Act. They have instead relied on rotational forces in going about such missions as NATO's enhanced Forward Presence in Poland and the three Baltic countries (see Lanoszka et al. 2020). Rotational forces may not necessarily suffer for fighting power. They can begin their deployment already on a high level of readiness such that they are prepared to fight if necessary. However, as John Deni (2017) shows, rotational forces have significant drawbacks. Beyond the stresses put on the families of the rotated personnel, rotational units suffer from lower manning units than permanent deployed forces and lack the local knowledge and familiarity that permanent forces would have with respect to the ground and the people they are supposed to defend.

A permanent military presence can be a strong commitment device, but withdrawing it unilaterally from an ally's territory can be destabilizing and accentuate abandonment fears. This is especially true if the ally is on the frontline and faces down a direct military threat from its adversary. Cold War-era West Germany and South Korea are cases in point. In 1956, West German Chancellor Konrad Adenauer read news reports indicating that the US Army would be subject to major restructuring and that major troop withdrawals from his country and elsewhere in Western Europe appeared to be in the offing. Given how the United States had embraced a new military posture that emphasized nuclear weapons at the expense of conventional military power, Adenauer interpreted the news report – which proved to be false – as an indication that Washington was giving up on containing Moscow. By the end of the following year, he entered his country into a trilateral initiative with France and Italy to develop nuclear weapons. Although this project went nowhere, doubts concerning West Germany's nuclear intentions carried over into the following decade and shaped negotiations over what would become the Nuclear Nonproliferation Treaty (Lanoszka 2018b: 48–78). South Korea exhibited a similar dynamic. Having believed that his country would be immune to whatever the Nixon Doctrine had in store for East Asia, South Korean President

Park Chung-hee felt blindsided when Nixon announced the withdrawal of one division from the Korean peninsula. Park probably believed that more withdrawals would eventually happen – a reasonable belief considering the Nixon Doctrine and the growing wariness among members of the US public about military engagement abroad. Within several years, Park had directed the establishment of a nuclear weapons program. Even though the United States eventually worked hard to curb this effort in the mid-1970s, South Korea's nonproliferation commitments remained suspect for several years thereafter (see Taliaferro 2019: 160–210).

### Can reliability be bought?

The discussion so far has focused on how a defender can convey credible security guarantees toward an ally. A question remains: can alliance reliability be bought? In other words, can a worried ally spend money on the defender in a way that enhances the guarantee? This question is timely. Over the course of his presidency, Trump repeatedly warned that allies that did not pay up might be left to their own devices. Though he issued such warnings in the context of ongoing burden-sharing debates, which will be covered in the next chapter, those admonitions suggest that providing economic benefits to the defender can increase the probability of intervention and thus enhance deterrence.

This view has some support. Paul Poast (2013) argues that military alliances that feature economic provisions are more likely to see treaty obligations fulfilled. The reasoning follows the logic of issue linkage. If one issue-area proves too difficult for negotiations, then tying it to another issue-area increases the probability of finding some sort of win–win solution for everyone. All parties will stick to the agreement in order to continue enjoying the benefits that they accrue from it. Poast offers the example of France's insistence on incorporating a commercial provision into the alliance treaty with Poland. As a result, Warsaw got the security guarantee it wanted from Paris, while Paris made money from helping to secure a newly created country ensconced in a precarious geopolitical situation. The alliance was consequently more credible. Along these lines, buying military weapons from the defender might also bolster the alliance. The defender, according to this reasoning, will be more likely to rescue an ally for fear of losing a customer.

The notion that reliability could flow from such exchanges has two problems. The first is that predicating an alliance agreement on commercial clauses can stoke resentment, raising the concerns that the alliance is nothing more than a racket whereby the ally pays tribute to receive protection from the defender. If the defender demands payment once, then it can just as well demand another, possibly greater, payment when the ally faces a perilous situation. The second, and more significant, problem is that any earnings that the defender makes from these commercial transactions might be insufficient for it to defend the paying ally. The costs of fighting on its behalf could still outweigh the benefits, even if the ally has spent money procuring weapons from the defender. Rationally, in fact, past benefits should not even factor into present decisions about whether to fight. Such is the sunken-cost fallacy. And in point of fact, the Polish example highlights these weaknesses of the argument. France's insistence on attaching commercial provisions embittered Polish business and political elites (Wandycz 1962: 221–2). More crucially, over the course of the interwar period, Warsaw came to perceive Paris as being increasingly unreliable because their interests diverged and France's military power had waned relative to Germany's (Wandycz 1988). The lack of a major French offensive against Germany in the autumn of 1939 proved the point.

## Complications with Reassurance

A number of factors affect the strength of a security guarantee, but there are two additional but related issues that the defender might need to consider in going about reassuring a worried ally. The first relates to the alliance dilemma. The second pertains to the alliance security dilemma. Glenn

Snyder (1997) conceived both of these concepts to highlight the difficult trade-offs that states must face when determining their alliance commitments.

The alliance dilemma is rooted in the observation that entrapment and abandonment are two sides of the same coin, at least from the perspective of the defender. Giving too weak a commitment might make an ally worry about abandonment and so could drive it to perform unwanted actions, but giving too broad a commitment could raise the risk of war and, consequently, make the defender fearful of entrapment. True to its name, the alliance security dilemma is a modification of the classic security dilemma. According to the security dilemma, two states favorably predisposed to the status quo could still be uncertain about each other's intentions and so misinterpret defensive measures as offensive ones out of fear. A spiral ensues in terms of an arms race, thereby heightening the risk of war (Jervis 1978). The alliance security dilemma thus holds that when two allies strengthen their ties to one another to augment their own security, the adversary might perceive this move as offensive when, really, it is defensive. One insight of the alliance security dilemma is that the requirements for reassuring an ally could not only undercut deterrence but also provoke an adversary into launching a pre-emptive war. After all, the adversary may fear that members of an opposing alliance are tightening their military links in order to mount offensive operations against it.

Put together, these dual dilemmas make life difficult for the defender because it has to work hard to assure and to deter both the ally and the adversary. That is, the defender may have to assure the ally of its support – what international security scholar Jeffrey Knopf calls alliance-related assurance – while also dissuading that ally from pursuing reckless actions like entrapment or an independent nuclear weapons program. The defender must also discourage the adversary from undertaking aggressive policies that undermine the alliance, while assuring that same adversary that its cooperation would be rewarded and not exploited, or what Knopf (2011: 380–1) calls deterrence-related assurance.

But do such dilemmas really exist? As noted in the previous chapter, even Snyder acknowledged that, under certain circumstances, one way to address an entrapment risk is to tighten, rather than reduce, the commitment. Such a move might secure the ally to the extent that it feels neither grave abandonment fears nor the need to resort to some sort of pre-emptive or preventive war to secure its own interests. Still, the institutional solutions for mitigating entrapment risks – precision of language, conditionality, and scope – are usually written into the alliance treaty. The fact that the treaty is signed in the first place should carry enough of a signal of commitment to offset any abandonment fears that the ally might have when the alliance is established. Nevertheless, the importance of the treaty itself as a commitment device will most probably dissipate over time, not least because political circumstances change. By the same token, any ambiguity that exists in the document might become magnified with age as military technology changes and states' interests evolve.

There are other reasons to suspect that the significance of the alliance dilemma is overstated. Abandonment fears are likely to exist no matter what, if the adversary is at least as strong as the defender in the theater of operations where the ally is situated. An ally that borders the adversary directly and is cut off geographically from its defender is especially prone to have persistent abandonment fears. Because the adversary could use its military power to isolate the ally, while using capabilities to keep the defender's reinforcements from providing relief in wartime, the ally can never be truly certain of the defender's support. Shared foreign policy interests and forward deployments can keep such abandonment fears at manageable levels. More importantly, as regards the alliance dilemma, they also lessen entrapment risks. After all, entrapment, by definition, is less probable the more that foreign policy interests overlap between the defender and the ally. And if the defender forward deploys its own forces to the ally's territory, then those forces would be training with the ally's own military and thus should have better intelligence and so be able to anticipate and prevent any undesirable behavior. In some cases, the ally's forces could even fall under the command of the defender, reducing even further the potential for unwanted behavior. The United States held the primary leadership role for both wartime and peacetime operations on the Korean peninsula for the entire Cold War, not relinquishing peacetime operational control until as late as 1994.

The severity of the alliance security dilemma depends on the nature of the adversary as well as on the rivalry. If the adversary has unlimited aims and a willingness to resort to brute force, then no dilemma exists. The alliance will need to be as strong as possible so that its members do not fall victim to the adversary's depredations. Thus, there was really no alliance security dilemma, or should not have been, between France and Nazi Germany in the 1930s because Hitler harbored extraordinarily revisionist aims that sought to upend the international order entirely. Only overwhelming military power would have likely dissuaded him from launching bold but successful campaigns against his neighbors throughout that decade. However, if the adversary has more limited aims and largely uses its military to defend its core values, then the requirements for deterrence should be much lower. In fact, exceeding those requirements for the sake of assurance could prove counterproductive. Concentrating a large military force – one capable of undertaking offensive operations – on the territory of a front-line ally can deepen the adversary's own insecurity and create pressure for it to launch a pre-emptive strike.

If the alliance security dilemma depends on the nature of the adversary, then understanding its intentions is imperative. This is easier said than done – hostile images of an adversary can sometimes come too easily, while policy disagreements can degenerate into mutual enmity. How we assess adversaries can often say as much about ourselves as about them. And yet the historical record indicates that there are states that really do have aggressive foreign policy goals. The current relationship between the West and Russia illustrates this conundrum (see Lanoszka and Hunzeker 2019: 7–20). One view is that Russia is an imperialist power eager to restore its influence and territorial control across Eastern

Europe and Eurasia. It will use military force to pursue this revanchist project, as it has already done by waging a war against Ukraine and subverting Georgia's territorial integrity little by little. No alliance security dilemma exists because the underlying problem stems from politics, not uncertainty as to what a military acquisition program represents. An alternative perspective is that Russia may simply wish to preserve its own territorial integrity and to prevent its encirclement by opposing alliances. It will use military force to assert its red lines, as it has already done in a bid to block Ukraine and Georgia from joining NATO. If this assessment is correct, then an alliance security dilemma would exist, provided, of course, that NATO does not have revisionist aims of its own, as Russian leaders and others sometimes allege.

Another way of looking at the problem involves considering the nature of the rivalry. The classic security dilemma postulates that insecurity primarily results from states' decisions to seek armaments as a bona fide way of safeguarding their own territorial integrity and political autonomy. At the root of the conflict is the uncertainty and the resulting fear about what a military build-up – however defensive in intent it may really be – means for others. But what if the conflict is instead about clashing political interests? Despite having sketched out the security dilemma in a seminal essay published in the late 1970s, Robert Jervis (2001: 58) famously declared much later that the Cold War was not a security dilemma per se because the conflict was ultimately a "clash of social systems." If true, then an alliance security dilemma logically cannot be operative if no security dilemma exists between the defender and the adversary. Actions that appear to manage the alliance security dilemma – like preventing allies from acquiring their own nuclear weapons – may have been borne out of other motives to maintain influence over the ally rather than avoid provoking an adversary like the Soviet Union.

Regardless of whether rivalries do feature security dilemma dynamics, some readers might offer the rejoinder that one cannot simply assume that an ally's own intentions and threat assessments are what the ally reports them to be. Because anarchy allows states to misrepresent their own

interests and resolve, an ally might overstate its own sense
of insecurity in order to extract as much support from their
defender as possible. They might, for example, exaggerate the
capabilities and aims of the adversary or argue that its goals
are much more expansive and hostile than what is really the
case. An ally that expresses abandonment fears could really
be an entrapment risk. Even undertaking a nuclear weapons
program, one might argue, could just as well be an effort
to grab the defender's attention and to manipulate it into
reaffirming its security guarantees.

A treaty ally will often want as much as it can get from
their defender, but the notion that it would go to such
great lengths to deceive the defender is unlikely. The ally's
ability to practice deception is limited. To begin with, trying
to grab attention by way of, say, nuclear proliferation
could backfire on the ally. If the adversary detects the
nuclear weapons program, then it could, at worst, launch a
preventive war or, at best, name and shame the ally and its
defender. Whether the nuclear weapons program will compel
the defender to reassert its security guarantees cannot be
assumed given the difficulties of prediction in international
politics. Most importantly, the defender is not blind. It will
have its own intelligence capabilities to assess the adversary's
military power and foreign policy intentions. It can judge the
adversary for itself and not have to take the ally's word for
it. By the same token, the defender will use those intelligence
capabilities to survey its own ally as well. It can independently determine the balance of power between the ally
and the adversary, and make forecasts accordingly. Burden-
sharing controversies emerge precisely because the defender
can monitor to some extent who spends money on what,
relative to what is needed against the adversary.

## Fearing Abandonment in the Early Twenty-First Century

Abandonment fears are natural and pervasive but rarely
intensify to the point that states dramatically change their
foreign and defense policies. The degree of convergence in

foreign policy interests, the military balance, and whether the defender has forward military deployments (and by what magnitude) are key factors that can affect the perceived strength of an alliance commitment. That said, some readers may argue that advances in technology and global governance are altering the strategies that adversaries use to undermine opposing alliances. By extension, those strategies affect what alliances must do in response to practice assurance. Countries are not so much worried about the prospects of being abandoned by their treaty partners while enemy military formations cross into their territories, these readers may argue, as they are about receiving inadequate support against subtler forms of aggression. After all, even NATO Secretary General Jens Stoltenberg (2019: 4) declared in 2019 that "a serious cyberattack could trigger Article V of our founding treaty."

As Mira Rapp-Hooper (2020: 179) cautions, in most US military alliances today, the bar for external aggression to trigger treaty obligations may be too high. In at least one case, the US alliance with South Korea, this high bar was by design. US negotiators inserted a statement of understanding on the part of their country that "neither party is obligated ... to come to the aid of the other except in case of an external armed attack against such party." The Washington Treaty also refers to "armed attack," but it does so without the modifier "external." In addition to clarifying its territorial scope, the Washington Treaty notes that an armed attack on a member can be "on the forces, vessels, or aircraft of any of the Parties." Tactics and strategies that operate below common thresholds for war – like those that do not involve major armed formations crossing internationally recognized boundaries but instead involve criminal activity or small, seemingly isolated armed incidents – complicate deterrence, the *raison d'être* of many military alliances today (see Gill and Ducheine 2013: 443–5). Eschewing more popular but problematic buzzwords like "hybrid warfare" and "gray-zone conflict," Rapp-Hooper (2020: 147) invokes the concept of "competitive coercion" to describe activities pursued by adversaries of the United States that deliberately avoid open conflict but can have a corrosive effect on defensive alliances. These activities are competitive, because they serve to advance political goals at the expense of their targets. They are also coercive, because they aim at changing the status quo while operating below recognized thresholds for war. What makes competitive coercion an enticing strategy are its cheapness and flexibility: competitive coercion can sometimes allow the adversary to plausibly deny its culpability as well as manage escalation risks (Rapp-Hooper 2020: 148). It can also aim at dividing allies from one another, whether to diminish their counter-balancing potential or to reshape their political preferences by supporting certain groups over others (Crawford 2011; Wigell 2019). Competitive coercion can encompass the use of disinformation campaigns and cyber operations, the deployment of military capabilities ranged at some allies but not others, limited border incursions, and the cultivation of friendly elites who can subvert the political institutions of a target state. Progress in international law, ironically, has perhaps incentivized certain subversive activities. Michael Poznansky (2020: 4) argues that states sometimes engage in "covert action" to "retain credibility and evade hypocrisy costs," the latter of which they would otherwise incur by flagrantly violating their international legal commitments regarding nonintervention in the domestic affairs of another state. Uncertainty abounds as to what exactly there is to deter, how to communicate those red lines, what responses are appropriate if deterrence fails, and what policy measures should be adopted to prevent the failure in the first place. Monitoring and the enforcement of commitments not to engage in such low-level aggression fall part. The alliance management problem, bluntly put, is that members of an alliance end up losing to an adversary without a shot being fired due to the successful use of competitive coercion.

This line of reasoning about competitive coercion is compelling and widely shared. Yet it suffers from two short-comings in such a way as to reinforce the argument that this chapter makes – namely, that abandonment fears are usually present but rarely become so intense as to push states toward neutralism and other dramatic policy changes.

The first problem is that competitive coercion could paradoxically be due to deterrence success. Adversaries may resort to tactics that fall under the threshold for war – assuming that a shared understanding of it exists – precisely because they are worried about crossing it. Such has been the case, arguably, with how Russia and China have behaved toward some of their neighbors in recent times. Following Russia's annexation of Crimea from Ukraine in 2014, the Baltic countries have been particularly unnerved by Russia. Although their political circumstances fundamentally differ from those of Ukraine, thanks to their membership in NATO and the EU, they have been concerned that they may fall victim to major Russian aggression. Lending justification to their worries is how Russia has mounted disinformation campaigns, made illegal incursions into their airspace, and sought to make connections in local Russian minority communities through its Compatriot Policy. For its part, China insists on the eventual reunification of Taiwan with the mainland under the control of the Chinese Communist Party, and has at times encroached upon Taiwanese airspace and waters with various military craft. But one reason why China and Russia have arguably refrained from undertaking bold military action (so far) against US allies is because they lack the military capacity to mount an outright seizure at their expense. Russia especially may worry about doing anything more because the potential costs of triggering Article V outweigh the benefits – an irony in light of concerns among NATO allies about whether Article V would amount to any meaningful response on their behalf. As a result, these states undertake competitive coercion to demonstrate their dissatisfaction with the status quo and their willingness to disrupt it. Hence adversaries may resort to competitive coercion because of deterrence success, not because deterrence has necessarily failed.

The second problem is that solutions offered to address competitive coercion may be unnecessary. Rapp-Hooper (2020: 179) notes that many US alliance commitments, such as NATO's Article V, may be outdated because they are too anchored in Article 51 of the United Nations (UN) Charter, which states that nothing in that document "shall impair the inherent right of individual or collective self-defense if an armed attack occurs against a Member of the United Nations, until the Security Council has taken measures necessary to maintain international peace and security." Accordingly, Rapp-Hooper argues that conflict thresholds can be revised by appealing to Article 2(4) of the UN Charter, which forbids "the threat or use of force against the territorial integrity or political independence of any state." Political independence is an elastic enough phrase to justify a lowered threshold, especially if a strong argument can be made that a competitive coercive effort constitutes a subterfuge and thus a form of intervention. To be sure, none of the key terms used in Article 51 – "attack," "armed attack," "collective self-defense," "international peace and security" – is clearly defined. The vagueness of these terms should in turn permit broader interpretations of international law that can accommodate technological developments and help push back against subversion.

Lowering the conflict threshold via international law may in fact be counterproductive, since doing so could have the unintended effect of increasing both entrapment risks and abandonment fears among some allies. Consider a situation similar to the major distributed denial of service (cyber) attacks that struck Estonian institutions in 2007. Many observers believe that state-sponsored or state-affiliated organizations operating in Russia were responsible for those attacks. This belief arose because they took place amid major protests by members of Estonia's Russophone minority over the relocation of a Soviet-era Second World War memorial (see Herzog 2011).

Had the attacks activated alliance obligations because they crossed a lower conflict threshold, a number of policy difficulties would have ensued. Some NATO members would have been uneasy about being potentially implicated in a major dispute with Russia if it meant puting Article V into play. (Recall that, in 2007, relations between NATO and Russia were souring but were nowhere near as tense as they would be a decade later.) To limit the force of their commitments in this crisis, those NATO members could highlight the uncertainty surrounding Russia's culpability. Some may even raise questions about the decision-making of the Estonian authorities that could have contributed to the crisis in the first place; arguably, for example, that they were insensitive to the needs and wishes of the local Russophone community. Questions about proportionality and response could also produce major disagreement. For those of the view that something must be done, differences of opinion on what exactly that something should be could arise. Naming and shaming could be sufficient for some NATO members, whereas others might argue that counter-cyber operations are necessary to show resolve and to reassert red lines. Yet others might favor minor economic sanctions. A lower conflict threshold could also, ironically, stir abandonment concerns, by creating the expectation that an aggression crossing it would generate some sort of response. To continue with the reimagined scenario, Estonia might be unimpressed by the reaction of its allies, worrying that displays of insufficient resolve and support could simply encourage more nefarious cyber operations by adversaries. Though not perhaps full-blown abandonment, perceptions of inadequate support can persist, with the result that the underlying alliance problem that lowering the threshold is supposed to address remains. Lowering the threshold for alliance activation could easily intensify inter-bloc security competition, and make alliances far more contentious on an everyday level. The credibility of the alliance suffers all the same.

A better solution would involve enhancing resilience and denial capabilities – things that a military alliance may not necessarily provide. Total defense against subversive activities is impossible. In the age of social media, for example, foreign disinformation campaigns will almost certainly find some audiences, whether they are receptive or simply unwitting. Not all malign cyber operations can be defeated, let alone detected. An illegal but limited territorial incursion – whether by land, sea, or air – is a nuisance, but may still be within the bounds of toleration. Allies may naturally fret about inade-quate support to tackle some of these challenges, but precisely because deterrence holds at higher levels, their abandonment fears remain manageable. An alliance's credibility will always have boundaries, and states may have to find some way of living with them. To try to plug all credibility gaps may very well be like chasing after the setting sun: a futile endeavor that ends in self-defeat.

Rather than consider lower thresholds, allies should develop capabilities and adopt measures that can curb disinformation, enhance cyber security, and immediately respond to incursions into their territory, thereby dulling whatever effectiveness these subversive activities might have. Some of these capabilities and measures are those that they have to do by themselves. It may not matter that a country hosts an alliance command center tasked with addressing such security challenges if its national politics are toxic and alienating to particular minorities. Local governments need at once to strengthen civil society, to develop intercultural links, and to boost intelligence if they genuinely worry that members of certain groups living within their borders will act maliciously to the benefit of an external power (Lanoszka 2016). Other capabilities may indeed have to be conventionally military in nature: having fighter jets available, for example, to scramble and to escort hostile aircraft out of national airspace soon after they are detected. Whatever the international law, nothing should prevent a state from calling a spade a spade. If an adversary is really undertaking competitive coercion out of weakness, then responding forcefully and immediately by using law enforcement and security services as appropriate can help deter future challenges, or at least keep them within tolerable levels. In some respects, this is why burden-sharing debates can become so intense within alliances. States want to see their allies doing their part so that none of them is the weak link. It is to this issue we now turn.

# 4

# Burden-sharing

The most significant controversy beleaguering US military alliances these days has revolved around the issue of burden-sharing – the notion that allies must contribute their fair share to collective defense. President Trump, in particular, chided treaty partners not only for failing to spend enough money on their militaries, but also for expecting that Washington would defend them against external aggression no matter what. Though his tone was uniquely acerbic – he threatened abandonment unequivocally as a way of inciting them to spend more (Sperling and Webber 2019) – many other presidents before him frequently criticized US allies for failing to carry their fair share of the common burden. Security analysts based in the United States have also criticized allies for allegedly free-riding. Frustratingly, although NATO countries have pledged to spend about 2 percent of their gross domestic product (GDP) on defense by 2024, only a handful of countries had, as of 2021, met this target, with very few of the others appearing to be on track to fulfill their promises. If allies seem uninterested in investing in their own militaries, then Washington might become even more disinclined over time to uphold those security relationships. It could even abrogate those alliances. Much is at stake with burden-sharing.

Scholars have advanced explanations for why burden-sharing controversies are likely to arise in military alliances and, specifically, why great powers like the United States often bear – to their exasperation – a disproportionate share of the defense burden. However, as this chapter argues, military technology complicates the issue of burden-sharing. On the one hand, the growing sophistication and complexity of conventional military technology create incentives for states to make persistent investments so that they do not fall behind their adversaries and allies. A state can no longer generate military power through a quick infusion of cash intended to pay for weapons and the military personnel needed to use them on the battlefield. Raising an effective army or navy might have taken years in the past, but now it could take decades. On the other hand, nuclear weapons have confounded the relationship between an individual ally's military contributions and the collective good – deterrence of the adversary – that springs from them. Spending a certain percentage of one's GDP on conventional military power may hardly be relevant if nuclear weapons are what prevent an adversary from attacking the alliance in the first place. Indeed, building up conventional military power can have contradictory effects: it can potentially undermine deterrence by signaling an aversion to using nuclear weapons; or it can be destabilizing by signaling a willingness to use conventional military power alongside nuclear weapons for the purposes of engaging in war. The relationship between military spending and deterrence is far from linear. The sophisticated nature of contemporary military technology at once encourages and discourages defense spending. A guideline like spending 2 percent of GDP on defense may be a useful heuristic for measuring defense contributions, but its utility is at best superficial.

To elaborate on this argument, this chapter outlines the theoretical reasons for why free-riding might occur in military alliances, before reviewing a history of burden-sharing debates. It then explains how conventional military power has become more complex, thereby necessitating enduring investments in defense on the part of those states that do wish to keep up with adversaries and allies. It then proceeds to explain how nuclear weapons confound burden-sharing. Before concluding, the chapter explains how US allies have responded to these contradictory incentives by reviewing the reasons why some of them spend more on defense than others. Note that this chapter will focus on burden-sharing mostly in financial terms. Of course, states can make important contributions to an alliance in ways that are not always counted in their defense budgets. Providing basing rights, offering Host Nation Support, imposing sanctions on third parties, giving foreign economic and military aid, or deploying troops more readily to combat zones could be more significant for the functioning of an alliance. The previous chapter concluded by mentioning how local efforts to boost civil society can help inoculate against foreign subversion. Burden-sharing debates are largely anchored in terms of defense spending, however. As one researcher observes, "the empirical relationship between defense inputs [i.e., money spent on defense, generally, and military equipment, specifically] and outputs is large, positive, and statistically significant" (Becker 2017: 135). This chapter will proceed accordingly and focus on burden-sharing in terms of defense expenditures.

## Burden-sharing in Theory and History

Burden-sharing purportedly matters in alliance politics for four related reasons. First, it reflects how much allies are willing to spend on their militaries to address common security challenges. Second, it is a sign of their commitment to collective defense and, more generally, the alliance. Third, alliances serve to aggregate capabilities; the more capabilities that an alliance can bring to bear, all things being equal, the more successful it will be in achieving its security goals. If war were to break out, then an alliance in which every state has done its part in peacetime will be more likely than not to prevail. Finally, a state that persistently bears a disproportionate share of the defense burden might decide that the alliance is not worth upholding. It may unilaterally decide to walk away in the belief that it can produce enough security for itself on its own.

At first glance, burden-sharing controversies and problems of alliance free-riding appear to be the result of a collective action problem. This social problem arises when members of a group want the benefits produced by their joint activities, but at the same time wish to minimize the amount of effort they put in. If any one member believes that it can derive the benefit despite not doing anything, then, rationally, that member would try to get away with doing as little as it possibly can: it would "free-ride" on the efforts of others. Unfortunately, if all members think this way, then nothing happens even though they would all be better off had they worked together to produce the good. What may serve the self-interest of the individual member could jeopardize the interests of the larger group. Accordingly, the collective action problem intensifies as the group membership grows because the marginal contribution made by any one member is harder to discern and unlikely to have much of an impact on the provision of the collective good (Olson 1971: 53).

Public goods are probably the most prone to these challenges, since they are neither non-rival nor non-excludable in terms of consumption. Public goods are non-rival – meaning that the consumption of the good by one individual member of a group does not preclude its being consumed by another member. They are non-excludable – meaning that one individual cannot be prevented from consuming the good. Clean air is the classic example of a public good. Breathing it in does not stop someone else from inhaling it, and someone from outside a group cannot be prevented from enjoying it – unless potentially lethal force is used against that person's respiratory system. Of course, groups are sometimes capable of mounting collective action, but that is likely because they contain members who are already highly motivated and capable of producing the collective good themselves as well as punishing potential free-riders.

The theory of collective action seems plausible enough with respect to understanding why burden-sharing controversies ensue in military alliances. One important insight of the theory is that larger – specifically, economically stronger – members would bear a greater share of the defense burden than smaller ones. As Wallace Thies (2003: 273) writes: "[P]recisely because it is large, wealthy, and powerful ... a state like the United States will have so much at stake that it will be highly motivated to contribute to the collective effort *and* have the resources to ensure that the collective effort is a success" (emphasis in original). Thus, unsurprisingly from this perspective, the United States has fretted the most about alliance burden-sharing.

Although burden-sharing controversies seem particularly intense today, discontent with allies' spending patterns has been a hallmark of US foreign relations since at least 1949, when NATO was established. In fact, the United States insisted on the inclusion of Article III of the Washington Treaty, which provides that "[i]n order more effectively to achieve the objectives of this Treaty, the Parties, separately and jointly, by means of continuous and effective self-help and mutual aid, will maintain and develop their individual and collective capacity to resist armed attack" (NATO 1949 [2019]). At the time, Secretary of State Dean Acheson justified Article III on the basis that "nobody is getting a meal ticket from anybody else so far as their capacity to resist is concerned" (quoted in Ringsmose 2010: 321).

Despite the inclusion of Article III, US decision-makers were often frustrated by what they perceived to be the lack of will on the part of their allies to invest in their own militaries. Discouraged by the inconclusive status of the European Defense Community, a proposed treaty that would have entailed a European army and, very controversially at the time, military contributions from West Germany, US Secretary of State John Foster Dulles asserted in a speech to the North Atlantic Council that its nonratification would "compel an agonizing reappraisal of basic United States policy" (*Foreign Relations of the United States, 1952–1954*, vol. V: 462–3). President Dwight Eisenhower was committed to European security, but he shared Dulles's frustration that NATO allies were not doing enough for their own collective defense. Eisenhower himself disliked "the European habit of taking our money, resenting any slight hint as to what they should do, and then assuming, in addition, full right to criticize us as bitterly as they desire" (quoted in Duchin 1992: 211). Ultimately, the French parliament failed to ratify the treaty to establish the European Defense Community and so both European military integration and West German militarization proceeded within a NATO framework. Later in his presidency, Eisenhower decried how, in shouldering "a large share of the infrastructure cost, we are bearing almost all the cost of the deterrent, and we are maintaining a large navy to keep the seas free" (*Foreign Relations of the United States, 1958–1960*, vol. VII: 508–9).

Subsequent US decision-makers voiced similar complaints. President John F. Kennedy inherited a growing balance-of-payments deficit whereby the United States suffered from major outflows of gold, mainly to those allies that had been hosting large numbers of US military personnel as part of its forward-leaning national security strategy. Those military personnel would earn pay in US dollars, which would be spent on allied territory and then used by the receiving ally to purchase gold. In the fixed exchange rate system that prevailed between 1944 and 1973, the US dollar was pegged to gold, at $35 per ounce, and served as the foundation of the international monetary order. Unfortunately, the balance-of-payments deficit meant that liquidity was leaving the United States. For Washington, such losses were unsustainable over the long term because it weakened domestic economic growth (Gavin 2001). As much as Kennedy recognized the importance of US military forces for allied security, he apparently noted in a 1963 National Security Council meeting that "we must not permit a situation to develop in which we should have to seek economic favors from Europe," adding that "we should be prepared to reduce quickly, if we so decided, our military forces in Germany" (*Foreign Relations of the United States, 1961–1963*, vol. XIII: 488–9). These frustrations continued throughout the 1960s, with US Secretary of Defense Robert McNamara emphasizing that he "wished to make clear that he was making no threats, but it would be absolutely impossible for the United States to accept the gold drain caused by the US forces in Germany if Germany did not assist through continuation of the Offset Agreements" (quoted in Zimmermann 2002: 165). This controversy over "offsets" was eventually settled through the Trilateral Agreements struck between West Germany, the United States, and the United Kingdom, but it loomed large in European security debates in part because it cast doubt on the US commitment to Europe and whether West Germany would remain firmly anchored in NATO (Gavin 2004).

Even so, the resolution of these balance-of-payment controversies did not put an end to burden-sharing debates. In the early 1970s, continued dissatisfaction with Western Europe's apparent unwillingness to bear the burden made itself felt in the US Congress when Senator Mike Mansfield (D-Montana) introduced resolutions calling for US military deployments abroad to be nearly halved in number. Capturing the sentiments of Mansfield's backers, Representative Otis Pike proclaimed: "I am not willing to help [Western Europeans] defend themselves when they think that we should spend 7.5 per cent of our [gross national product], and they can get away with 2, 3, or 4 per cent because they know that the taxpayers of America will take care of them" (quoted in Williams 1976). Initially pro-NATO in his presidency, Nixon grew frustrated with treaty partners for failing to appreciate his successful efforts in defeating these congressional efforts aimed at limiting overseas deployments. By the time he resigned the presidency in 1974, he considered European allies to be largely ungrateful (Sayle 2019: 167–90). Congress never let go of the notion that West European countries could be doing much more. Just as the Cold War was ending, debate continued over whether Europe was contributing enough to the collective defense burden (see Steinberg and Cooper 1990). These conversations were not unique to Europe. In addition to his concerns about the US allies' human rights record, President Carter sought to withdraw troops from South Korea in order to force Northeast Asian allies to spend more money (Oberdorfer 1999: 87–91).

Burden-sharing controversies continued into the 1990s and the 2000s, but because the United States was economically and militarily far superior to any potential adversaries, these debates never seemed very consequential. There was, of course, some embarrassment over how Western European countries lacked the capabilities in going about military interventions in the Balkan region (see Chalmers 2001). But the collapse of the Soviet Union meant that no major power posed a serious threat to continental Europe, thereby allowing many European countries (and the United States, for that matter) to reduce their defense spending and enjoy a peace dividend at a time of economic prosperity (see Figure 4.1).

The old burden-sharing controversies became salient again during the Obama years, however. Venting his frustration with how some NATO countries failed to provide desirable levels of military support in out-of-area operations in Afghanistan and Libya, US Secretary of Defense Robert Gates famously warned in 2011:

> The blunt reality is that there will be dwindling appetite and patience in the US Congress – and in the American body politic writ large – to expend increasingly precious funds on behalf of nations that are apparently unwilling to devote the necessary resources or make the necessary changes to be serious and capable partners in their own defense. (US Department of Defense 2011)

Despite this stern warning, European defense expenditures remained low, not least because many states embraced austerity in their efforts to weather the Eurozone crisis that was unfolding at the time (Gordon et al. 2012). Even so, Gates issued his warning after the United States had expended much blood and capital in Afghanistan and, especially, Iraq, which, for better or for worse likely made the burden-sharing problem appear much more acute from Washington's perspective. President Obama even declared to one journalist that "free riders aggravate me" (quoted in Goldberg 2016). Between 2001 and 2014, the US share of allied spending within NATO grew from 63 percent to 72 percent (Belkin et al. 2014: 1).

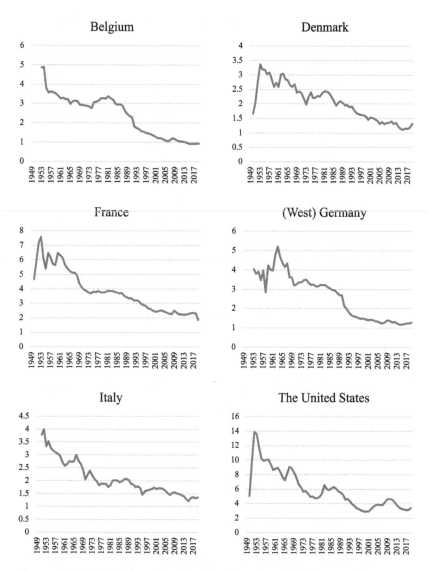

Figure 4.1: Defense spending of select European NATO countries and the United States as a percentage of GDP (1949–2019).

*Note*: 2020 is excluded because the SARS-CoV-2 pandemic sharply reduced economic activity that year, thus distorting defense burdens. Note the different y-axes.

*Source*: Data from Stockholm International Peace Research Institute.

Table 4.1: NATO military spending as percentage of GDP in 2019

| Country | % | Country | % |
|---|---|---|---|
| Albania | 1.26 | Lithuania | 2.03 |
| Belgium | 0.93 | Luxembourg | 0.56 |
| Bulgaria | 3.25 | Montenegro | 1.66 |
| Canada | 1.31 | Netherlands | 1.36 |
| Croatia | 1.68 | Norway | 1.80 |
| Czech Republic | 1.19 | Poland | 2.00 |
| Denmark | 1.32 | Portugal | 1.52 |
| Estonia | 2.14 | Romania | 2.04 |
| France | 1.84 | Slovakia | 1.74 |
| Germany | 1.38 | Slovenia | 1.04 |
| Greece | 2.28 | Spain | 0.92 |
| Hungary | 1.21 | Turkey | 1.89 |
| Iceland | N/A | United Kingdom | 2.14 |
| Italy | 1.22 | United States | 3.42 |
| Latvia | 2.01 | | |

*Source*: Estimated data from NATO (2019).

Russia's aggression toward Ukraine in 2014 brought deterrence and defense back to the NATO agenda. At that year's Wales Summit, where NATO leaders gathered together for the first time since the Russian annexation of Crimea, NATO members reaffirmed their 2006 pledge to spend 2 percent of their GDP on defense, with additional commitments to do so by 2024 as well as to devote 20 percent of that expenditure to the research, development, and procurement of defense equipment. Such pledges are nonbinding and would trigger no sanctions in the event of failure. Perhaps unsurprisingly, by 2019, just before the SARS-CoV-2 pandemic hit, only eight of twenty-eight European NATO members reached that threshold. As Table 4.1 shows, most of the other allies made modest increases that fell well short of the NATO guideline. These yawning gaps between commitment and reality proved to be rhetorical fodder for President Trump. Although the view that US allies could and should do much more in bearing the military burden has been a mainstay among presidents since Truman, Trump had a different, more assertive tone, going as far as to threaten wholesale abandonment if allies failed to increase their military expenditures. He even spoke of NATO members not paying their dues – which do not exist if taken literally – while showing a clear preference for those countries that have met the 2 percent guidelines.

To be sure, burden-sharing debates have not been unique to US-led alliances. Shades of such controversies arose within the Warsaw Pact considering that members like Czechoslovakia, East Germany, and Poland received large subsidies from the Soviet Union in order to retain political authority and to deliver material welfare to their citizens (Bunce 1985: 29). The Warsaw Pact did not have the same sort of discussion on how best to approporionate military contributions as NATO did; the influence of Communist Party politics on military institutions in the Soviet bloc precluded such talk. Nevertheless, in mounting a leadership challenge to General Secretary Mikhail Gorbachev in the twilight years of the Soviet Union, Boris Yeltsin espoused a form of Russian nationalism, one that drew on the sentiments of many Russians who had believed that their own personal sacrifice underwrote Soviet support for republics and Warsaw Pact countries (Tuminez 2003: 129). After all, the Russian Soviet Federative Socialist Republic represented the largest and most economically powerful part of the Soviet Union, which was, of course, the leader of the Soviet bloc.

Collective action theory thus appears to illuminate why burden-sharing controversies arise in alliance politics and why the strongest ally is most likely to accuse its partners of making inadequate contributions to collective defense. But military alliances are not just any type of collective action. Critically, a military alliance is not a public good but a private good. It is, by its nature, exclusive because allies deter and defend against adversaries. If the security generated by being in a military alliance were not exclusive, as the theory must assume, then abandonment fears would be entirely irrational. Alas, we saw in Chapters 1 and 2 that alliance treaties often feature enough uncertainty to inject doubt about the provision of military support in a crisis. We also saw in Chapter 3 that countries have had good reasons to fear abandonment. More importantly, in surveying the historical record, earlier references to burden-sharing controversies in peacetime are difficult to find. One possible explanation is that alliances have lasted much longer since 1945 than before. According to one dataset, a terminated alliance forged after 1945 lasted on average about fourteen years before ending. Some, like NATO, have not yet ended. Prior to 1945, the average lifespan for an alliance was about eight years (Leeds et al. 2002). There was just not enough time for a burden-sharing controversy to develop, either because a war would break out or because allies' foreign policies had changed and the alliance came to an end without being renewed.

Still, the difference in lifespans raises a new question: what exactly changed between the pre- and post-Second World War periods? In light of how burden-sharing is largely a story driven by Washington, one possibility is that the United States moved beyond its reservations about foreign entanglements to embrace a strategy of forward defense (Rapp-Hooper 2020: 51–2). This strategy meant not only that the United States would have military alliances and a large standing army in peacetime, but also that it would deploy its forces to theaters of operations located abroad. As such, the United States expected its allies to do their share by contributing to this forward defense posture. However, that is not all. As explained below, much has to do with the nature of military technology.

## How Advances in Military Technology Shape Burden-sharing

A military alliance is a grouping of states that strive to create security for themselves against shared threats. Because security – specifically, deterrence – is the collective good that most military alliances produce through their members' joint activities, the key question as regards burden-sharing is how states' individual defense contributions affect the overall security that their alliance generates. Presumably, the failure of at least one state to provide its equitable share – however defined – undermines the alliance's overall security. The bigger the alliance, all things equal, the less clear it becomes as to how impactful any individual contribution would be on the overall production of deterrence. And indeed, a classic view of alliances is that they aggregate capabilities. Any absence of capabilities suggests that a military alliance is not fulfilling its true potential.

Is that really the case, though? The first part of the discussion below argues that conventional military power has become much harder to generate than in the past. As such, concerns about underspending are legitimate because persistent spending on conventional military power has become even more important as military technology grows in complexity. Nevertheless, as the second part of the discussion below argues, the reality of alliance politics is much less straightforward than what the theory of collective action and the capability aggregation model would imply. For one, nuclear weapons have rendered obsolete the view that alliances serve to aggregate military capabilities. For another, the impact of any country spending more on its conventional military power would be limited and potentially counter-productive because of the nature of nuclear war.

### The growing complexity of conventional military power

Having some level of conventional military power is important for any ally. All wars fought since 1945 involve it, and all military operations undertaken by NATO and coalitions of security partners after the Cold War ended have relied on it. Out-of-area operations, to varying degrees, still depend on ground, naval, and maritime power, and such operations may rebound to the collective interests of the alliance even if, by definition, they do not implicate its territorial integrity. China and Russia have all made strides in developing their non-nuclear forces since 2008, leading some observers to claim that those countries could launch major attacks on US allies and achieve a fait accompli in taking their territory (see, e.g., Shlapak and Johnson 2016).

Burden-sharing controversies have intensified since 1945

in part because the requirements for generating conventional military power have become much more demanding and military technology much more complex than in previous historical epochs. In other words, "the rate at which wealth can be transformed into power" has slowed down, at least with respect to military power (Brawley 2004: 80). Although any new technology may seem complex to producers and consumers when it first appears, weapons and organizational practices have become steadily more technically demanding since the early twentieth century than ever before. They require much more than quick infusions of cash to be adopted and used effectively. Their complexity can be broken down into three dimensions: platform, organizational, and individual skill.

*Platform complexity* refers to the technical nature of a military platform, whether it is an aircraft carrier, jet fighter, main battle tank, or something else. One measure of a platform's complexity is how many component parts it contains. The greater the number, the more likely that problems will arise in their design, manufacture, production, operation, and maintenance. To quote Andrea Gilli and Mauro Gilli (2019: 150): "As the number of components expands, the number of potential incompatibilities and vulnerabilities increases geometrically. Ensuring the proper functioning and mutual compatibility of all the components and of the whole system thus becomes increasingly difficult." Individual components themselves have become more advanced and on average much smaller, requiring advanced know-how and competence in electronics, engineering, and the material sciences to be able to produce them. The growing use of software, too, adds a further complication. For example, first flown in 1958, the F-4 Phantom II had about one thousand software lines of code. The contemporary F-35 has almost six million lines of code (Gilli and Gilli 2019: 151). Compounding matters is the way in which platforms have become increasingly integrated with one another. A drone capable of hitting targets requires a sophisticated kill chain that in turn relies on data links to transmit information as quickly and voluminously as possible. Extensive infrastructural support is often necessary. To invoke another example, aircraft carriers, to be at their most defensible and effective at projecting power, require groups of other platforms like destroyers, frigates, submarines, and supply warships to operate alongside them (Gilli and Gilli 2016: 61).

*Organizational complexity* refers to the difficulty (or ease) involved in adopting military technology for operational use. Specifically, it encompasses the range of concepts, practices, skill sets, and doctrines – the software – that an organization should have in order to use platforms – the hardware – most effectively. According to Stephen Biddle (2004), with respect to land warfare, the modern system of force means that soldiers could best mitigate the challenge of industrial-scale firepower by operating in small, dispersed groups that engage in cover, concealment, and suppression on the battlefield, while using combined arms at the tactical level. Having come into maturity during the First World War, the modern system represented a major shift in warfare, since, hitherto, armies relied on concentrated mass to maximize their lethality on the battlefield. Though countries that adopt it may be more likely to prevail over opponents that do not, many countries cannot embrace the modern system because it demands civilian trust in military authorities, organizational flexibility, and rational performance standards that are free from politicization and cronyism (Talmadge 2015). For military alliances, the modern system also means that capability aggregation per se may no longer matter for winning on the battlefield because of the premium it places on how military force is used rather than on how much of it is used.

Finally, *individual skill complexity* refers to the extent to which a high level of human capital is required for service in the armed forces. Historically, the intellectual requirements for effective service were not very high, since the use of most weapons largely depended on physical force and dexterity. Over the course of the twentieth century, warfare became more capital-intensive, which in turn has led to changes in the sort of personnel that militaries now need. Given the growing complexity of military platforms, however, high-skilled individuals who can operate them become much more coveted and, when armies no longer rely on conscription, harder to recruit. As one team of researchers finds:

> The increased sophistication of modern tactics and doctrines, the growing set of threats that armed forces face at the tactical level, the higher level of complexity of modern weapon systems and the need for synchronization and coordination required by advanced technologies have made warfare more difficult and thus have raised the requirements in terms of cognitive, non-cognitive and physical abilities of recruits. (Asoni et al. 2020: 39)

Modern war certainly now involves much more than giving a foot soldier a pike and using drill to impart a set of tactics. What makes individual skill complexity an especially acute problem is that the cost of labor has shot up, with many national militaries shifting away from conscription. Pay and benefits comprise, for example, an increasingly larger share of the US defense budget in order, in part, to boost recruitment and retention (Williams 2013: 56–8; see also Bury 2017).

These forms of complexity – platform, organizational, and individual skill – interact with one another such that shortcomings in any one domain can seriously undermine overall combat effectiveness. What might seem like a trivial flaw in design could lead to major cost overruns and delays because the entire design might be compromised. From an alliance perspective, these observations suggest that states can easily fall behind in their contributions to the common conventional defense burden because continuous investment is necessary. Military modernization programs can take decades, not years, to develop. Problems of interoperability are inevitable between allies – that is, allies would come to experience more technical and organizational challenges in working together because they are located at different points on the technological curve. Such challenges were already in sharp relief in 1999 when allies of the United States experienced basic problems with systems integration and interunit communication during NATO's bombing of Yugoslavia

(Lambeth 2001). Considering that the United States has had a persistently large defense budget since that campaign even as its European allies kept military spending low to enjoy the post-Cold War peace dividend, such gaps have likely persisted, sometimes even widening. Problems of operational readiness and personnel shortages have become notorious in the German armed forces, with many – if not most – weapons systems not available for use at any given time because they are under maintenance (German Bundestag 2020).

Note that many of the foregoing challenges have little to do with money per se. As a general rule, having more money to spend is better than not having enough. However, meeting financial targets may be less relevant if a state spends money on outdated equipment, inappropriate operational concepts, and ill-trained personnel. The example of China suggests that cash alone does not solve the underlying challenges that come with contemporary military technology. Making reliable but relatively inexpensive component technologies – such as single-crystal turbine blades, which can range from about 30,000 to 50,000 US dollars per unit – has proven elusive for China despite its efforts at industrial espionage and reverse engineering (Lindsay 2015; Horowitz et al. 2019: 191). One problem is that China has only relatively recently aspired to produce such technologies. For its part, the United States has been tapping into a deep reservoir of expertise and tacit knowledge that took decades to develop. Skill sets can atrophy easily if neglected. Long a seafaring nation that has come to rely on ballistic submarines for nuclear deterrence, the United Kingdom itself faced major difficulties in the earlier design phases of the Astute-class of nuclear-powered fleet submarines simply because it lacked designers who could use 3D-CAD software (Jinks and Hennessy 2015: 617). In the case of Germany, a parliamentary report identified excessive regulation as being one obstacle that prevents the Bundeswehr from achieving operational flexibility (German Bundestag 2020: 14). And so, for a state willing to keep up with adversaries and allies that do invest in their militaries, persistence and institutional fitness have now become necessary.

### The paradoxes of nuclear weapons

The growing complexity of conventional military power suggests the need for continuous investment by states in their militaries, especially if they wish to deter and to defend against their adversaries. Yet there is a serious complication that confounds the role that conventional military power plays in deterrence: nuclear weapons. The view that military alliances serve to aggregate capabilities might have been appropriate for understanding such security arrangements prior to the nuclear age. Before the August 1945 atomic bombings of Hiroshima and Nagasaki, the side that would prevail in a major power war was the one that could generally mass, and effectively employ, lethality on the battlefield. Because lethality usually entailed the use of metal, whether in the form of blades, bullets, or artillery, capability aggregation really meant bringing more metal to bear on an opponent. Nuclear weapons are decidedly different: they are lethal because of the immense energy that nuclear reactions generate as well as secondary effects like radiation exposure. If nuclear weapons are the most powerful military capabilities that a state can possess, and alliances serve to aggregate capabilities, then members of an alliance should all acquire them so as to maximize their lethality and firepower in addition to complicating the targeting options of an adversary. Contrary to the capability aggregation model of alliances, however, unrestrained nuclear proliferation does not occur. Washington and, to a lesser extent, Moscow have generally sought to limit the nuclear ambitions of their formal allies (Coe and Vaynman 2015; Lanoszka 2018c). The advent of nuclear weapons thus has led to several paradoxes: they seem to be the most effective deterrent because of their destructive potential, but that very destructive potential makes promises to use them hard to believe, especially on behalf of an ally in a crisis; increasing the size of a nuclear weapons arsenal could signal a willingness to use nuclear weapons, but so does increasing conventional military power; and nuclear weapons can stabilize a rivalry, but they also offer fresh incentives for rivals to engage in risky competition.

The influence of nuclear weapons on collective defense burdens is more profound than commonly understood. Consider again how, at least nowadays, military alliances largely serve to deter aggression. Since the early part of the Cold War, extended deterrence has had a significant nuclear dimension. That is, deterrence is not so much about mustering more soldiers and more steel against an adversary as about using the destructive power of nuclear weapons to threaten unacceptable costs on adversary. Because it faced a much larger conventional military force led by the Soviet Union in Europe, the United States relied on the threat of nuclear weapons to discourage communist aggression at the highest spectrum of conflict against its allies. In East Asia, too, the United States forward deployed nuclear weapons in South Korea, Taiwan, and even some outlying Japanese islands to make nuclear deterrent threats more credible (Jones 2010). One problem with an overreliance on nuclear deterrence is that it was inherently unbelievable in those situations that did not feature a large-scale attack. Would the United States, for example, really have used nuclear weapons against the Soviet Union in response to a limited border incursion? Mindful of this problem, the United States and its allies needed to develop conventional military capabilities – ironically, more metal – so that they could plug any gaps in their deterrent posture vis-à-vis the Warsaw Pact. Hence US decision-makers insisted that West Germany had to rearm if containment of the Soviet Union were to be effective. As US nuclear superiority eroded while the Soviet Union expanded its arsenal of nuclear weapons and means of delivering them, NATO had to shore up its conventional capabilities to ensure stability across different rungs of the escalation ladder. But as nuclear parity between the two competing superpowers started to emerge in the early 1960s, and the condition of mutually assured destruction subsequently took hold, many observers started to question whether a war fought in the heart of Europe could ever stay conventional. When the Kennedy administration adopted the doctrine of flexible response, leveraging recent technological advances to provide more military options should a conflagration break out with the Soviet Union, leading decision-makers in West Germany questioned – correctly as it turned out, in view of US nuclear war plans – the assumption that nuclear weapons would not be used any time soon (see Sagan 1990; Bluth 1995: 111–13; Gavin 2001).

Boosting conventional military power in the shadow of nuclear weapons was problematic for two, somewhat contradictory, reasons. The first is that decision-makers in France and West Germany – especially in the 1960s – worried that increases in conventional military power undermined the threat of nuclear escalation. By making such investments, NATO risked signaling an aversion to using nuclear weapons – an aversion that could embolden Warsaw Pact countries into launching an attack (Duffield 1995: 156–7). This concern gave way to its opposite later in the Cold War. At least from the European perspective, the acquisition of conventional military power could convey a willingness to fight nuclear wars, thereby raising their likelihood. Of course, if mutually assured destruction were truly operative, then greater, or even fewer, conventional military investments should not change the underlying balance of power between the rival blocs. The costs of war would remain unacceptable and unalterably high (Jervis 1989). More conventional military investments could, however, signal greater resolve and risk-taking, especially if those investments came with parallel improvements in nuclear forces that, together, would increase the ability to wage war rather than to prevent it. In the early 1980s, new conventional defense concepts in NATO suggested the alliance was no longer sticking to forward defense whereby it would concentrate its efforts in limiting losses of territory along the eastern border of West Germany. To many observers, including a large number of West German citizens, the United States appeared to embrace a more aggressive posture that envisioned the practice of striking targets deep into Warsaw Pact territory through the use of high-technology conventional arms. Fueling these concerns was the US Army's adoption of a new battle doctrine called AirLand Battle (Monson 1986: 620–2).

Paradoxes thus arise with respect to burden-sharing.

Nuclear weapons arguably provide an alliance with the security that it covets. In reducing the risk of major war, this sense of security should dampen whatever interest that allies might have in conventional military power, at least as far as deterrence and defense are concerned. What difference does it really make if West Germany spends this much or that little when forward deployed nuclear weapons are what keep Warsaw Pact forces at bay, assuming, of course, that those forces are otherwise willing to invade? However, by spending an insufficient amount on conventional military power, those allies risk incurring the dissatisfaction of Washington, which may become reluctant to provide them with support in a time of grave need. Although this dissatisfaction may arguably be a result of their own stinginess, they might subsequently fear abandonment from the United States and perceive themselves vulnerable to the adversary, suggesting that the chance of war could be higher than initially believed. This conundrum was what dogged West German decision-makers early in the Cold War.

Of course, nuclear deterrence does not resolve all the security challenges that an alliance might face, even against an adversary that has its own massive nuclear weapons arsenal. Decision-makers might believe that the stalemate associated with mutually assured destruction is in fact unstable and thus cannot be taken for granted (Green 2020). Some argue that nuclear deterrence can create new avenues for conflict (Snyder 1965: 198–9). The so-called stability–instability paradox holds that if both sides believe that war is too costly at the strategic level, then one side might still engage in conflict at lower levels of violence, thinking that the other side would be too fearful to retaliate in kind. Strategic stability could in fact encourage instability at the lower end of the conflict spectrum. To be sure, with mutually assured destruction, whereby both sides have survivable second-strike capabilities, one could argue that the risk of miscalculation should generally be large enough to deter aggression at those lower levels of violence (see, e.g., Jervis 1989: 21–2). One could also claim that nuclear deterrence has been exaggerated in its importance because other factors could explain the absence of war between major powers since 1945 or because a taboo makes the use of nuclear weapons normatively unacceptable (Mueller 1988; Lebow and Stein 1995; Tannenwald 2007). Against such uncertainty, states might nevertheless still invest in conventional military power for added insurance.

But if those allies were to spend a lot on conventional military power, then other alliance management problems would arise that stand apart from those relating to nuclear escalation. For one, states might be more likely to use their military power against the adversary in ways that could generate entrapment concerns among their allies. What if, for example, Taiwan sought to use its military power to launch a cross-strait invasion against mainland China – a fear that US decision-makers had in the 1950s and 1960s? For another, some allies might be less likely to find their security ties with the United States useful if they feel that they have sufficient power to deter an adversary on their own. Taken at its word, the ideal ally that the United States purportedly wants is one that does not need it. Washington might be more wont to reduce its military commitments vis-à-vis those allies it deems to be powerful enough to deter the adversary single-handedly. A more equitable distribution of the defense burden could in fact create more insecurity, especially if those allies genuinely believe that they cannot stand up to adversaries by themselves. This disagreement may be most pronounced if the conventional military burden is split equitably, the nuclear arsenal is concentrated in the hands of a small part of the alliance, and the adversary has its own nuclear weapons. In fact, a state has incentives not to do what its stronger ally might ask of it if spending more on defense could hasten the latter's disengagement. One way to square the circle is for the ally to participate in nuclear decision-making, whether through sharing arrangements or nuclear proliferation. Yet, as discussed in Chapter 3, such concessions could either undermine the defender's ability to control escalation or deepen the anxieties of others. Consultations of the sort discussed in Chapter 3 are better for exchanging views and managing these disagreements.

Put together, what these observations suggest is that

the relationship between alliance membership, an ally's individual contribution, and collective security is not at all linear when nuclear deterrence is operative. Much confusion and uncertainty arise when trying to determine the precise role of conventional deterrence. In the pre-nuclear world, all things equal, an alliance produced collective security by way of accumulating relatively more military power over adversaries. If one ally neglects to invest in its own army, then the loss could undermine deterrence, especially when the result is fewer troops and weapons in the theater of operations where war could conceivably break out. Of course, this rule may not always hold true. Under Chancellor Otto von Bismarck's leadership, Germany had alliances with Austria-Hungary and Russia, but did not necessarily want to see their military power grow. Given the relatively short lifespan of alliances in Bismarck's time, the concern that one day's ally could be another day's enemy really did have foundation.

In the nuclear area, much depends on the sorts of beliefs that leaders have about nuclear deterrence, war, and military power. If allies believe that the threat of nuclear escalation is sufficient, then conventional military investments in the area of defense and deterrence may be undesirable and possibly counterproductive. Those allies might even want a greater control of nuclear decision-making, as was the case for West Germany in the 1960s. However, if allies believe that the threat of nuclear escalation is insufficient, or disagree as to the appropriate threshold for when nuclear weapons should be used, then conventional military investments should still matter for shoring up any vulnerabilities.

In this last case, whereby conventional military power remains important for deterrence and defense, what sort of rule allies should use to determine how they can equitably contribute to the collective burden is unclear. Presumably, such a rule should be based on the threat assessment that allies share of the security challenges that they jointly face. Put differently, it should revolve around the intentions and capabilities of potential adversaries, the most dangerous and most likely scenarios in which they might undertake aggression, and how those very intentions, capabilities, and scenarios affect allies directly at the individual and collective levels. It should also consider when conventional deterrence ends and nuclear deterrence begins, if that is at all possible.

Unfortunately, this rational procedure may require frank discussions that allies might not wish to have with one another. For example, an alliance might face multiple threats that receive different levels of priority and attention from its members. A wide-ranging threat assessment could bring those disagreements out into the open. And so, in the Cold War, the default method for measuring defense contributions involved examining the percentages of countries' GDP spent on defense – a heuristic practice that has largely continued into the present day with NATO's 2 percent guideline. As the NATO's Defense Review Committee observed in 1988, this measurement strategy "is the best-known, most easily understood, most widely used and perhaps the most telling input measure. It broadly depicts defense input in relation to a country's ability to contribute" (quoted in Ringsmose 2010: 324). Still, European countries have offered other measurements in order to deflect criticism that they have not been contributing their fair share: foreign aid flows to strategically important countries, participation in out-of-area deployments, and the hosting of bases and facilities for alliance use (Thies 2003: 135). Yet none of these methods for evaluating individual contributions to collective security gets at the deeper issue: what does an equitable contribution mean in the context of nuclear (extended) deterrence?

## Burden-sharing Controversies in the Contemporary Era

Nuclear deterrence makes war between major powers unlikely and so, theoretically, decreases the incentives for investing in conventional military power as far as deterrence and defense are concerned. In the atomic age, conventional military technology itself has become much more sophisticated and more challenging to operate effectively. Despite the disincentives that nuclear deterrence might create, states have to make sustained investments in conventional military power if they want to overcome the challenges that could arise with platform and organizational complexity. They also need to achieve the necessary level of human capital with their recruits. With such contradictory pressures at play, why do some US allies spend more, or less, than others?

The simple explanation – one that suggests limits to the effectiveness of nuclear deterrence – is that states do invest in conventional military power when confronted with near-term security challenges. Japan, under Prime Minister Shinzo Abe's leadership, reinterpreted a constitutional provision that suggests that it could maintain military forces so as to be better positioned to strengthen its international security partnerships and address international threats. This constitutional reinterpretation, and the military spending it presumably allows, comes at a time when North Korea has engaged in ballistic missile tests and China has been building up its military and increasing its activities in the East and South China Seas (Auslin 2016). For much of its post-war history, it has spent no more than 1 percent of its GDP on defense. Interestingly, despite these constraints, Tokyo had, until recently, robust enough military capabilities appropriate for its environment (see Lind 2004). Spending over 2.5 percent of its GDP on its military, South Korea retains a strong military precisely because of North Korea's bellicosity and weapons program amid concerns about US reliability (Kwon 2018; see also Bowers and Hiim 2020/21).

Consider also NATO and the data reported above in Figure 4.1. In 2019, outside the United States and the United Kingdom, all the countries meeting the 2 percent threshold were those located along the Alliance's eastern frontier in Europe (see Christie 2019: 82). These countries were Bulgaria, Greece, Estonia, Latvia, Lithuania, Poland, Romania, and Turkey. All but Bulgaria and Greece consider Russia to be their most serious geopolitical challenge following the annexation of Crimea and the instigation of war in eastern Ukraine. Nevertheless, these countries are all concerned more about low levels of subversion (i.e., the competitive coercion discussed at the end of Chapter 3) than about the sort of major Russian assault that would probably put nuclear weapons in play, although that possibility cannot be entirely discounted (Lanoszka and Hunzeker 2019). Greece has kept high defense expenditures because of ongoing maritime disputes regarding fellow NATO ally Turkey. Exceptionally, Bulgaria, which does not see Russia principally as a threat, experienced a dramatic increase in spending when it purchased eight F-16 Block 70 fighter jets from the United States as part of its military modernization effort. To be sure, the majority of NATO members have upped their defense spending since 2014. Germany, frequently lambasted for spending relatively little on its military, has seen modest increases in its defense spending (NATO 2019).

Russia's ability to project military power fades the further one is from its borders; in the same vein, an ally's suspicion that Washington might not come to its aid increases the further away it is from the United States. Canada, for example, is able to get away with spending relatively little on its defense. A large proportion of its population resides near the US border, making Canada a beneficiary of an "involuntary guarantee" from the United States that more far-flung allies do not have (Jockel and Sokolsky 2009: 308). Even Western European countries like Belgium are far enough away from Russia that they do not share the threat perceptions of their more eastern counterparts (Jakobsen 2018: 502–13; Haesebrouck 2021). Indeed, they enjoy the strategic depth afforded to them by NATO enlargement. Free-riding is thus an option only available to those that face no threat or can rationally depend on a much stronger state for their security. Chances are, however, that if a state faces a significant threat, it cannot assume that a defender would come to its aid given the costs involved with protection (Lanoszka 2015).

Besides the severity of its threat environment, other factors can shape a state's willingness to invest in its own military. Jordan Becker and Edmund Malesky (2017) determine that, among European NATO countries, countries with an "Atlanticist" national strategic culture are more likely to have higher defense expenditures than those with a "Europeanist" one. Jo Jakobsen and Tor Jakobsen (2019) find that hosting US forces might discourage a state from bearing its share of the defense burden, however measured. Specifically, they note that an ally with as few as 100 soldiers on its territory would reduce its citizens' willingness to fight. Germany, Japan, and, to a lesser extent, Italy do fall into this category. All three had fought on the losing side in the Second World War, with the former two known for having developed pacifist national security cultures. This observation raises the possibility that historical legacies influence countries' willingness to spend on their militaries. West Germany was not pacifist at the start of the Cold War (Berger 1998); such values took root over time and many decision-makers spanning the East–West divide worried about its potential militarization and foreign policy orientation. Although US decision-makers did want West Germany to contribute militarily to NATO, they too sought to enmesh West Germany in various institutions and agreements that would curb its interest in the use of force. To a degree, Germany's current lack of spending reflects the success of those efforts, even though it did muster a large tank fleet toward the end of the Cold War despite allegations of free-riding (Chalmers and Unterseher 1988: 8). Japan, as mentioned, is a similar case.

Finally, and related, another factor could be the beliefs of political leaders. As mentioned earlier, some leaders might have their own beliefs about how the conventional military balance affects nuclear deterrence. Other beliefs could also be operative. In his study of NATO members' military spending throughout much of the alliance's history, international security scholar Matthew Fuhrmann (2020) uncovers evidence that heads of government with previous business experience are more likely to spend less on defense and to rely instead on the United States because of their tendency to be selfish and unconcerned with fairness. That may be so, but France, the United Kingdom, and West Germany all bear a major influence on the results of this analysis. Because France and the United Kingdom both have nuclear weapons, it is unclear how either of them can free-ride on the United States. In fact, in the early 1970s, French President Georges Pompidou, a leader with previous business experience, saw value in nuclear weapons as a means of safeguarding French interests, particularly when he was nervous that the United States and the Soviet Union might strike a deal at Europe's expense (Trachtenberg 2011: 41–2).

Whatever states' reasons for meeting or failing to meet spending guidelines, fulfilling them does not necessarily add to the collective security of an alliance. Neither does failure to do so necessarily subtract from it. If allies have widely divergent foreign policy goals, then underspending may actually enhance collective security because it could even reduce the scope for mutual insecurity to emerge among treaty partners. Theoretically, a state that fulfills its spending pledges by purchasing offensive capabilities would be seen as a potential entrapment risk. And so the United States has been inconsistent when it comes to burden-sharing and its allies. The Trump administration made Germany and South Korea its favorite targets in burden-sharing debates, but those countries spend very different proportions of their GDP on their militaries. Had Germany devoted as much of its wealth on its military as South Korea has done, then it would be by far the biggest European spender in NATO. But with South Korea, the issue that the Trump administration stressed centered on the degree to which South Korea would directly cover the costs associated with the US military presence on its territory. One might be forgiven for thinking that burden-sharing controversies are really about other political issues, not least because the Trump administration had ordered the redeployment of troops posted in Germany to countries that spend even less on their militaries (Lanoszka and Simón 2021). In Germany's case, the problem that truly vexed the Trump administration might have been about trade, immigration policies, energy policies, and China; in South Korea's case, it was likely to be trade and the desire to resolve the enduring problem of North Korea once and for all. One wonders whether burden-sharing controversies are just a red herring.

# 5

# Warfare

As a general rule, states form alliances to deter adversaries and thus to prevent war from breaking out. The peacetime management of alliances may be costly for reasons relating to entrapment, reassurance, and burden-sharing, but being at war is costlier still. Lives are lost, physical property gets destroyed, and the risk of miscalculation sometimes has the potential for turning small wars into much bigger and more devastating wars.

Historically, military alliances have participated in numerous conflicts. The Peloponnesian War (431–404 BCE) was a contest between two rival leagues led by Athens and Sparta. Six coalitions had to form against Napoleon Bonaparte before he was finally defeated by one in the suburbs of Paris in 1814. Formal allies Germany and Austria-Hungary went to war in 1914 against the Triple Entente – France, the United Kingdom, and Russia. Although the notion that war is on the decline is a popular one, the fact is that combat operations remain a key part of what military alliances do. This is true even if they are engaged in armed conflicts that have at best a tenuous connection to the founding obligations of their alliance treaty. For example, so far in the twenty-first century, different subsets of NATO countries have participated in out-of-area military operations in Afghanistan and Libya as well as in joint military exercises and strategies aimed at mounting effective territorial defense against Russia. For its part, Russia has undertaken large-scale military exercises with Belarus aimed at testing the readiness of their forces in fighting high-intensity wars, presumably against NATO members. South Korea has contributed forces to peacekeeping and reconstruction tasks in Iraq and elsewhere, but its military plans mainly for contingencies involving North Korea.

At first blush, belonging to a military alliance should boost a country's chances in war. If alliances aggregate capabilities, then having a greater sum of military power ought to make defeating an adversary on the battlefield more likely. Reality is much more complicated, however. In light of his experience in the First World War as Supreme Allied Commander, Ferdinand Foch remarked that he lost some respect for Napoleon Bonaparte's military abilities when he realized just how difficult managing a wartime coalition can be. Perhaps, as Foch implies, Napoleon would have proven to be less of a military genius had he not faced so many coalitions that floundered in trying to achieve their strategic objectives. After all, members of an alliance might disagree on their wartime goals and how to go about a military campaign. They might even withhold resources, thereby preventing the alliance from realizing its true potential. Alternatively, allies could have trouble fighting together, whether because their units do not communicate well with one another or because their armaments are incompatible. Some allies might even defect during the campaign, deciding unilaterally not to fight any longer. Such tensions could create opportunities for an opposing side to try to divide and conquer the wartime coalition.

This chapter addresses several key questions in turn. First, what exactly are the types of conflicts that might implicate military alliances? Second, why would states take part in multinational military campaigns, regardless of whether alliance obligations are truly at play? Third, what makes for a militarily effective alliance or coalition? These questions are pertinent in today's security environment. The Baltic countries have been anxious, especially in the immediate aftermath of the annexation of Crimea, that their stronger allies within NATO would abandon them in the face of a determined Russian aggression. Still, some of these countries have participated in ad hoc coalitions organized around out-of-area operations – operations that risk taking their attention away from territorial threats closer to home and may even require very different capabilities.

A clarification of terms is necessary before proceeding. In war, coalitions of states do the fighting, but these coalitions may not coincide fully with a formal treaty alliance to which at least some of those fighting states may belong. All NATO countries contributed to the International Security Assistance Force (ISAF) in Afghanistan to some extent, but not all NATO countries participated in the 2011 military intervention in Libya. On the eve of the First World War, Germany, Austria-Hungary, and Italy were still all part of the Triple Alliance, originally formed in 1882, but rather than join its allies in the fighting, Italy adopted a policy of neutrality when hostilities broke out and, a year later, broke ranks and joined the Triple Entente. Confusing matters further is that ostensibly nonaligned countries sometimes participate in an alliance's military operations. Sweden and Finland – two non-NATO countries – provided forces to ISAF, while several Arab countries contributed to NATO efforts in Libya. Notably, the United States fought as an Associated Power alongside France and the United Kingdom in the latter stages of the First World War. The US-led "coalition of the willing" against Iraq in 2003 drew members from various alliances and partnerships that the United States was able to cobble together. Thus, although military alliances are groups of states joined by formal treaties, coalitions are groups of states that may or may not be formal allies but are engaged in a specific multilateral military operation. Coalitions often disband when the military operation around which they are organized concludes (Mello 2020: 48). Some do sign formal agreements in wartime, as various members of the coalition did against Nazi Germany in the Second World War, but such arrangements rarely last beyond the military conflict at hand unless a new treaty subsumes them or takes their place. An illustrative example is the 1941 Ogdensburg Agreement concluded between the United States and Canada during the Second World War. Those two countries went on to help found NATO in 1949.

## What Is War and What Are the Trends in War?

War itself is a rare event. Consequently, an ally will likely face a very limited number of occasions when it must actually determine whether or not to fulfill a commitment. To be sure, war is an ambiguous concept and can be used to describe military confrontations as varied as the First World War, the Soccer War fought between Honduras and El Salvador in 1969, the invasion phase of the Iraq War in 2003, and the Donbas War fought between Ukraine and Russia after 2014. Notwithstanding such diversity in form, war is ultimately the mutual use of violence on the part of belligerents in the pursuit of their political interests. War is also costly and risky: soldiers and civilians die, physical property gets destroyed, and events can spiral out of decision-makers' control. States generally prefer to settle their disputes peacefully and avoid such pains (Fearon 1995). They tend to establish alliances to avoid armed conflict altogether rather than just to litigate it, hoping that a more powerful grouping of states will present itself as a credible enough fighting force that others would be dissuaded from attacking any of its members. That said, some argue that newly formed defensive alliances can put states on the war path, partly because they can cause greater insecurity among adversaries via the alliance security dilemma (discussed in Chapter 3), leading to a spiral of hostilities (Kenwick et al. 2015).

To rise to the level of reciprocal lethal force that characterizes war, states have to decide whether to go beyond mere enmity, whether to ratchet up a full-blown political crisis, whether to use physical violence, and then whether to retaliate further if violence provokes more violence. In selecting each of these escalatory options, states bypass multiple opportunities for defusing tensions at each step of the way. How alliances – more precisely, the states that make them up – go about these stages of selection can turn on various factors. Military balance might count as one factor. One side might be losing a major strategic advantage, creating pressure on it to exploit the closing "window of opportunity" by attacking the other side. Similarly, fears of falling victim to an impending attack could lead one side to launch a pre-emptive attack of its own, although such pre-emptive wars are empirically very rare (Reiter 1995). In another scenario, states might exploit a favorable imbalance of power or the support that they receive from the alliance and so increase hostilities in such a way as to make war likely. Entrapment concerns could be salient here, but, as Chapter 2 explains, states should be able to find ways to restrain a pugnacious ally or to withhold critical support if they wish not to fight. Resolve may be yet another factor that drives selection into war. One side might be more willing to accept costs and risks in pursuit of its political interests and so becomes more combative toward its adversary. This risk-taking may not necessarily result in war: the adversary could offer concessions for the sake of peace. Nevertheless, the underlying issue of contention might be so intrinsically important that it is worth risking blood and money.

Since the end of the Second World War in 1945, however, wars between states – let alone those between opposing alliances – have apparently declined in number. This empirical observation has prompted John Mueller (1989) to argue that war has become so costly and unattractive as to become nearly obsolete. States are presumably more willing to de-escalate than in the past. Steven Pinker (2012) goes further to argue that violence in general has declined thanks largely to high literacy and improved government administration. Norms regarding territorial integrity may also be part of the explanation (Fazal 2007), and many observers have written about new wars, hybrid wars, or gray-zone conflicts to try to explain those transformations in military conflict that they believe are taking place (e.g., Hoffman 2009; Kaldor 2012). Tanisha Fazal (2018) shows that, with the proliferation of international humanitarian law, states have grown reluctant to declare war formally or to sign peace treaties in order to avoid the consequences that might come with noncompliance. Indeed, the frequency of limited land grabs like Russia's annexation of Crimea in 2014 has not seen much change historically (Altman 2020). Nuclear weapons might also have something to do with the waning number of interstate wars and the reduced war proneness of alliances (Kenwick et al. 2015). Thanks to mutually assured destruction and how major military conflict has become unacceptably high for those armed with nuclear second-strike capabilities, so the argument goes, the incentives for cooperation outweigh those for conflict (Jervis 1989). These observations aside, the thesis that war has been in decline is controversial; the reduced number of interstate wars may simply be due to chance or the fact that advances in military medicine have made armed conflicts result in fewer battlefield deaths – the benchmark often used by scholars for measuring war (Braumoeller 2019; Fazal 2014). That wars happen rarely indicates that states are selective when it comes to engaging in them: they do so when they believe that the odds strongly favor them or that the alternative is much worse.

Some scholars argue that the decline in the number of wars is largely the case only in the developed world; when the most advanced industrial countries do participate in conflicts, these generally take place across the Global South (Mann 2018). The involvement of these countries tends to take the form of multilateral military operations, even implicating those military alliances whose main areas of operation are found in Europe or in Asia. These conflicts have included military interventions in Afghanistan, Iraq, Libya, Syria, and Mali. Taking place far from their own home territories, these interventions constitute out-of-area operations for many countries participating in them, and may require different military capabilities from those that are useful for territorial defense. Especially if they are focused on defeating an insurgency, out-of-area operations generally involve expeditionary forces that are relatively light on armor and more suited to low-intensity conflict. In contrast, territorial defense often requires greater firepower and lethality, especially if the adversary is strong and capable of engaging in high-intensity conflict – in other words, a great power. Of course, the trade-off is not absolute: military interventions can involve complex military operations involving a wide spectrum of capabilities, especially if the goal is to unseat a ruling government and to defeat its military. Still, out-of-area operations can risk escalation and mission creep, whereby participating states progressively take on more tasks beyond the original mandate in the hopes of achieving success (see Taliaferro 2004). They might fear that they will become ensnared in the mission, which would hurt their reputation if they wish to back out of it before it is officially complete. And so, whether with respect to territorial defense or out-of-area operations, taking part in a multilateral military operation has its costs and risks. In most cases, it is not a given as to whether a state should participate unless its own territory and existence are directly threatened.

## Why Take Part in Multilateral Military Operations?

Estimates vary on how often – or how seldom – states decide to fulfill their alliance obligations by fighting wars alongside their treaty partners. As mentioned in Chapter 3, a team of scholars finds that allies act as promised about three-quarters of the time (Leeds et al. 2000). Others have, more pessimistically, reported estimates as low as 23 and 30 percent of cases (Sabrosky 1980: 164; Siverson and Sullivan 1984: 11). A recent study finds that, between 1816 and 2003, the alliance fulfillment rate was about 50 percent (Berkemeier and Fuhrmann 2018: 2). But in breaking down the period under review into the pre- and post-1945 eras, that same study also finds that alliance commitments were fulfilled, respectively, 66 percent and 22 percent of the time.

To be sure, there may be instances when a state does not want an ally to contribute to the fighting. One reason is that an ally might be at a high risk of suffering battlefield defeats such that its territory and resources could fall into enemy hands relatively easily. Despite its alliance with the

United Kingdom, the longest-lasting partnership of its kind in Europe, Portugal remained neutral for much of the Second World War. Its nonparticipation was desirable partly in order to reduce the likelihood of Germany attacking it and being able to acquire from it too much tungsten – a chemical element useful for ammunition capable of penetrating armor. Portuguese nonparticipation also helped to keep Francoist Spain neutral and the Azores out of German control (Wheeler 1986; Crawford 2008). Pre-war Poland had an alliance with Romania, but its leaders preferred that Romania not fight against Germany in September 1939 so that they could use Romanian territory as an escape route. Another reason for not necessarily wanting commitments upheld is that other states might fear that the ally could pick its own fights mid-war, thereby causing new campaign difficulties that would divert critical resources away (see Edelstein and Shifrinson 2018). This sort of ally might be valuable in peacetime for the diplomatic support that it can provide, but it could be a liability in times of war. Fascist Italy is one such example, as it invaded Greece against Germany's wishes in October 1940 (Kallis 2000: 175–6). Italian forces eventually encountered such stubborn Greek resistance that Germany had to intervene to help them.

Scholars have identified which factors correlate with whether states fulfill their alliance promises in wartime. Building on the finding that alliance promises are kept three-quarters of the time, Brett Ashley Leeds (2003) postulates that most alliances will prove reliable because states make peacetime investments that at once demonstrate their sincerity and screen out potentially unfaithful allies. Certain factors are common among those that do not act as promised toward its allies. One is when a state has experienced at least a 10 percent change – positive or negative – in its power capabilities following the formation of the alliance. Another is that major powers are slightly less likely to fight than their weaker counterparts. This latter result may not be surprising, since major powers tend, all things being equal, to have more flexibility in choosing their foreign policy engagements. In contrast, weaker states might feel compelled to join the fray

regardless of whether their vital interests are directly implicated in that conflict. Another factor identified by Leeds is
whether a state has experienced a major change in the make-up
of its domestic political institutions, by becoming appreciably
either more democratic or more autocratic (2003: 820–2).
Scholars often assess democracies as much more reliable with
respect to their promises to fight than nondemocracies, but
others contend that democracies may in fact be more likely
to renege on their commitments. Specifically, Erik Gartzke
and Kristian Gleditsch (2004) argue that because democracies can expect turnover in their governing coalitions, those
leaders forming the alliance will likely be different from those
called upon to defend the alliance militarily. The resulting
commitment gap is too difficult to bridge given the nature
of democratic politics, and can only be partially mitigated
by way of a treaty. Still, others like Michaela Mattes (2012)
assert that the evidence does not bear out such skepticism
because democracies resort to institutional measures to offset
these risks.

Yet identifying correlations is not enough – they do not
get fully to the root of the question of why states fulfill their
commitments and undertake military operations, let alone
participate in such common endeavors when alliance obligations are not even at stake. After all, multilateral military
operations are examples of collective action and may accordingly be prone to free-riding. One solution to the collective
action problem inherent in multilateral military operations is
that like-minded states will take part in light of their common
interests, threat perceptions, political ideologies, and values
(Davidson 2011; von Hlatky 2013). Without formally
declaring war, Warsaw Pact members Poland, Bulgaria,
Hungary, and the Soviet Union invaded Czechoslovakia in
1968 out of a shared concern regarding the liberal reform
process initiated by leaders in Prague (Crump 2015: 215–57).
Another solution involves the use of coercion by powerful
states that wish to boost the numbers of a coalition, whether to
aggregate military power, enhance the campaign's legitimacy,
or both. A powerful state can use its superior capabilities to
compel countries to join its coalition or, in the case of treaty

allies, to fulfill alliance promises. Alternatively, these junior partners could simply "comply ... with commands not only out of shared interests or threatened punishments but also because they respect and comply with the authority of the dominant state" (Lake 2011: 173).

A more compelling explanation ties coercion, interests, and legitimacy together. Marina Henke (2019) argues that, because multilateral military operations can suffer from collective action problems, states interested in forming a coalition to confront a particular security challenge must try to persuade others to join it. To do so, these states must identify others who could plausibly take part, and, if those potential partners have reservations, bargain with them, at times even providing side-payments and making arrangements around their deployment preferences in return for their participation. To ease the negotiation process, states organizing the coalition lean on what Henke calls "diplomatic embeddedness" – the set of bilateral and multilateral diplomatic ties that two countries can have with one another at a given time. Diplomatic embeddedness creates opportunities for building trust and more enduring agreements, creating access to private information, and providing the space for negotiations to unfold in the first place (Henke 2019: 19–26). For example, in learning through local contacts the priorities of the Nigerian government, the United States recruited it into a UN-authorized coalition to stabilize war-torn Darfur by removing sanctions imposed on Nigeria and reducing its debt (Henke 2019: 106–9). One surprising finding that Henke uncovers concerns the role of alliances in the formation of multilateral military operations. She observes that "roughly three-quarters of coalitions that intervened in crises during the late twentieth and early twenty-first centuries involved no allied states, and of those coalitions that did involve allies, most also included non-allied partners" (2019: 5). Such a finding invites the question of why have a formal alliance in the first place, if membership in one does not necessarily translate into coalition participation.

Alliance politics is not unimportant to this story, however. On some occasions, states have participated in multilateral military operations to create diplomatic embeddedness (Gannon and Kent 2021). Many European members of the "coalition of the willing" that the United States pulled together against Iraq in 2003 were relatively young democracies eager to align their defense policies with one another and, significantly, with the United States. As Marcin Zaborowski (2004: 12) notes: "Poland's support for the United States during the Iraq Crisis appears, in fact, aimed at developing a sense of obligation and responsibility for Poland's security in America." Polish President Aleksander Kwaśniewski declared: "We bet on a strategic partnership with the United States, because without it we would surely be in a lot worse situation" (quoted in Wągrowska 2004: 10). By strengthening relations with the United States, Polish leaders believe that they can create a better balance against the long-term threat posed by Russia to its political sovereignty and territorial integrity (Zaborowski and Longhurst 2007: 12). As part of its campaign to cultivate good standing with the United States in its pursuit of NATO membership, Georgia participated in various interventions, even contributing forces to Iraq amid the deepening threat presented by Russia (Kyle 2019: 238). Estonia has sent troops to join French anti-insurgent operations in Africa's Sahel region in part to diversify its defense relationships and to convey support to EU defense initiatives. France, in turn, has contributed rotational forces to Estonia (see Stoicescu and Lebrun 2019).

## Why Military Effectiveness Is Hard for Military Alliances to Achieve

But, given these bargaining dynamics, how militarily effective can these coalitions be? Military effectiveness refers to how well basic tactics and higher-level complex operations are performed in combat. Although alliances purportedly serve to aggregate military capabilities against shared threats, and although states nevertheless have to surmount collective action problems when building multilateral coalitions, the actual military effectiveness of those wartime coalitions is open to question (Bensahel 2007: 187–90; Schmitt 2018). As Sara Bjerg Moller (2016: 27–36) explains, the capability aggregation model makes several problematic assumptions about the military effectiveness that alliances purportedly have – namely, that coalition membership is additive in military power (that is, the military power that allies bring to bear simply added together) and that allies reap economies of scale. Ideally, a militarily effective alliance (or coalition) would be one in which equipment is standardized and plentiful; supply and logistic chains are resilient and efficient; inter-unit communication is secure and understandable; key intelligence on enemy intentions and capabilities is shared; and unity of command exists with integrated staffs available to coordinate national deployments and operations. Some national armed forces do not even approach this ideal themselves; the following discussion examines how and why coalitions often fall very short of it.

Much of what follows turns on the concept of alliance interoperability. NATO offers perhaps a good definition of it:

> Interoperability refers to the ability of different military organizations to conduct joint operations. These organizations can be of different nationalities or different armed services (ground, naval and air forces) or both. Interoperability allows forces, units or systems to operate together. It requires them to share common doctrine and procedures, each others' [sic] infrastructure and bases, and to be able to communicate with each other. It reduces duplication in an Alliance of 26 [as of 2006] members, allow [sic] pooling of resources, and even produces synergies among members. (NATO 2006: 1)

These issues need not come down to differences in military equipment, for problems of interoperability can derive from strategic, organizational, and technical factors. Politics runs through all of them. Choices over which rifle to use can be just as contested as decisions about whether to subordinate national forces to an alliance command or whether to continue fighting at all (see Ford 2017).

## Strategic factors

If hostilities with an adversary intensify so much or a security challenge becomes so pressing that a coalition must be put together to engage in military operations, various strategic factors will come into play that shape how that coalition will perform throughout the campaign. Differences in threat perceptions are one such factor. Some members of a treaty alliance will have to decide whether they are to use force against an adversary, regardless of what promises they might have made previously in peacetime. Alliance commitments are never automatic. Though many observers often regard Article V of the Washington Treaty as the gold standard of all alliance commitments, in that it provides for how an attack against one NATO member is an attack against all, nothing about Article V compels any sort of military response in the event of hostile action. As mentioned, some allies may need to be cajoled or given compensation before they join the fray. Those that do join have to grapple with at least two questions.

First, do coalition members have compatible aims? They need not have the same exact goals. What is important is that their objectives are complementary. The United Kingdom and Russia had their own reasons to fight against Germany in the First World War. For London, it was to forestall, in part, the emergence of a regional hegemon that could dominate Europe, as well as to protect British prestige and to abide by promises to defend Belgian territorial integrity. For Moscow, war aims not only included the weakening of Germany, but also the dislodging of Austria-Hungary from the Balkans and acquiring control of the Dardanelles. These different war aims were not at all harmonious, but they overlapped sufficiently for each of these two members of the Triple Entente to fight Germany simultaneously once mobilization orders were issued and declarations of war were made. As this historical example indicates, geography has some influence in shaping the war aims that states have. Not only did the two allies have different types of empires – one on land and the other maritime – but they also found themselves confronting Germany from different directions. They varied in their aims as well as in their vulnerabilities and resource constraints, to say nothing of their political systems and values.

This observation brings us to the second question: how can coalition members manage the threat of defection? Coalition warfare is much like a stag hunt, a dilemma often invoked by game theorists to illustrate certain problems that stymie social cooperation. The situation is as follows. Several hunters are pursuing a large stag that they may or may not catch. If they work together, are patient, and avoid detection by the stag in their hunt of it, then they most likely can kill the stag and enjoy its meat. But if a hare comes along, offering some prospect of meat but certainly not enough to feed the entire hunting party, one hunter may be tempted and unilaterally decide to take it while the rest go hungry, facing even worse odds for catching the coveted stag. Members of a multilateral military campaign can find themselves confronting similar incentives. Their chances for achieving complete victory over an adversary are greatest if they all stay together in the fight for as long as it takes. Nevertheless, some states might be satisfied if they fulfill some but not all of their aims. Or they might eventually come to feel that they have put in enough effort to prove that they are reliable to their partners but that the costs of participation have become too high to continue.

Goals themselves change over the course of any war, often as a result of intra-coalition bargaining. In general, belligerents should rationally adjust their war aims based on their performance on the battlefield and whether events confirm or not their expectations for how the war will play out (Ramsay 2008; Friedman 2019: 161–86). The worse things get, the more moderate their aims should become. Some coalition members may be more sensitive to battlefield outcomes than others. Romania entered the First World War on the side of Germany, only to be defeated shortly thereafter when Russia mounted the Brusilov Offensive in the summer of 1916. Yet coalition politics can also distort the relationship between battlefield outcomes and war aims. The United Kingdom, for example, escalated its war aims and military engagement in the opening months of the First World War. Mira Rapp-Hooper (2014) explains the United Kingdom's behavior by pointing to the Treaty of London. This agreement tightened the Triple Entente – an arrangement made up of France, Russia, and the United Kingdom that did not feature formal defense ties prior to the war – by obliging the signatories not to pursue separate peace negotiations with Germany. Rapp-Hooper's data reveal that just fewer than 10 percent of all alliances concluded since 1816 feature promises not to reach separate settlements with the adversary. Half of these pledges were invoked in wartime and rarely have they ever been broken. States with roughly similar economic and material capabilities have tended to sign them, suggesting that concerns about abandonment in war are relatively less acute in unequal relationships where a strong state can more effectively manage a weaker ally.

The reasons for signing these agreements are severalfold. One is to create reputation costs associated with breaking an agreement and to manage intramural differences in the coalition, thereby addressing the problem highlighted by the stag hunt dilemma described above. Another is to improve the wartime coalition's own bargaining position vis-à-vis the adversary by making it much more cohesive and thus less prone to fracture. But to realize these benefits, states might have to accept each other's war aims so as to prevent defection. If war is ultimately a violent process by which states bargain with one another to find some sort of mutually acceptable settlement, then the expansion of war aims for these alliance reasons can perversely narrow the opportunities for diplomacy, making the conflict more intractable. Perhaps it is small wonder that, even if the two world wars – which did see the use of these agreements – are excluded from the count, wars that have not allowed separate peace treaties were much bloodier than wars where that was not the case (see Rapp-Hooper 2014: 817–23).

The risk of defection is real in multilateral military

operations. In some cases, an adversary is able to practice such skillful diplomacy that it can realign members of an opposing alliance. In 1915, the Triple Entente successfully enticed Italy away from its alignment with Germany and Austria-Hungary by promising Rome a privileged position in the Adriatic Sea as well as control over various territories located in southeastern Europe and elsewhere. For the Triple Entente to make these concessions, Italy had to be valuable enough as a partner for its perceived potential to tip the balance (Crawford 2014: 135–42). In other cases, domestic political factors can influence whether a state sticks to a multilateral military operation. The degree of elite consensus – the extent to which members of the ruling and opposition parties agree on a policy – can shape coalition participation (Kreps 2010). Absent such consensus, right-wing governments might be more concerned about their reputation for reliability and so will remain in a coalition. Left-wing governments might be more reluctant to deploy military forces in the first place and so could defect from a coalition upon coming to power (Massie 2016: 90). To be sure, the decision to defect is usually multifaceted. A combination of international and domestic factors is often at play. Even a right-wing government might defect if it has decided that it has done its fair share and that battlefield conditions have become unacceptable (Mello 2020). Domestic factors themselves are complex, particularly in democracies. In a presidential system, ideological disagreements matter most when the executive and legislative branches of government are under the control of different, opposing parties, which in turn reduces the ability of leaders to make such major policy changes as a premature withdrawal from a military commitment. In a parliamentary system, ideological disagreements matter most when the executive draws not on a single ruling party, but on multiple political parties as a result of some sort of domestic coalition arrangement. These disagreements can lead to defection from a military campaign if one political party demands it in exchange for approving another policy that a different party really wants to implement.

Even if defection is not a salient concern, seeing an ally

absorb massive losses on the battlefield can compel a state to re-evaluate its own military operations. Austria-Hungary fared poorly against Russia in the opening stages of the First World War, prompting the Austrian Chief of the General Staff Franz Conrad von Hötzendorf to appeal for German support. He got it, but at the expense of Germany assuming a more dominant role in the command and control structure on the Eastern front. Plans for an offensive that would simply relieve pressure on Austria gave way to more expansive objectives in light of a series of victories in the area around Gorlice and Tarnów in what had been, before the war, Austrian-controlled Galicia, which is now southern Poland (Foley 2005: 132–42). The outcome turned out to be a major victory for the two Central Powers because it compelled the strategic withdrawal of the Russian 3rd Army. The British and the French faced similar pressures in 1917 but experienced a very different result. Hoping to make the long-awaited breakthrough, the commander of the French armies on the Western Front, Robert Nivelle, planned a major offensive to break through German lines. But his strategy failed and French casualties were so high in the fighting that took place in April and May 1917 that many French infantry divisions ceased to abide by new orders to attack, effectively triggering a mutiny. The British subsequently launched limited offensive operations near the village of Messines in June 1917 in order to draw out German reserve forces, to relieve pressure on the French, and to boost morale (Philpott 1996: 139–40).

## Organizational factors

In agreeing to participate in a multilateral military operation, countries must determine what sort of command and control arrangement they would use in going about the campaign. The US Department of Defense's Dictionary of Military and Associated Terms defines command and control as:

> The exercise of authority and direction by a properly designated commander over assigned and attached forces in the accomplishment of the mission. Command

and control functions are performed through an arrangement of personnel, equipment, communications, facilities, and procedures employed by a commander in planning, directing, coordinating, and controlling forces and operations in the accomplishment of the mission. (US Department of Defense 2004: 101)

As a senior British Army officer, who took part in US-led operations against Iraq in the early 1990s, observed: "The most contentious aspect of coalition operations is command and control" (Rice 1997: 152). Governments have good reason to be wary about how their armed forces might be used by an allied commander from another country; sovereignty concerns loom large. Governments do not want to see, for example, their own soldiers being cynically deployed in dangerous missions that are out of step with their own country's goals and interests. At the same time, if governments jealously protect the use of their own forces too much, then the coalition might not be able to draw effectively on its members' contributions. It can even be vulnerable to divide-and-conquer tactics by the adversary if each coalition partner fights separately.

Command and control arrangements in wartime partnerships vary in their level of integration – that is, "the degree to which different military activities [at the strategic, operational, and tactical levels] are internally consistent and mutually reinforcing" (Brooks 2007: 10). At the one end, countries fight as allies but nevertheless conduct their operations independently of one another. Forces are subject exclusively to their own national chains of command. An example is when South Korea sent a large contingent to fight in the Vietnam War but refused to subordinate its soldiers formally to US command (Cosmas 2009: 434–5). At the other end, there is unified integration whereby one ally exercises authority over the armed forces of another. Ironically, South Korea provides an example of a country that is subordinate to the command of its treaty ally – the United States – by way of the ROK/US Combined Forces Command (CFC), established in 1978. Commanded by a four-star US general, the

ROK/US CFC has more than 600,000 active-duty military personnel under its operational control, representing all services and both countries. Each position in a staff section is manned binationally, such that a Korean chief would have an American deputy, and vice versa. The US and South Korean militaries have been engaged in joint exercises for most years since 1978 (United States Forces Korea n.d.). Recent years have seen a debate arise as to whether South Korea might repatriate at least peacetime control over its own forces. In the meantime, the structure is a hybrid of an independent and a unified form of command and control. Combined command and control structures can still differ in terms of how centralized and how divided the authority may be across military services or geographical areas (Moller 2016: 87–8).

In most cases, alliance command and control structures are complex and convoluted. Consider NATO. Control of its multinational operations falls under four authoritative levels. Operational Command (OPCOM) allows a commander to assign missions or tasks as well as to delegate operational and/or tactical control to subordinate commanders. OPCOM also permits a command to deploy units and to reassign forces. Operational Control (OPCON) denotes the authority granted to a commander to direct fighting units in carrying out missions or tasks that are defined in terms of their function, time, or location. Neither OPCOM nor OPCON covers responsibility for administration or logistics. Instead, both are concerned with the planning and execution of the operational process undergirding a military campaign. Tactical Command (TACOM) and Tactical Control (TACON) relate to the actual fighting or execution of particular missions. TACOM allows a commander to assign tasks to forces under their command so as to achieve a specific mission assigned by a higher authority. TACON grants commanders the narrow authority to direct and to control the maneuvers of their units in a specific operational area (Young 2001/2: 41; Moller 2016: 71–3).

For civilians, as much as this alphabet soup of command levels can be bewildering, theory is still cleaner than reality. In practice, actual campaigns in which NATO countries have participated deviated from this already complicated model. Take the example of the United Nations Protection Force (UNPROFOR), which was the first UN peacekeeping force deployed in the early 1990s in Croatia and in Bosnia and Herzegovina during the Yugoslav Wars. Before its operations were replaced by NATO and EU missions in 1995, the command and control arrangement for airstrikes was dual-key – meaning that both the UN and NATO would have to grant authorization for an airstrike. Myron Hura et al. (2000: 27) nicely illustrate how this political compromise slowed decision-making and handicapped military effectiveness:

> A request by ground troops [for an airstrike] typically went through Lt. Gen. Sir Michael Rose, the ground commander for U.N. forces in Bosnia, to Gen. Jean Cot, the French officer in Zagreb (who commanded all U.N. troops in the former Yugoslavia), to Yasushik Akashi, the U.N. special envoy with the authority to command a strike. In other words, U.N. procedures required that NATO strikes against ground positions attain approval from Rose's Bosnian military command in Sarajevo; the request would then be relayed to the UNPROFOR commander in the Balkans before reaching special envoy Akashi. In the case of NATO close air support to help defend UNPROFOR ground troops, a dual-key approach was also found wanting, because it generally resulted in aircraft arriving on scene and having to loiter while authority was sought from U.N. civilian authorities to provide support.

Although the dual-key approach was rooted in the different strategic approaches that the United States and its NATO allies had for addressing the conflict, the situation turned out to be too unwieldy to be viable (Bensahel 2007: 193). NATO made clear its preference that no parallel chain of command should exist such that it eventually acquired full authority for UNPROFOR's replacement, Implementation Force (IFOR).

Members of a coalition often attach so-called caveats that place limits on how their forces are to be used over the course of a military operation. The issue of caveats was especially salient in ISAF – the NATO mission in Afghanistan that lasted from 2001 to 2014 (NATO took command of it in 2003). Whether official or unwritten, caveats can place restrictions on the geographic areas or types of operations in which military forces from a particular country can be deployed. Sometimes caveats can dictate the rules of engagement by which those forces must abide – for example, not opening fire unless attacked (Saideman and Auerswald 2012: 70; Mello 2019: 47–9). Caveats can undermine overall military effectiveness and cause resentment among those coalition members who believe that they are bearing a disproportionate share of the costs and risks. In the initial phases of the campaign, during Operation Enduring Freedom, Canadian commanders in Afghanistan had to confer with Ottawa before undertaking any mission that risked collateral damage. Such micro-management was relaxed over time and Canadian forces contributed to some of the more dangerous missions overseen by ISAF. In contrast, several key NATO allies – like Belgium, Germany, and Italy – had put in place various restrictions on their contingents throughout ISAF's operational history. German forces could barely operate beyond Afghanistan's northern region – an area that was mostly peaceful. This limitation created friction and undermined effectiveness, since they could not be deployed outside the ambit of their regional command even if it meant being alongside the Afghan forces that they had mentored. Caveats also played a role in the NATO intervention in Libya. The Netherlands withheld the use of its F-16 fighter jets for airstrikes (Coticchia 2011: 57). International security scholars Stephen Saideman and David Auerswald (2012) find that the use of caveats partly reflects domestic political institutions rather than public opinion or even threat perceptions. Countries that have strong majoritarian parliamentary or strong presidential systems are less likely to place caveats than those systems that usually feature a coalition parliamentary system like Germany.

Caveats aside, trade-offs often abound in how alliances can achieve integration. Allies tend to vary in their military skill sets and capabilities. Accordingly, it may make sense to distribute their national forces across different geographical sectors so that they complement one another and achieve some efficiency. One disadvantage of this division of labor is that the adversary would be able identify the weakest geographical sector and try to exploit it (Bensahel 2007: 194). Allies could also exchange liaison teams between them in order to coordinate functions and operations. However, liaison teams can be resource-intensive, lack specialized knowledge, and create new bureaucratic demands upon already overwhelmed military personnel (Bensahel 2007: 195). Finally, information-sharing can prove vital for alliance effectiveness as partners learn crucial details about combat operations and enemy capabilities. Alas, states might sometimes be too hesitant to release intelligence to even their allies, lest it is leaked to third parties. A consequence of the United Kingdom being part of Five Eyes – an intelligence "alliance" comprising five members of the Anglosphere – is that it is restricted from sharing certain information with France despite their common membership in NATO and their pledge to deepen bilateral security cooperation following the 2010 Lancaster House Treaties (Pannier 2020: 106–7).

## Technical factors

Technical factors can also hamper interoperability and, by extension, the military effectiveness of a wartime coalition. One such factor is the diversity of equipment. For many observers, the very concept of interoperability conjures up differences in weapons platforms, communications equipment, and information systems that can inhibit connectivity between units drawn from multiple countries and services. The well-founded conventional wisdom is that standardization of equipment benefits a coalition. If states use the same platforms and the same equipment, then they are able to use the same ammunition and fuel types, thereby alleviating burdens on the supply chain and simplifying military logistics. Sometimes having multiple configurations of the same platform is enough to deprive states of the ability to share interchangeable parts when their equipment suffers inevitable wear and tear. That said, using the same equipment does not automatically eliminate interoperability issues. If users cannot operate equipment because they are unfamiliar with it, for example, then interoperability issues will remain. During the Korean War, the United States supplied its partners with everything from uniforms to vehicles to weapons. Unfortunately, some partners lacked the requisite experience to use properly, and without accident, the equipment they had received (Moller 2016: 40).

Numerous examples abound of how equipment differences between coalitions have undermined their joint military effectiveness. At the beginning of the twentieth century, the Canadian government was denied a contract to acquire Lee-Enfield rifles from the United Kingdom in part because the British Army had its own equipment shortfalls following the Boer War. And so, in April 1915, Canadian infantry fighting at the Second Battle of Ypres used the made-in-Canada Ross rifle – a cumbersome and defective weapon that often jammed and thus was very badly suited to the rigors of high-intensity trench warfare on the Western Front. Worsening matters was that the Ross rifle could not use British-made ammunition, which had been of lower quality than Canadian-made ammunition but was nevertheless usable in the Lee-Enfields that Canadian soldiers ended up using later in the war (Nossal 2016: 33–7). Sometimes it is not so much about equipment differences as it is about supply. European NATO members constantly suffered capability shortfalls during military interventions in the Balkans and sub-Saharan Africa in the 2000s (Menon 2011: 80). Even the United Kingdom, which typically spends much more on defense than most European countries, saw its own stockpile of precision-guided munitions run embarrassingly short during the 2011 air campaign over Libya (Goulter 2015: 181).

Communication problems also arise. Language barriers, unsurprisingly, can hamper mutual understanding. A correspondent for *The Times* noted that the lack of a common language was "a real hindrance to relations" between the British and the French at senior military and political levels during the First World War (quoted in Greenhalgh 2005: 9).

The US-led coalition in Korea wrestled with language barriers as well. Mismatched cryptographic equipment and insecure communications can also cause problems. Considering the importance that the modern system of warfare accords to dispersal, small-unit maneuver, cover, and conceal, units need to be able to talk to one another without being jammed or giving away their location. In Afghanistan, NATO countries had to buy the same radios that US forces had been using in order to achieve some interoperability. Otherwise, countries might have to bridge the gap between noninteroperable radios by changing the voice output from one radio into a voice input for another radio, which risks being compromised if the radio networks are insecure or have different security classifications (Johannes 2018: 5–6). Sometimes countries use different frequencies. During the Second World War, a strike force comprising British and American bombers incurred major casualties during a raid at a German training base in Mailly-le-Camp, France, for this very reason. They were picking up music by Bing Crosby and Glenn Miller rather than being able to talk with one another (Nichol 2020: 61).

Mobility problems deserve a mention as well. A problem recently vexing NATO defense planners is how to ensure that armed forces can move across Europe to provide reinforcements and support to the Baltic countries in case they come under Russian attack. Although civilians and civilian goods do not have to clear customs when crossing most national borders within the EU, the movement of military personnel and equipment has been subject to stringent regulations and procedures, which in turn can create major delays that could leave the Baltic countries hapless against a major assault. The problem is not just legal – it is also tied to physical infrastructure. Different rail gauges, limited road networks, and the lack of depots, vehicle parks, and fueling facilities would also hamper any effort by NATO forces to surge into the theater of operations (Hodges et al. 2020: 8). Furthermore, moving military forces from their host territory into a war zone requires lift capabilities that allies might wish to use sparingly. In 1943, a major controversy between the United

States and the United Kingdom centered on the production of landing craft. US senior military leaders believed that the United Kingdom could have been doing more to produce landing craft, especially as British leaders were at the time insisting on Mediterranean operations – operations that risked diverting such hardware from being used in a cross-Channel invasion (Harrison 1951: 62–8). During the Cold War, the United States invested significantly in sea and air lift, not least because of concerns that it would have to surge forces into Central Europe in the event of a Soviet attack. Since the end of the Cold War, disinvestments in lift capabilities have meant that even the US military forces can experience major delays and high costs when moving, for example, an army brigade from the continental United States to northeastern Europe (Owen 2017: 104–5).

## Coalition Warfare in the Contemporary Era

In the early decades of the twenty-first century, perceptions regarding the nature of military conflict have already changed dramatically. The security challenges posed by civil war and terrorism have been the most acute, pushing states to engage in "out-of-area" operations in the Middle East and Africa, taking them into conflict zones geographically removed from where their alliances – to the extent that they have any – would be facing their most direct territorial threats. Popular for much of this time has been the notion that war between states is on the decline and that most threats had more to do with ethnic violence and weak state capacity than with rival great powers. Many states have thus felt that they would be better served investing in light expeditionary forces and not in the heavy military hardware more suited to the high-intensity combat operations characteristic of major power war. And yet, after 2008, threat perceptions and priorities began to shift. Territorial defense slowly came to dominate defense planning amid concerns relating to the rise of China and the revisionism of Russia. States now are not only worried again about threats from the major powers; they are also fearful that others will not back them up in case fighting does break out for some reason.

These observations about contemporary warfare speak to the questions addressed in this chapter. Which countries fulfill their alliance commitments in wartime? Which countries take part in multinational military operations at all? Why do they get involved, given the risks and costs involved? And when they are in a coalition, what shapes their military effectiveness? What factors impinge upon alliance interoperability?

One striking empirical observation is how increasingly uncommon it is for allies to fight alongside one another, despite their commitments. Estimates do vary, but the latest research finds that alliance reliability – defined in terms of fighting alongside an ally in wartime – has in fact been on the wane since the dawn of the nuclear age. Democracies and weaker alliance members are most likely to fulfill their commitments. To be sure, selection effects are operative: states do not randomly decide to go to war so that their commitments get tested. By virtue of not fighting wars, the most reliable alliances do not figure in these statistics, thereby distorting their results (Cohen and Lanoszka n.d.). Nevertheless, as discussed above, Henke (2019) finds that alliance membership is not a significant predictor for a state to get involved in a multinational military operation. States interested in cobbling together a coalition have to woo others to join them, often appealing to interests and networks that may seem peripheral to the conflict at hand. It makes one wonder about why formal military alliances exist at all if participation in an actual campaign needs to be negotiated – until, of course, one remembers that the purpose of most alliances is not to fight wars, but to prevent them.

Even when allies do get involved in a campaign, their military effectiveness is hardly assured. The conventional wisdom is that an alliance can aggregate military capabilities and thus bring greater force to bear on its adversaries, thereby upping the odds of victory. Though intuitive, this view underestimates the difficulties that coalition partners encounter when engaging in multinational military operations. Coalition partners have to wrestle with war aims and interests that could possibly diverge over the course of the campaign and even result in separate peace treaties and unilateral defections. They have to decide which command and control arrangements should govern their operations, and reckon with national caveats that some partners can impose on the use of their own forces. Equipment differences, unequal military supplies, communication problems, and mobility challenges can also limit the effectiveness of partners fighting together.

Does this all imply that military alliances are much less important in international politics than is often assumed? After all, if their entire purpose is to deter war, and thus to offer a vehicle that raises the military effectiveness of joint operations lest deterrence fails, then what are we to make of the fact that alliances tend to fall prey to unfulfilled commitments and numerous strategic, organizational, and technical challenges in wartime? Or of how not being a member of an alliance does not preclude participation in a multinational military operation?

One should surely not exaggerate the difficulties of fighting in coalitions. States do join formal military alliances because, in the end, they believe that they stand to benefit from such arrangements. Strategic, organizational, and technical problems do arise. Some of them come with trade-offs, but they are not always intractable. They just cannot be wished away, as some accounts of how alliances serve to aggregate capabilities might imply. It is thus worth recalling Winston Churchill's observation: "There is only one thing worse than fighting with allies, and that is fighting without them!" Many states – especially small ones – share these sentiments. The Baltic countries of Estonia, Latvia, and Lithuania would of course prefer to be within rather than outside NATO, despite all the risks of abandonment and the military challenges that their membership would engender in the event of a serious crisis with Russia. Being in a treaty alliance at least offers opportunities for enhancing military effectiveness on a much more consistent basis than what more tacit or flexible alignments could provide. By the same token, Taiwan covets a rekindling of its security and political ties with the United

States as it faces an increasingly unfavorable balance of power vis-à-vis China. A US military intervention on its behalf may very well be unsuccessful and may never be assured in the first place, regardless of whether there is a signed commitment. But in the end, for many security partners, it is arguably better to be in a formal military alliance than not, precisely because of their potential deterrent value, even if the war-fighting value may in reality prove suspect.

# 6

# Termination

We often take it for granted that the United States leads major military alliances in Europe and East Asia and that these alliances remain relatively strong despite their age. The fact that they have lasted as long as they have should be surprising to us. Prior to the Second World War, the average lifespan of a military alliance was scarcely ten years. Based on the historical records available to them at the time, the European and Asian leaders who helped establish formal alliances with the United States in the late 1940s and early 1950s would probably be astonished to learn just how resilient many of those arrangements have proven to be; they would be impressed by the fact that most of them survived the Cold War and outlived some of their rivals.

The end did appear to be nigh, however, following Trump's surprise win in the 2016 US presidential election. Although he did not campaign explicitly on ending any one military alliance, his stinging criticisms of NATO and a select set of treaty allies left many friendly governments worried that he would pursue an isolationist foreign policy. Over the course of his single term in office, he withdrew the United States from the Paris climate accords, the Trans-Pacific Partnership, and various arms control agreements, all the while refusing to soften his rhetoric against US alliance treaty obligations. Rumors abound that he did seek to pull the United States out of NATO in 2017 but was convinced not to do so by his political and military advisors. Acrimonious negotiations with South Korea over the cost of military bases also fueled speculation that this particular bilateral alliance would end. Of course, no alliance actually ceased to exist during Trump's controversial tenure; on the contrary, two new formal allies were added under his leadership, when Montenegro and North Macedonia joined NATO in 2017 and 2020, respectively.

Trump was uniquely critical of US alliances, but debates about their sustainability will endure as the United States and its treaty partners have to face hard choices about their defense budgets and foreign policies. What lent some credence to the notion that the age of Trump would mean the end of alliances were the deeper trends that seemed to push for their demise. Some observers argue that the United States is facing "strategic insolvency," whereby its international commitments far exceed its capabilities (Mazarr 2012). Others highlight power shifts in international politic that lead the United States to see China as a peer competitor and to regard Europe as relatively less important (Simón and Fiott 2014). Yet others point out that US alliances have, to a degree, become a victim of their own post-Second World War success and that complacency has at last set in (Rapp-Hooper 2020: 2–3). These considerations will still matter in Trump's wake: the economic aftermath of the SARS-CoV-2 pandemic, the rise of China, and persistent worries of US retrenchment will continue to strain some relationships.

Under what circumstances, and how, do military alliances in fact come to an end? Notwithstanding the extraordinary durability of most US alliances, all military alliances eventually do cease to exist. Few, if any, last forever. Even the United States has abrogated some treaty partnerships (e.g., the Sino-American Mutual Defense Treaty) or has let some arrangements slowly wilt before finally annulling them (e.g., the Southeast Asian Treaty Organization), although, in the latter case, its founding treaty – the Manila Pact – remains operative between the United States and Taiwan.

To understand these processes, this chapter outlines five different forms of alliance termination and, by extension, discusses how a military alliance can end. It does so after reviewing discussions within alliance treaties themselves of how the commitments they embody might eventually expire. The first form of termination occurs when the alliance has successfully fulfilled its purpose, whether in war or in peace. A second is that alliances meet their demise as a result of military defeat. A third occurs when at least one member decides that the alliance no longer serves its interests and so abrogates it in peacetime in order to pursue other foreign policy objectives. From the perspective of the withdrawing ally, those objectives would simply be impossible to realize if the alliance were to continue existing. A fourth form of alliance termination involves downgrading. In some ways, this is akin to the zombification of an alliance relationship. Rather than abrogate the treaty commitment outright, members simply let it exist on paper while avoiding making any meaningful investments that would maintain their major security ties. In this scenario, political and military leaders grow increasingly estranged from one another but the costs of rupture are too high for it to be done openly. The fifth and final form of alliance termination is transformation. This type of termination is a bit of a misnomer, since it may be the case that one military alliance is supplanting another. Transformation can happen if allies agree to become a union state or if a bilateral alliance becomes enfolded in a larger multilateral alliance.

This chapter brings us back full circle to an earlier discussion on alliance formation. Presumably, explanations that identify the factors that drive states to establish military alliances can also illuminate what leads them to renounce those arrangements. That said, such decisions are rarely monocausal – different factors are often shaped by major foreign policy decisions. It is possible, too, that a key variable that explains why states formed an alliance offers limited insight on how that alliance endures over the long term. For example, the Soviet threat pushed North American and European countries to form NATO, an alliance that

continues to exist despite the collapse of the Soviet Union
in 1991. Each type of alliance termination has its own logic,
thereby complicating any effort to provide a unified account
of why or how any one alliance begins, endures, and ends.

## How to Get Out of an Alliance via the Alliance Treaty Itself

Many international agreements forged by states have escape
or withdrawal clauses. Escape clauses allow some flexibility
in case a state experiences unforeseen shocks in its domestic
and international circumstances (Koremenos et al. 2001:
773). For example, the legal doctrine of *rebus sic stantibus*
("things standing thus") allows for a party to withdraw
from an agreement in light of fundamentally altered circumstances that make the original deal too difficult to respect or
to enforce. Indeed, escape clauses can suspend obligations
without necessarily being in violation of the terms of the
agreement. They might have the effect of watering down an
agreement by creating opportunities for a state to threaten
its withdrawal in order to resist a specific commitment that
it does not want to make. Nevertheless, their insertion may
be essential for getting a state to agree to the treaty in the
first place (Rosendorff and Milner 2001: 831–2). Military
alliances are, of course, not based on just any type of
treaty. Their activation implicates both blood and money,
with sometimes existential consequences for members of
the alliance themselves. In the nuclear age, as discussed in
Chapter 1, states have inserted deliberately vague language
so as to leave indeterminate the exact conditions under which
they would honor a treaty commitment.

Although alliance treaties may not contain escape clauses
per se, they do often feature clauses that touch on the
matter of termination. Interestingly, the time horizons
of alliance treaties grew longer as warfare became more
complex. Negotiated in part by German Chancellor Otto
von Bismarck, the League of the Three Emperors and the
Reinsurance Treaty of 1873 and 1887, respectively, were
originally written to last at least three years. The 1879 Dual

Alliance signed by Austria-Hungary and Germany was to last five years and, provided that neither party sought to negotiate the agreement, would thereafter be renewed for another three years. Those two countries signed the Triple Alliance with Italy in 1882, which was initially set to last for five years as well. An expanded version of this alliance agreement, signed in 1912, was to last six years. Barring any renunciation by any one member, it would be automatically renewed for another six years. Like other agreements of its era, the 1914 Treaty of Alliance Between Germany and Turkey also specified a duration of five years. The secret 1892 pact, the Franco-Russian military convention, was exceptional in its vagueness, declaring that "it shall have the same duration as the Triple Alliance" (see Brigham Young University Library 2020).

Time horizons became longer over the course of the twentieth century. The Polish–French accord of 1921 in fact made no mention whatsoever of its expected length. France's 1924 alliance treaty with Czechoslovakia was similarly indefinite in its duration. France's other treaties – with Romania and Serbia – did specify a duration of ten and five years, respectively. The two separate mutual defense treaties that the United States has with South Korea and the Philippines commonly state that each agreement "shall remain in force indefinitely. Either Party may terminate it one year after notice has been given to the other Party" (Yale Law School 2008b; Yale Law School 2008c). The Japan–US Security Treaty contains a similar provision, but with the preamble that it "shall remain in force until in the opinion of the Governments of Japan and the United States of America there shall have come into force such United Nations arrangements as will satisfactorily provide for the maintenance of international peace and security in the Japan area" (Ministry of Foreign Affairs of Japan n.d.). NATO's founding treaty is also indefinite and assumes, perhaps ironically, constant US participation. However, Article XIII does provide that: "After the Treaty has been in force for twenty years, any Party may cease to be a Party one year after its notice of denunciation has been given to the Government of the United States of

America, which will inform the Governments of the other Parties of the deposit of each notice of denunciation" (NATO 1949 [2019]). The founding treaty of NATO's Cold War rival – the Warsaw Pact – had a more robust discussion of termination. Similar to NATO, the Warsaw Treaty was to be in force for twenty years, adding that, absent any one-year notice to withdraw, it would remain in place for another ten. Perhaps to signal benign or defensive intentions to domestic and international audiences, it stipulated that the alliance treaty "shall cease to have effect as from the date on which [a General European Treaty concerning collective security] comes into force" (United Nations 1955: 32).

Variation exists in how long military alliances have really endured. The Warsaw Pact saw its withdrawal clause invoked – first with Albania in 1968 and then with its final dissolution in the early 1990s. In the interwar period, France's alliance commitments came to an end with the territorial conquests of Nazi Germany against Czechoslovakia and, later, Poland. NATO still exists. Alliances can thus meet their demise in different ways. The discussion below describes a set of outcomes for how alliances can end.

### Fulfillment

An alliance can simply come to an end if it has fulfilled its original purpose – the *casus foederis* ("case of the treaty") that brought the alliance into existence in the first place. Recall the reasons why states form alliances. They primarily do so to counter some shared threat, but, because their interests are not perfectly aligned, they opt for a formal – but often deliberately ambiguous – arrangement to signal their common aim to each other and to adversaries. That shared threat could be a great power, a rival coalition or alliance of states, a transnational ideological movement, or some combination of these challenges. If that shared threat lessens markedly in intensity, whether because of military victory or a major shift in the balance of power, then the alliance might outlive its usefulness and so would eventually cease to exist (Walt 1997: 158–9). Alternatively, states might use alliances to manage disputes among themselves; this is what Prussian chancellor Otto von Bismarck hoped to achieve with the League of Three Emperors with regards to the problem of great power competition in the Balkan region. If the dispute finds some sort of resolution – one that can transform a rivalry into a more cooperative relationship – then the treaty alliance may lose its significance given the feelings of greater amity.

How many alliances have actually ceased to exist because they had achieved their core aims? Surprisingly, the answer is not many. One statistical study of alliance termination reveals that about 16 percent of alliances end for more or less this reason (Leeds and Savun 2007: 1119). Successful wartime coalitions, by their very definition, fit this model. The Grand Alliance between the United States, the Soviet Union, and the United Kingdom is one such example. It fell apart shortly after the Second World War even though the two great powers had negotiated an alliance treaty in 1942 that stood to last at least twenty years. Even so, the demise of the Grand Alliance was largely due to the way in which the defeat of the Axis Powers allowed pre-existing tensions to sharpen. Disagreements flared up between the Soviet Union and its erstwhile partners over the post-war settlement for Europe (see Trachtenberg 1999). Success can just as easily produce new problems that go on to undermine cooperation.

There are at least three reasons why fulfilling foundational objectives is a rare way for alliances to end. The first is that the problems that states seek to address by forming alliances are uniquely difficult to resolve. Great power adversaries hardly ever collapse in peacetime, whereas transnational ideological challenges tend to be enduring, though variable in intensity, in an era of mass politics. The disintegration of the Soviet Union was an exceptional geopolitical event, one produced by a unique confluence of factors relating to the structure of its economy, interest group politics, and nationalist mobilization (Beissinger 2002; Miller 2016). Typically, however, ailing great powers retrench in much less spectacular fashion, cutting commitments selectively in order to regroup and to go about long-term military and political competition more efficiently (see MacDonald and Parent 2018).

The second reason why successful alliances might persevere is that achieving a core aim can sometimes suggest to members of an alliance that their cooperation has been effective and worth keeping for other common projects. In other words, successful cooperation begets more cooperation. This may be due to what Glenn Snyder (1997: 8) calls the "halo" effect, whereby allies "expect their partners to support them on a variety of issues, including diplomatic crises, even though there is nothing in the alliance treaty requiring it." But it could have less to do with alliance psychology and more to do with how institutionalized and bureaucratized the alliance has become. Such is the basic argument that some experts have made to explain NATO's continued existence after the Soviet Union's collapse. Celeste Wallander (2000: 711–12) argues that, over the course of the Cold War, NATO developed institutional assets that facilitate coordination and negotiation among its members. Those assets were also useful for going about new security missions that went beyond the Alliance's initial anti-Soviet mandate. Because such assets are costly to produce, members of a successful alliance like NATO may not want to jettison them and run the risk of having to create them all over again if a new security challenge were to emerge (see also Haftendorn, Keohane, and Wallander 1999). Institutions, simply put, can alter the incentives for cooperation by widening the range of agreements and expanding the time horizons such that members think more long term rather than get carried away by short-term expediencies (Oye 1985: 16–18). Other alliances may fit this pattern. The Anglo-Portuguese Alliance came into being in 1386 out of a mutual desire to keep in check Castilian and French ambitions. Although the agreement was disrupted in 1580 when Portugal and Spain formed a dynastic union that would last sixty years, this alliance still exists to this very day, making it the oldest of all time. Common interests between Lisbon and London alone do not explain its remarkable endurance in light of their imperial policies and, eventually, major disagreements over the slave trade. Portugal was able to use arbitration and other emerging international legal norms to help smooth over the irksome asymmetries in their relationship (Paquette 2020).

Others could more cynically argue that the institution becomes a constituency in its own right such that the military alliance endures longer than what is rational from a security perspective. Using NATO as an illustrative example, realist scholar Stephen Walt (1997: 166) argues:

> [I]f the alliance generates a large formal bureaucracy, this will create a cadre of individuals whose professional perspectives and career prospects are closely tied to maintaining the relationship. Such individuals are likely to view the alliance as intrinsically desirable and will be reluctant to abandon it even when circumstances change. The longer the alliance lasts, the more numerous and influential its advocates will be.

The problem with this explanation for alliance persistence, of course, is that groups should be lobbying for the alliance's demise as well. If the alliance becomes more disconnected from the national interest, whatever that may be, then those opposition groups should be stronger because they ought to have the more compelling argument. Moreover, an alliance secretariat that enjoys too much policy autonomy can provoke backlash from its membership if states feel that the secretariat is acting contrary to their own interests (von Borzsyskowski and Vabulas 2019: 348n.65). If the secretariat does not receive pushback, then it is just as possible that its members still see the alliance as useful in a way that is independent of its bureaucratic strength. That an alliance can fool states on the account of the transnational networks it embodies does not comport well with the realist view that states have their own agency and remain the most important actors in international politics.

### Military defeat

Another reason why alliances end is because they fail to deliver military success in wartime. The alliance between

Austria-Hungary and Germany ended just shy of its fortieth anniversary when both, as the losing side, signed separate armistices that helped conclude the First World War in November 1918. Intended to last at least ten years, the 1939 Pact of Steel between Germany and Italy effectively came to a premature end in 1943. Not long after the Allied invasion of Sicily, leading government and military officials overthrew Italian leader Benito Mussolini and formed a new post-fascist government that went on to sign an armistice with the Allies before declaring war on Germany itself.

The winning side can still see its alliances fall apart in wartime. During the First World War, the Franco-Russian alliance, and thus the Triple Entente, came to an end when a succession of major battlefield defeats helped bring about the collapse of Tsarist rule in Russia as well as that of the subsequent provisional government. The Bolshevik revolutionaries who seized power in November 1917 subsequently renounced the war and agreed to sign a punitive separate peace with Germany. Although the Bolsheviks did request military assistance from France, which the French general staff was in fact willing to accommodate, the political leaders in Paris found the new revolutionary regime so distasteful that they eventually launched an armed intervention in the Russian Civil War in support of its anti-communist opponents (Carley 1976: 426–8). In 1939, France and the United Kingdom declared war when Nazi Germany invaded Poland, but they did little else to save their beleaguered ally. The Polish government-in-exile operated out of London for the rest of the war, to be sure, but it was ultimately unable to restore political sovereignty and to assert territorial control given the might of the Red Army in Central and Eastern Europe following the defeat of Nazi Germany. French and British alliance commitments to Poland effectively ended. In each of these cases, military defeat helped bring about regime change, which itself can sometimes finish an alliance (Walt 1997: 162; see also McKoy and Miller 2012).

Besides failing at their core purpose, another reason why alliances do not survive military defeats – to the extent that such arrangements cannot be reconstituted shortly thereafter – is that the conclusion of wars can lead to a reordering of regional or even global politics. In the peace conferences and settlements that follow major wars, leaders craft new sets of institutions and collective agreements in an effort to regulate their interactions and to ensure lasting peace and stability. Some of these political orders may be more consent-based than others (Ikenberry 2001). New alignments may form, with the vanquished now working alongside the victors in a way that transcends whatever interests those states might have had before. Whereas the Treaty of Versailles failed to give the newly created German republic a stake in its success, the post-war order that emerged in the wake of the Second World War saw all major defeated Axis powers – Germany, Japan, and Italy – become gradually integrated in institutions created by their erstwhile adversaries to help secure democracy and to prevent the spread of communism. Moreover, military defeat can discredit or disempower the ruling authorities, leading sometimes to revolutions that bring to power leaders with radically different political sensibilities and ideological leanings than those who ruled before them. As the Russian case from the First World War indicates, such regime changes can stir anxiety and even hostility amongst erstwhile allies (see Walt 1996).

Military defeat has not been a reason for why alliances that practice nuclear deterrence have ended. This observation raises an interesting, if startling, question: could alliances survive an armed conflict that involves the use of nuclear weapons? Hopefully, the answer will never be known. Cold War military alliances in East Asia and Europe did plan for nuclear war under the belief that it could be winnable. Throughout the first half of the Cold War, both NATO and the Warsaw Pact still had objectives that they wished to achieve in war even though their use of nuclear weapons would be especially calamitous for those societies caught in the conflagration. By the late 1960s, however, NATO defense planners concluded that the notion of victory in a high-intensity military conflict no longer made sense. They increasingly saw nuclear escalation as being only useful as a threat, inasmuch as this served to induce caution among

Soviet decision-makers and to prevent war from breaking out in the first place. Despite US perspectives on this matter, nuclear escalation was no longer part of a war-winning doctrine for NATO. It was used, if anything, to reinforce the status quo, which suggests that alliances could remain intact. In contrast, owing somewhat to the insistence of Marxist-Leninist theory that communist triumph was a historical inevitability, the Warsaw Pact adopted strategies that envisioned so-called annihilation battles and the use of strikes deep into NATO territory. Thus, the two opposing alliances in Cold War Europe had contrasting perspectives on nuclear war, with Warsaw Pact forces holding more stead-fastly to the view that political goals were possible to fulfill despite a major nuclear exchange. If realized, one alliance – the Warsaw Pact – would remain standing, while another would surrender (see Heuser 1998). Whether this theory of victory has any validation in practice was thankfully never determined, but the Cold War case does reveal that decision-makers do not necessarily think that nuclear war would mean an end to all participating alliances.

### Downgrading

Military alliances are not cheap. Formalizing a security partnership via a public treaty that is visible to international and domestic audiences alike can create reputation costs if a state later decides to renege on that agreement, whether because it no longer sees its values or because there are other relationships it wishes to pursue instead. Adversaries can be emboldened upon observing that a state is backtracking on its commitments. Future allies might demand more assurances and thus more concessions in order to be confident that they would not be betrayed at a later date. Within the reneging state itself, opposition parties and members of the public may question whether any disengagement or alliance violation serves the national interest. Furthermore, to make such an alliance effective for deterrence and war-making, states often invest in coordination bodies and various defense planning efforts as well as perform joint military exercises.

These benefits accrue with time and may be hard to give up suddenly. Renouncing a treaty outright may be too damaging reputation-wise, especially if the justification for it is dubious, and can expose the repudiating government to too much criticism at home and abroad. The quiet alternative is to let the alliance go adrift, downgrading its importance but not rejecting it entirely. The alliance increasingly becomes no more than a mere "scrap of paper."

This sort of outcome is surprisingly common in world politics as regards the fate of international organizations. Julia Gray (2018) finds that over a third of international organizations – which can encompass such issue areas as regional integration and financial cooperation – are what she describes as "zombie." As she explains it, "[z]ombie organizations maintain a level of semi-regular operation, but output in terms of progress on their goals falls below expectations" (2018: 3). On occasion, they seek to revitalize themselves by taking on new missions, but nevertheless can stagnate even if they are successful in taking up those additional tasks. Such stagnation, Gray finds, can be the result of the organization having insufficient autonomy or an inability to attract a skilled staff for its own secretariat. These factors may not be germane with respect to military alliances, however. Their functional specialization lies in the security domain where existential stakes may be involved and the arena can be highly competitive and unforgiving (Jervis 1982).

Some military alliances may nevertheless become zombie. In 1985, late in the Cold War, the United States suspended some of its obligations to New Zealand over major differences regarding nuclear strategy. Partly in response to public opinion, Wellington espoused increasingly antinuclear sentiments and adopted a nuclear-free zone, going as far as denying access to US Navy ships that either carried nuclear weapons or relied on nuclear propulsion (see Hensley 2013). That said, New Zealand remains part of ANZUS (Australia, New Zealand, United States Security Treaty) to this day and still cooperates with the United States on defense and intelligence matters.

Paradoxically, North Korea's treaty alliance with China

is another such example. Pyongyang depends on Beijing for the vast majority of its foreign trade. North Korea also benefits from the diplomatic shelter that China provides in international negotiations with the United States and other regional stakeholders over the status of its nuclear weapons program. Still, international security scholar Youngjun Kim (2019: 16–17) reports that "North Korea engaged in little military cooperation with China since the withdrawal of the Chinese People's Volunteer Army from North Korea in the 1950s," adding that, "officially, there have been very few educational exchanges, combined exercises, or other activities between North Korea and either country's military." Indeed, North Korean leaders sought to diminish the importance of this alliance almost as soon as they signed its founding treaty in 1960, jealously guarding their national sovereignty and trying hard not to become overly reliant on any great power. North Korea's alliance with the Soviet Union operated similarly. Ties between the two communist countries had been strained throughout the 1960s and 1970s. Moscow rejected Pyongyang's request for assistance in building nuclear power plants, in part because of Soviet mistrust over North Korean intentions (Szalontai and Radchenko 2006: 11–12). Cooperation between the two countries stayed limited for the remainder of the Cold War. Elsewhere in the "socialist camp," the Soviet Union's alliance with China also became zombie. Ideological disagreements and geopolitical discord began to rankle the relationship between them by the late 1950s (Lüthi 2010). The schism widened so much throughout the following decade that, in 1969, the two nominal allies had a series of border skirmishes. Tensions eventually abated, but competition between them continued. The Soviet Union tried to put pressure on China by signing a new alliance with Vietnam in 1978, but the effect was negligible: Beijing allowed its alliance treaty with Moscow to lapse finally at its expiry date (Elleman 1996).

Perhaps the most archetypal example of a downgraded or zombified alliance is the Southeast Asia Treaty Organization (SEATO). Formed in 1954, this alliance brought together Australia, France, New Zealand, Pakistan, the Philippines,

Thailand, the United Kingdom, and the United States with the goal of blocking the further expansion of communism, especially in Indochina. However, disagreements quickly arose as to what would qualify as a threat meriting great power intervention or the activation of alliance commitments. Internal disputes brought on by disparate political interests would continue to beset SEATO over the next few decades. Aggravating the disunity within its ranks was the question over how to handle a major political crisis in Laos in the early 1960s. By the next decade, SEATO had become moribund as the United States and several of its local allies began to pursue dialogue with China, a goal that became more pertinent as Washington began to disengage from Indochina amid the political failures that attended its war in Vietnam (see Buszynski 1981). Pakistan even withdrew from the organization after its defeat in the liberation war in Eastern Pakistan (Bangladesh) and the Indo-Pakistani War of 1971. SEATO finally gave up the ghost and expired in 1977.

Other Southeast Asian alliances may find themselves meeting this category of fate. Some observers might argue that Philippine President Rodrigo Duterte is currently striving to downgrade his country's alliance with the United States. Amid concerns of entrapment and his wish to pursue a more independent foreign policy, he has sought to vitiate the mutual defense pact by abrogating from the 1999 Visiting Forces Agreement (Cruz De Castro 2020: 18). This agreement provides the legal framework for US military forces operating on Philippine territory, allowing, for instance, the US government to have jurisdiction over US military personnel accused of committing crimes in the Philippines. Duterte eventually reversed course on his Visiting Forces Agreement decision, partly perhaps as a result of domestic pushback, but he had already made clear his preference for charting a more independent course. Had his presidency continued past 2022, the US–Philippine Mutual Defense Treaty might have been at risk of zombification. Elsewhere in the region, the United States still retains an alliance with Thailand. This partnership was founded with the Manila Pact, which had launched SEATO, and remains in force on the basis of the Thanat–Rusk communiqué of 1962 and the 2012 Joint Vision Statement for the Thai-US Defense Alliance. Although Thailand received the status of non-major NATO ally from the United States in 2003, which facilitates US weapons sales, the vitality of the alliance has been suspect owing to a lack of common interests and threat perceptions (Ciorciari 2010: 120). Thailand, for example, has shown reluctance when it comes to labeling China as anything other than a strategic and development partner (Chongkittavorn 2020).

Is NATO at risk of being downgraded? Although the alliance meets very regularly and has a robustly institutionalized character, some critics claim that it is falling well short of expectations and that it might be outliving its usefulness. These critics have included Donald Trump and French President Emmanuel Macron. Trump lambasted many NATO members for not only contributing less than their fair share to the collective defense burden, but also for simply assuming that the United States would support them in a militarized crisis no matter what. With slightly more nuance, Macron infamously described the alliance in an interview with *The Economist* (2019) as being "brain dead" – that is, too dependent on a fickle United States, too hesitant to pursue a more autonomous direction in its own security affairs, and too unwilling to embrace dialogue with other great powers like Russia. As rumors of its demise have been recurrent throughout its history, NATO will likely survive such criticisms one way or another. Nevertheless, European members of NATO have taken to partner more with like-minded states within that alliance to focus on shared security challenges, at times using existing subregional formats or even launching new initiatives at the bilateral or "minilateral" level that fall outside NATO's ambit. The result is growing fragmentation, with NATO providing an overarching multilateral framework that lends a veneer of cohesion to European security efforts (Simón et al. 2021).

In fact, some members have previously unilaterally downgraded the importance of NATO in their own security policies. France withdrew from the alliance's integrated structure in 1966 and expelled all NATO institutions and allied forces from its territory. For the French President at the time, Charles de Gaulle, NATO seemed increasingly out of synch with his own foreign policy goals. He had sought to put France on an equal footing with the United States at least as far as Western European security was concerned. He distrusted, too, the strategic concepts that Washington had been pushing, made all the worse by how those very concepts were gaining traction among other NATO members. Moreover, the threat environment had subsided in its severity, not least because France could avail itself of its own nuclear weapons arsenal (*force de frappe*). A new European order was de Gaulle's ambition, and France's membership of NATO's military command simply did not fit those plans (Haftendorn 1996: 2–4). France did remain within NATO, in part because Article XIII of the Washington Treaty forbade members from leaving the alliance within twenty years of its founding. France would go on to participate in NATO exercises and procurement projects, as well as to host, on occasion, its civilian conferences in the time between its withdrawal from NATO military command and its return in 2009 (NATO n.d.).

## Unilateral abrogation

Sometimes it is not enough for a state to reduce a military alliance to a mere "scrap of paper"; the state may need to abrogate it altogether so that it no longer exists in any form. Why might an ally ever do such a thing?

One reason why states might unilaterally go down this road relates to the signaling logic of military alliances. Recall that states write down and formalize their military and political commitments in order to convey to audiences – domestic and international – their seriousness in addressing a particular security challenge. Although some degree of vagueness is often embedded in the language of alliance treaties, alliance members expect potential adversaries to see the treaty as evidence of their unity and willingness to take risks in the pursuit of collective defense. Those adversaries will thus be more circumspect in challenging the alliance, creating a deterrence effect that bolsters the security of those states party to it (see, e.g., Morrow 2000).

Over time, however, the foreign policy goals among members might evolve so as to produce an increasingly untenable – maybe even intolerable – divergence of interests. Allies might grow apart as a result of major shifts in the balance of power, significant alterations in the make-up of their domestic institutions or societies, or some major crisis that causes leaders to rethink their international strategies. These sorts of changes might encourage leaders to reach out to an adversary and to pursue a much more cooperative relationship with it. Perhaps an adversary could be useful for balancing against another, more menacing adversary. Perhaps the benefits of cooperation in the non-security domain are too high to forgo, as in the case of significant trade opportunities. Yet, in creating a more cooperative relationship with an adversary, the alliance commitment could become a liability. Due to the uncertainty of intentions engendered by the international condition of anarchy, the adversary may worry that any cooperative gesture on its part would make it vulnerable to being cheated or exploited. It cannot be sure if the member of an opposing alliance is acting in good faith. Not wishing to be suckered, the adversary seeks assurances that any cooperation will be credible and reciprocal. Renouncing a formal alliance is a strong form of assurance in this type of situation. By unilaterally abrogating it, the state is demonstrating its willingness to forgo the benefits of alliance, especially if doing so creates some risk of being exposed to the adversary potentially acting in bad faith (Yarhi-Milo et al. 2016).

The United States renounced its alliance with Taiwan in the late 1970s to achieve such ends with China. The original purpose of this alliance was not only to defend the island country from communist attack, but also to have a mechanism in place for restraining Taiwan's leadership from launching unwanted offensive operations against the mainland. Although these objectives were largely constant throughout much of the Cold War, other priorities came to dominate Washington's policy toward the Taiwan Strait. For

one, the Sino-Soviet split described above created opportunities for the United States to ratchet up pressure on
the Soviet Union. President Nixon was worried about his
country's weakened international position, not least because
the Vietnam War had sapped its resources and had torn its
society apart. Nixon feared that Moscow would use détente
– defined as the easing of tensions between the two superpowers – to exploit this weakness. Normalizing diplomatic
relations with China was part of a competitive strategy
intended to outflank the Soviet Union. For another, Nixon
hoped to save face in withdrawing the United States from
Vietnam. He believed that some outreach to China was
necessary for resolving that war. The problem, however,
was a key demand made by Chinese leaders if diplomatic
relations were to be established at the time: the United States
must loosen its relationship with Taiwan – a demand that
Nixon and his National Security Advisor Kissinger were
generally willing to fulfill (Shen 1983; Tucker 2005: 121–5).
The logical end of this initiative came a bit later when
President Carter abrogated the alliance treaty unilaterally on
New Year's Day 1980, one year to the day after the United
States had established diplomatic relations with China, and
gave notice to end the treaty as per its terms.

Sometimes countries do switch sides by withdrawing from
one alliance and joining another. Consider members of the
Warsaw Pact. Albania had already decided to withdraw
from the alliance in 1968 and to realign itself ideologically
with China. The two communist countries did not end up
concluding a new treaty alliance and, within a few years,
Albanian leaders became dissatisfied with China as well
(Mëhilli 2017). More significant is what happened with the
rest of the Warsaw Pact two decades later. Throughout 1989,
the ruling communist parties in Central Eastern Europe
gradually lost their monopoly hold on power, giving way
to democratic opposition groups that had long chafed at
Soviet rule. The Soviet Union had dominated the Warsaw
Pact since its inception in 1955, but its satellites eventually
became more efficient at using the alliance to articulate their
own policy concerns and disagreements (Crump 2015). With

such dramatic change afoot across the Soviet bloc in 1989 and 1990, the Warsaw Pact suddenly found itself facing an existential crisis from within. Leaders of Czechoslovakia and Hungary quickly moved to request the withdrawal of Soviet troops from their territories. Poland was initially reluctant in view of its concerns regarding German reunification. Shortly thereafter, however, Soviet satellites began to demand a watering down of alliance military structures before asking to disband them outright. In 1991, the Warsaw Pact met its demise and was officially disbanded, to the chagrin of the Soviet military (Matějka 1997). Within several years, some former members of this defunct alliance began to seek NATO membership. Still, to go about this process, and to achieve greater integration in Western institutions more generally, these countries had to make a number of costly reforms, especially with respect to civil–military relations, in order to become suitable members (Epstein 2005).

Signaling logics need not always account for why a state unilaterally annuls an alliance treaty. Domestic politics could also be a deciding factor. The Anglo-Japanese alliance is a case in point. Signed in 1902, and renewed twice, in 1905 and 1911, this alliance with Japan brought the United Kingdom out of its so-called "splendid isolation" to help protect its interests in China and India as well as to balance against Russia and, eventually, Germany. Alliances often benefit from commercial linkages: the wealth generated can potentially be used to purchase military power that benefits the alliance as a whole (Gowa 1995). Nevertheless, some British merchants had to stomach arguably unfair Japanese trade practices and government subsidies that made them less competitive in the Far East. The Japanese textile industry proved very competitive to the British one as well. Over time, protests grew in Parliament. When the alliance-skeptical Liberal Party came to power, thanks in part to support drawn from the British working class, British leaders began to leverage the alliance and, in 1910, extracted – successfully – tariff concessions from Japan in a new commercial treaty in 1910 (Davis 2009: 171–2). But British economic displeasure with Japan only intensified after the First World War.

Although Japanese leaders still supported the alliance even as the foreign policies of the two partners were starting to diverge, the commercial rivalry between British and Japanese business interests impelled London to end the relationship. The alliance became officially defunct with the 1921 Four Power Treaty, signed by the two erstwhile partners along with France and the United States to maintain the status quo in the Pacific. The alliance formally ended in 1923.

### Transformation

Another way for an alliance to end is through a transformation that fundamentally enhances the security relationship. Transformation can unfold in two ways. The first is that the allied states agree to become a unified single state. States might unify consensually for several reasons: a shared cultural identity, a desire to exploit economies of scale, or a powerful interest to pool sovereign resources in a way that would not otherwise be possible. The second is that the alliance becomes subsumed within a much larger alliance framework, making the original one effectively less important. A bilateral alliance, for example, could be incorporated into a multilateral one that, by default, features more partnerships.

Erstwhile partners have unified throughout history. The Kingdom of Poland and the Grand Duchy of Lithuania may have been separate countries, but they were already allied by way of a personal union. With the 1569 Union of Lublin, however, the two countries were now joined as a real union in the form of the Polish-Lithuanian Commonwealth. One impetus for this transformation was the lack of success that Lithuania had in fighting the Livonian War against Muscovy. Its elites exchanged political autonomy for Polish military support (Bardach 1970: 75–6). Similarly, Scotland and England had been joined by personal union when King James VI of Scotland acceded to the throne of England and Ireland in 1603. Over a century later, in 1707, this personal union became a real one in the shape of Great Britain, thereby helping not only to ensure that Scotland could not support the French in an invasion of England but also to husband much-needed resources for the War of the Spanish Succession (Macinnes 2007: 277). Throughout the Cold War, some members of the Arab League attempted to build upon their pan-Arabist identity to found new federal or confederal states. These attempts to unite all failed, with the exception of North and South Yemen becoming Yemen in 1990. In Europe, Belarus and Russia pledged to become a union state in 1999, but both states remain separate due to profound disagreements over its institutional character and policy priorities, to say nothing of the toxic relationship that developed between President Alyaksandr Lukashenka of Belarus and President Vladimir Putin of Russia (Marin 2020: 4; Gould-Davies 2020).

Transformation can also result from a new alliance taking precedence over an older one. Of course, such an event would not mean the end of an alliance per se. It would instead entail a fundamental alteration of how security ties are patterned between a group of states. That is not to say that the bilateral relationships underpinning the new arrangement are any less important, though. One such case of transformation is where a bilateral alliance gets engulfed by a multilateral one. Germany and Austria-Hungary complemented their own alliance by forming the Triple Alliance with Italy in 1882. The Anglo-Portuguese alliance effectively became multilateralized in 1949 when both parties became founding members of NATO. The same was true for Canada and the United States with respect to the 1941 Ogdensburg Agreement. This sort of transformation is also what the United States has long aspired to do with its individual alliances with Japan and South Korea. Both of these East Asian countries are now liberal democracies with market-oriented economies. They each have, since the early 1950s, their own bilateral alliance with the United States. Despite these commonalities, Washington has met with little success in getting its two treaty partners to form ever stronger security ties with one another. They have refused to multilateralize the alliance commitments and to deepen the cooperation that already does exist between them (see Jackson 2018a). Problematically for US decision-makers, Seoul and Tokyo appear to get along best when neither seems to be getting along well with Washington (Cha 2000).

## The Analytical Importance of Understanding Alliance Termination

That alliances can cease to exist for a number of different reasons suggests that a degree of skepticism is warranted with respect to any single factor, or monocausal, explanation of alliance politics. Military alliances may be established in response to a particular security challenge amid a specific set of strategic circumstances, but much can happen over the course of their existence. They might outlive their original functions, as in the case of NATO, or they might be outlived by their primary concerns, as in the case of the Reinsurance Treaty and Germany's late nineteenth-century grand strategic need to keep France and Russia separate. States might establish alliances in order to deter threats, but deterrence can still fail and military defeat could end up being their fate. Sometimes, cooperation is so successful, however, that it begets more cooperation.

Grasping the complexity of alliance termination is important for reasons that go beyond assessing the power of any one explanation. Some observers might argue that the collapse of alliances, especially in the US context, could create more uncertainty and thus greater conflict. Those making such arguments expressed alarm over Trump's nationalist rhetoric and its implications for global order and stability (see Brands 2017). Others have welcomed the possibility that the Trump administration might pull back from long-standing commitments, arguing that it was time for the United States to rationalize both its foreign and defense policies so as to avoid so-called "strategic insolvency." According to this view, the risks for post-alliance conflict have been exaggerated and are truly low (Gholz et al. 1997). In fact, conflict can ensue as a result of alliances. And even if conflict does break out when an alliance ceases to exist, it does not follow that the withdrawing partner – in this case, the United States – has vital enough interests at stake to get involved (Posen 2014: 34).

These positions are polar opposites of one another, but the problem with evaluating either perspective is that an alliance commitment is not really an explanatory variable in its own right. Put another way, an alliance commitment does not exist independently of the interests that states have, the overall military balance, and the beliefs that leaders have about reputation as well as about the use of force. George Liska (1962: 3) declared: "It is impossible to speak of international relations without referring to alliances; the two often merge in all but name. For the same reason, it has always been difficult to say much that is peculiar to alliances on the plane of general analysis." Further muddying the waters is that each of those factors can affect others. To say that maintaining or retracting an alliance commitment has an effect on stability obscures some of the more fundamental issues involved in international relations. For example, the US unilateral decision to abrogate its mutual defense treaty with Taiwan in 1980 did not result in a war in East Asia, but the French decision to let Germany annex territory from its ally Czechoslovakia in 1938 proved to be a prelude to world war. In the former case, China might have had revisionist intentions toward Taiwan, as it still does, but it lacked the means to mount military operations across the Taiwan Strait. The United States eventually availed itself of the right to provide Taiwan with defensive weapons despite the abrogation of the treaty. This was not by intentional design, to be sure, as Congress legislated the 1979 Taiwan Relations Act out of frustration with how the Carter administration handled the island country (Romberg 2003: 107). In the latter case, Germany had revisionist intentions toward Czechoslovakia and other Central Eastern European states, but, by the late 1930s, it had developed a major military force that it could wield effectively against its neighbors. Unfortunately, France had become too hamstrung by various domestic political and economic difficulties, which, in turn, affected its military power and willingness to fight, instilling a strong feeling of diffidence in its president – Edouard Daladier – at the infamous Munich Conference despite his understanding of the existential challenge posed by Nazi Germany (see Butterworth 1974).

Pinning either success or failure on the demise of the alliance commitment alone is at best misleading. Doing so requires overlooking the complex set of factors that shape both the reasons why the alliance ended in the first place and the effects of its termination. This observation is worth bearing in mind when assessing the health of alliance commitments today. A number of stressors now exist that could put some alliances at risk. For example, cutting-edge technologies like precision strike have matured and proliferated so that potential adversaries of the United States can now add them to their arsenals (Mahnken 2011). In East Asia, the rise of China means that the costs of defending an ally have increased, especially as China has converted some of its wealth into military power. Rather than incur the expenses that come with containment, a state might cut a deal with China in order to diffuse its threat, which in turn could result in a downgrading or even a termination of an alliance treaty. The United States could just as easily seek some grand bargain. Its allies might fear, rightly or wrongly, that such a grand bargain could come at their expense. And, indeed, the United States has steadily turned inward as its decision-makers have begun to prioritize domestic political agendas over international ones – a process that the economic fall-out of the SARS-CoV-2 pandemic may accelerate. Other countries grappling with similar economic challenges could also choose to recalibrate their foreign and defense policies in a way that puts further strains on their alliance relationships. If some alliance relationships do somehow meet their demise in the near future, then one must take into account the set of circumstances that produced this outcome.

Do these observations imply that the effects of alliance politics – even if they concern alliance termination – are ultimately unknowable and thus perhaps even benign? Not necessarily. Kaiser Wilhelm II's decisions to dismiss Chancellor Bismarck and not to renew the Reinsurance Treaty helped set in train a blundering German foreign policy that would antagonize both France and Russia, thereby bringing the two together as eventual treaty allies that would fight on the same side decades later in the First World War. The crisis that saw France withdraw from NATO's military command structure pushed the alliance to create new consultative processes as well as to embrace new ideas regarding its military and political strategy (Wenger 2004). Although it may have paid geopolitical and even economic dividends, the US decision to repudiate its alliance with Taiwan has made the latter insecure. About forty years later, Washington's subsequent policy of strategic ambiguity with regard to the Taiwan Strait has come under strain in view of China's growing military arsenal and deep-seated intention to unify the island with the mainland under its control. Amid outcry over China's policies, especially in the wake of the SARS-CoV-2 pandemic, some observers have called for a rekindling of security ties between the erstwhile allies (Glaser et al. 2020). Actions like terminating alliances can still have negative consequences, even if they are sometimes diffuse and run along paths that are hardly linear.

# Conclusion

If the alliance politics that characterized 2008 were subtle but perceptibly tense, then the alliance politics on display in 2020 were visceral and unmistakably toxic. In the last year of his controversial term as US president, Trump appeared poised to upend many of his country's military alliances. Without consulting any European member of NATO, his administration announced its intention to withdraw about 12,000 military personnel from Germany, with some of those forces returning to the United States and others to be co-located with other units and headquarters in Europe. A feeling of dread hung in the air during the November 2020 election. Some observers speculated that Trump would be even more unhinged if he were to be re-elected, going so far as to take the audacious step of pulling the United States out of NATO in his second term as president. Negotiations with South Korea over the costs of military bases remained fractious and the Trump administration appeared to have given up on trying to curb North Korea's nuclear weapons and missile programs. Japan under Prime Ministers Shinzo Abe and Yoshihide Suga had tried its best to manage Trump, but patience was wearing thin in light of the White House's erratic messaging on East Asia – trying to build an anti-China coalition, while repudiating a regional economic bloc involving only US allies and partners – amid its costly trade war with China. Contradicting the Pentagon, Trump downplayed concerns about Philippine President Rodrigo Duterte's effort to end their countries' Visiting Forces Agreement. The haltingly uneven international cooperation in overcoming the SARS-CoV-2 pandemic could have been a prelude for even greater protectionism, which Trump would have embraced with little hesitation.

But by early 2021, the storm clouds seemed to be dissipating. Throughout his presidential campaign and in the opening days of his administration, Joseph Biden reiterated his desire to repair and to strengthen US military alliances and global partnerships. In a *Foreign Affairs* article, Biden (2020: 65) pledged that, "as President, I will take immediate steps to renew US democracy and alliances, protect the United States' economic future, and once more have America lead the world." He reiterated this point in his inaugural address with members of his cabinet following suit in their own official statements. Almost immediately after being confirmed by the Senate, Secretary of Defense Lloyd Austin proceeded to call NATO Secretary General Stoltenberg as well as his counterparts in the United Kingdom, Japan, South Korea, and other allied countries. During his Senate confirmation hearings, Secretary of State Anthony Blinken approvingly observed that membership in NATO was a strong explanation for why Russia had not attacked European countries and he welcomed the possibility of other countries – specifically, Georgia – joining the alliance so long as they met its criteria (Prince 2021). At the June 2021 NATO summit in Brussels, Biden declared that "the U.S. commitment to Article 5 of the NATO Treaty is rock solid and unshakable. It's a sacred commitment" (White House 2021). The shift in rhetoric between the Trump and the Biden administrations could not have been more stark.

It would, of course, be naive to think that, in the contemporary era, alliance politics would be no more, largely wrapped up in some long and unique crisis that spanned the years between 2008 and 2020. It would also be naive to think that US military alliances have come full circle, with yet another Democratic president arguing that their Republican predecessor did not manage them very well, to the detriment of global security. The point here, instead, is that some skepticism is appropriate when leaders promise to revitalize alliances – not because they are insincere, for they may genuinely be well-intentioned, but because of the challenges that doing so involves. As instruments that states use to advance their foreign and defense policy interests, military alliances are difficult to understand, let alone to manage. No matter how earnestly a state tries to rebuild or strengthen a global network of alliances, resource constraints and policy priorities can pull in such different directions. Some allies naturally end up being disappointed, while others may find themselves pleasantly surprised. Contradictions are rife in how military alliances operate, from when they are first negotiated to when they meet their eventual demise.

The purpose of this book is to expose this complexity and murkiness. Of course, the real world is complicated: our theories and concepts in the study of international security should aspire to simplify it rather than to emulate it. Yet in the field's pursuit of theoretical rigor and parsimony, its dominant concepts increasingly gloss over crucial nuances, generate contradictory predictions, and ignore important outliers. As a result, they offer poor guidance to policymakers and alliance leaders as they try to navigate today's increasingly complex and volatile environment.

Consider again the pieces of conventional wisdom on alliance politics that were mentioned in the introduction.

### Conventional wisdom #1: States form alliances to balance power, and/or to gain influence over other states

An intuitive set of explanations holds that states form military alliances as a means of creating a balance of power in face of threats, of gaining influence over other states, or both. There are several problems with this particular standard claim. One is that many shared threats, even grave ones, do not provoke states enough to form military alliances. Another is that those objectives – balance of power and control – should not require a written treaty. Some scholars are aware of these issues and so argue that an alliance on paper generates reputation costs that would be incurred if that commitment is violated, thereby strengthening the deterrence signal to allies and adversaries alike. But these qualified arguments themselves raise new questions. Is violating an alliance commitment really that costly if, for instance, doing so might serve the national interest? Would the strength of the deterrence signal weaken over time as interests, political leaders, and resource availability all change?

As Chapter 1 argued, having a written alliance commitment is helpful not just for providing clarity, but also, ironically, for allowing enough ambiguity that states can backtrack on their promises if things do not go according to plan. Common interests are essential for an alliance to form, but so are disagreements – alliance treaties thread this needle, or at least try to. Indeed, states will very seldom agree about exactly what goals, actions, and policies are worth pursuing at any given moment. The natural question that flows from this observation is why more alliance treaties are not signed. Yet that very question is itself the point: the decision to sign an alliance treaty is ultimately based on how leaders perceive the benefits, costs, and risks of such an arrangement. These perceptions must be sufficiently aligned. Certain factors like shared threat make states more likely to sign an alliance treaty, but the actual decision to do so may be idiosyncratic. There is no neat mathematical formula for it.

To take one example, Russia and China have stepped up their military cooperation significantly since the 1990s, leading one observer to conclude that they are "on the verge of an alliance" (Korolev 2019). Their leaders share similar antidemocratic impulses and a fundamental dislike of the United States and its foreign policy choices. But they have also stopped well short of forming an alliance. Presumably, this disinclination is due to how they both participate in various territorial disputes in their respective neighborhoods, making it hard to have a written alliance that would become redundant as soon as it is signed. For the same reason, NATO may not be welcoming either Georgia or Ukraine anytime soon because their membership and their ongoing territorial disputes with Russia could automatically entail an Article V situation. Nevertheless, this point should not be overstated: ongoing territorial disputes have not stopped other alliances from forming in the past. Early in the Cold War, West Germany, Japan, South Korea, and Taiwan all had territorial disputes when they acquired their defense pacts with the United States. The same was true for North Korea when it concluded its alliance treaties with China and the Soviet Union in 1961. This should not be a surprise: expectations of conflict encourage states to forge alliances, and much conflict around the world centers on territory. What it would take for Moscow and Beijing to sign one remains frustratingly unclear.

### Conventional wisdom #2: The alliance dilemma is a fundamental problem shared by all military alliances

Another common refrain in discussions about alliance politics is how endemic the alliance dilemma is. A broad commitment creates perverse incentives for an ally to behave more aggressively than it otherwise would, thereby creating the risk of entrapment for its defender. Yet weakening that commitment could stoke worries of abandonment, which in turn can lead the fretful ally to engage in dramatic foreign and defense policies that could destabilize the alliance and regional security. Hence the dilemma: the trade-offs are inevitable and decision-makers can choose only from a set of bad options.

In examining entrapment and abandonment, respectively, Chapters 2 and 3 revealed that, on closer inspection, the dilemma is not really much of a dilemma. First, scholars have identified entrapment risks that spring from a wide variety of sources. These can relate to the alliance treaty itself, systemic factors like polarity and the offence–defense balance, reputational concerns, or transnational ideological networks. Some of these purported risk factors contradict one another. Entrapment should be much less common under bipolarity because, for example, no ally can tip the balance of power when only two great powers exist. Some scholars have still argued that US leaders have been obsessed with the country's national reputation during the Cold War, which should have increased the risk of entrapment despite bipolarity. Others postulate that states that supposedly behave most like reckless drivers – for example, Israel – are those that do not have any alliance commitments, which in theory should make them much less reckless than those that do have one. The internal logic of these arguments can be suspect, as the implication is that weak states successfully deceive their great power allies. Somehow weak states can have more agency than strong states when the latter can insist on precise language, treaty loopholes, and conditionality in order to temper a commitment and, by extension, manage perceived entrapment risks.

Second, abandonment concerns are natural when an ally faces some security threat. It can never be fully certain that it would receive much-needed assistance from its treaty partners. Interests are never fully aligned; fighting is destructive, especially on the behalf of another state. However, abandonment concerns do vary in their intensity. States do not always have enough of them to merit engaging in dramatic foreign and defense policy changes designed to improve their security situation. Acting on abandonment fears can be costly, too, for example with respect to a nuclear weapons program or accommodation of the adversary. States thus evaluate their received security guarantees by referring to the degree of interest overlap with their allies, the overall military balance, and whether their allies deploy their own military assets in or around their own theater of operations. Of course, the credibility of an alliance will always be limited. Part of the problem that some contemporary alliances have is that they can be very successful at deterring large-scale territorial aggression but less good at more subtle forms of aggression that add up to what Mira Rapp-Hooper (2020) calls competitive coercion. By the very nature of those threats, it may be up to the target states themselves to develop the wherewithal to neutralize them.

Simply put, entrapment concerns can be mitigated and abandonment fears always exist, even though they vary in their intensity. If the ally and its defender have highly convergent interests and share similar attitudes toward their common adversary, then worries about entrapment and abandonment alike will be minimal. The dilemma mostly exists if interests and attitudes sharply diverge.

*Conventional wisdom #3: Members of US alliances must do more to bear their fair share of the common defense burden*

Perhaps the alliance problem that grabs the most headlines concerns burden-sharing. As president, Trump castigated those NATO members that did not spend 2 percent of their GDP on defense while demanding that South Korea pay more to cover the costs of US bases. He called them all free-riders. The intuitive reason for insisting on greater defense spending is clear enough: if allies spend more on their militaries, then the alliance in aggregate will be more powerful and, for its part, the United States will not be uniquely responsible for trying to plug all of its capability shortfalls. The allies themselves will benefit from being stronger themselves vis-à-vis their own adversaries.

Chapter 4 demonstrates that the relationship between defense spending and alliance security is hardly linear. For one, the notion of free-riding presumes that states have enough belief in their received commitments that they can underspend relative to a threat. Such beliefs are irrational, especially if they face major threats and nothing truly obligates their defender to come to their rescue. For another, states might conclude that, in light of nuclear deterrence, more defense spending, at worst, can run the risk of undermining alliance security or, at best, be unnecessary. During the Cold War, some allies took the view that making investments in conventional military power signaled a willingness to fight nuclear wars when the point of the alliance was to prevent them. Indeed, alliances in the Cold War would generally last longer than what had, beforehand, been the historical norm. This longevity has created contradictory incentives for how states should allocate resources toward their militaries. Generating conventional military power has become more difficult, owing to the growing technical, organizational, and individual skill complexity that it now involves. States may wish to continue spending money so as not to fall behind both their allies and their adversaries. And yet, if alliances serve to deter, and nuclear weapons offer the ultimate deterrent, then the likelihood of high-intensity conflict goes down and states might believe that they have a lesser need to invest in their militaries. The 2 percent guideline is a heuristic that NATO has embraced precisely because evaluating defense contributions is too difficult, but it is just that: a heuristic.

### Conventional wisdom #4: Military alliances aggregate capabilities and thus allow their members to confront security challenges more effectively

Another piece of conventional wisdom is that alliances aggregate capabilities, which in turn makes them into more effective military organizations. This claim relates to the first – that balancing power is a major motivation for why states sign alliances. The problem with the capability aggregation model, simply put, is that members of a military alliance – or, more specifically, a coalition – can encounter many difficulties over the course of a campaign. Just as the relationship between defense spending and alliance security is hardly linear, so the relationship between alliance membership and military effectiveness is also uncertain. In fact, the historical record reveals that most multinational military operations feature treaty partners working alongside states with which they have no formal alliance.

Chapter 5 shows that a number of complications can arise for any coalition of states mounting a multinational military operation. At the strategic level, states might be working for different political aims or participate with varying degrees of resolve, making them liable to defect from the mission. At the organizational level, members of a coalition must agree upon command and control arrangements. Some might jealously guard their sovereignty and so opt to go their own way over the course of a campaign, creating friction with other states. They could even attach caveats on how their own national forces will be used, whether with respect to the geographic sectors in which they will operate or the rules of engagement with which they would abide. At the technical level, coalition partners could suffer from a lack of standardized equipment as well as from cumbersome supply chains. Communication problems and mobility challenges can also hurt effectiveness. The capability aggregation model simply does not withstand scrutiny. That said, many fearful states may prefer to be in a treaty alliance than not because it entails far more opportunities for enhancing joint military effectiveness, however imperfect it may ultimately be in wartime.

*Conventional wisdom #5: Military alliances are only useful for as long as the strategic circumstances that led to their emergence hold*

The realist school of thought takes the view that states will find alliances useful only to the extent that their interests are advanced in a particular set of circumstances. If those circumstances change, then military alliances will find themselves obsolete and states will use new arrangements in their stead so as to address new problems. As British Prime Minister Lord Palmerston said of his country in 1848: "We have no eternal allies, and we have no perpetual enemies. Our interests are eternal and perpetual, and those interests it is our duty to follow." This view flows naturally from arguments that emphasize balancing; whether to balance power or confront a threat, the alliance will last only as long as the situation demands it.

This view is wrong for at least two reasons. The first is that states find alliances to be useful beyond the specific circumstances that give rise to them. Even Lord Palmerston admitted on another occasion that "constitutional states" were "natural" allies of Britain (quoted in Cannadine 2017: 184). This observation relates to the second reason: that alliances can meet their demise in a variety of ways. As recounted in Chapter 6, an alliance can end in five different ways. One is that they disband after fulfilling their core mission. This particular outcome is rare because successful cooperation tends to beget more cooperation, especially if the alliance has developed institutional assets that are useful for addressing future security challenges and are too costly to repudiate. Another way for an alliance to end is military defeat on the battlefield. A third way is if the alliance is downgraded. In some situations, explicitly ending an alliance could prove too harmful for a state's leadership and so it lets the security arrangement gradually weaken and go "zombie." A fourth way is when the repudiating state has no such reservations and decides to abrogate an alliance unilaterally, perhaps to convey its bona fide interest in securing the cooperation of an erstwhile adversary. The last possible way for an alliance to terminate is by transformation. In this case, an alliance becomes incorporated into yet another arrangement, thereby losing its visibility even if it is still active. To be sure, some of these outcomes do correspond with the realist view that alliances last as long as the core problem exists. Sometimes, however, the problem that the alliance was intended to solve outlives the alliance itself.

## Military Alliances and World Order in the Twenty-First Century

Dysfunction is a permanent feature of alliance politics, not a temporary bug. After all, alliance politics involves the interaction of diverse military powers and distinct political willingness to address common, but not necessarily identical, security concerns. Alliance politics is often emotional, not least because the stakes can be high. States very rarely suffer the dramatic fate of Poland in 1939, but they do, as a general rule, prize their independence, sovereignty, and territorial integrity. Being potentially exposed to physical harm or to political blackmail on the part of an adversary can trigger a range of sentiments: the sense of dread that the adversary could seize something of value; the feeling of alarm that enemy forces could use military power against fellow citizens; the rush of indignation felt upon the betrayal by an ally no matter how righteous their intervention would be; the bitterness of the realization that high expectations of support turned out to be false; the bitter fruit of that resigned under-standing that, in the end, not much more could be done. Because each of these feelings is harmful in its own right, much of alliance politics turns on trying to avoid them, at best, or to mitigate them, at worst.

This view of alliance politics contrasts with popular impressions of it. Cooperation, solidarity, jointness, and like-mindedness often typify what many think when it comes to military alliances. These values are, of course, significant: alliances do serve to facilitate cooperation; alliances do undertake actions to demonstrate their internal solidarity; members of alliances do aspire to achieve jointness in under-taking operations with one another; and alliances do consist of partners that are like-minded, at least on several key policy dimensions. However, in contemporary international relations, the problems created by anarchy and modernity put a premium on the need for security. Differences in interests, priorities, and threat assessments make discord inevitable even when allies' goals are similar enough for them to be in a military alliance in the first place.

This sort of discord will affect many alliance relation-ships in the years ahead in light of the deep trends that mark international politics. Controversies over the direction of NATO will endure, concerning, for example, what should be done about Russia, or what could be done about China, or how to handle more nontraditional challenges like climate change, pandemics, and instability in the Middle East and North Africa. Burden-sharing controversies will likewise persist, especially as those challenges mount. Despite these centrifugal forces, however, NATO will continue to bear core institutional assets that will be valuable to its members. If this alliance continues to fragment as subgroupings of states within it take on particular tasks that are more pressing from their point of view, NATO will continue to offer a layer of multilateralism to those efforts and allow for broad coordi-nation over complex issues. Elsewhere in the world, the rise of China is inciting previously disconnected countries to forge ever closer ties, as in the case of the Quad between Australia, India, Japan, and the United States. Still, even if those closer ties result in new military alliances, variation in their security needs, geographical exposure, political systems, and leaders' beliefs will complicate their cooperation at multiple levels of decision-making. This is already the case in existing bilateral alliances that the United States has with Japan, the Philippines, South Korea, and Thailand.

For its part, the United States will remain a fickle partner. The structural reasons for this fickleness are apparent: Washington has commitments around the world despite having lost a major share of power, however defined, relative to other members of the international system. To be sure, this point should not be overstated. Each era features its own challenges, some of which are particular to the prevailing level of technology. Early in the Cold War, when the United States held a preponderance of military and economic power, its treaty allies harbored doubts as to whether it would truly aid them in a militarized crisis involving the Soviet Union, China, and even North Korea. Part of the problem back then was the uncertainty of how to deal with the major technological changes that came with nuclear weapons and missiles. Given the massive costs of war that would ensue with nuclear weapons use, many states – ignorant as they were at first with respect to US capabilities and doctrine – felt acutely vulnerable to the military might of their adversaries amid doubts as to whether Washington would really fight alongside them.

Such uncertainties still exist today. Aside from ongoing concerns about extended nuclear deterrence, newer technologies are likely to open up further avenues for aggression and also challenge prevailing notions about thresholds for war that adversaries can exploit.

Complicating matters further is the internal cohesion of the United States. Trump's presidential campaign in 2016 and his single term in office gave a cold shower to those long accustomed to the US executive branch projecting stability and having a certain degree of predictability, despite at times embracing policies at odds with allied interests. Trump proved to be too much of a wild card – an inexperienced leader who clung to nationalist rhetoric and yet flitted between various policy positions in a way that perplexed, and troubled, both longstanding international partners and members of his own administration. Despite his defeat in the 2020 presidential election, the angry populism that Trump embodied may yet linger for a more competent politician to exploit. Whether such a leader could become president is open to question, but in some sense, it may be beside the point. The Trump historical moment – culminating as it did in the events of January 6, 2021 on Capitol Hill – highlighted the deep polarization, the potential for democratic backsliding, and the violent underflow that are current in US domestic politics. And indeed, if the 2008 financial crisis generated doubts about US strategic solvency, then the SARS-CoV-2 pandemic may amplify those concerns even more in its aftermath. Stated briefly, the United States may be so preoccupied with its own problems that having a steady leader at the helm might only provide limited relief to those allies counting on its support.

There are reasons, however, not to be too pessimistic about the value of the United States as a security guarantor. First, US alliances did survive the Trump presidency even though Trump himself never came around to the view that alliances can benefit US security interests. Of course, we will never know what would have happened in a second term. It is possible that certain relationships would have been abrogated. But the US state itself is bigger than whoever is occupying the Oval Office. Relatively strong bipartisan support, for instance, exists within Congress for facing down the perceived challenges posed by China and Russia. Even within the executive branch itself during the Trump presidency, different factions had their own views on how best to address those concerns, with implications for alliance relationships (Rogin 2021). Second, important differences existed in how some alliance relationships fared under such a mercurial leader. Poland, for example, did improve its ties with the United States at both the military and the political levels under the Trump administration, at some risk to its relationship with its successor (Lanoszka 2020a). Others, like Germany, saw a sharp deterioration instead. This may in part be due to how complementary the political interests and values of the governments were. Such variation is unsurprising: as argued, states sign alliance treaties precisely because they are aware of their political differences and thus expect interests to clash eventually. And third, although questions will abound as to how the United States might allocate its geopolitical attention and military resources to address those security concerns, especially in the post-COVID era, these questions are not entirely new. Allies are not blind to these matters. With its insistence on China as being the primary threat, the Trump administration may have crudely highlighted a potential trade-off between what it can provide for Europe and what it can do for East Asia. Yet during much of the Cold War too, US allies saw Washington alternate between which regions received its priority, as when the Vietnam War channeled attention and resources away from Europe. Besides, if they truly fear an adversary in whatever region they are situated, then they will complement the alliance with their own armament efforts regardless of what the United States is doing. Fear of abandonment is always rational. Nevertheless, for its part, the United States has enduring interests in Europe and in Asia – chiefly to prevent their domination by another great power – and therefore has strong incentives to maintain some level of military and political engagement in both. Even the Trump administration pursued this strategy.

Another reason for some optimism about the United States is that, even though it has its problems, so too do China and Russia. There is nothing inevitable about China's rise, and the United States may not have to compromise its own alliances to accommodate its emergence by striking some sort of grand bargain with it (Beckley 2018). A slowing economy, looming demographic crisis, tightening authoritarianism, growing international opposition, and environmental degradation may limit Beijing's potential to be a true peer competitor to Washington. To date, China only has one treaty ally – North Korea – and seems unable to attract more. Of course, as Thomas Christensen (2001) once noted, China can still pose problems without catching up to the United States given its improved capabilities and political goals – an observation that applies just as well to Russia, which also faces various constraints. Economically, Russia's growth is anemic and overly reliant on natural gas and oil; politically, its leadership has only become more afraid of its own population and thus more autocratic under Vladimir Putin. Most of its own allies are authoritarian, located as they are in Central Asia. One exception is Armenia, a partly free state that wagered unsuccessfully on receiving Russian support in its ongoing conflict with neighboring Azerbaijan. The United States may appear to be an unreliable security guarantor in Europe, but Russia is hardly a ten-foot giant either. Adding to this optimism is Matthew Kroenig's (2020) observation that autocracies are at a disadvantage when they engage in great power rivalries with democracies, not least because autocracies tend to repel potential partners and to struggle at innovation over the long term. Democracies may very well backslide, but autocracies simply fail.

China and Russia may yet forge ever closer ties to make up for their own shortfalls and to strengthen themselves against the United States and its allies and partners. But even if they do sign a written alliance commitment, such a treaty would hardly guarantee stability over the medium to long term in their diplomatic relations with one another. Moscow and Beijing signed a mutual defense pact in the early 1950s only to have a public falling out within one decade, followed by major border skirmishes. US alliances are prone to dysfunction, being largely composed of unevenly sized democratic states with relatively open and transparent political systems, but two great powers that have closed autocratic regimes, relatively large militaries, revisionist intentions, and different political and economic goals should be equally inclined, if not more so, to distrust one another. A formal alliance concluded by China and Russia would certainly be a major event, but the resulting partnership would hardly be monolithic. It could very well impress upon the United States and its allies the need to tighten their own security cooperation even more, which in turn could cause fissures between Moscow and Beijing by heightening the risks of unwanted conflict.

In making these observations, one recalls how the great Russian writer Leo Tolstoy began *Anna Karenina*: "Happy families are all alike; every unhappy family is unhappy in its own way." If formal military alliances are families – and note that I have likened them already to legal marriage – then Tolstoy's famous line does not entirely hold up. There is no such thing as a happy alliance; they are all unhappy to some extent, in their own way.

# References

Abadi, J. (2019). Saudi Arabia's rapprochement with Israel: The national security imperatives. *Middle Eastern Studies*, 55(3), 433–449.

Alexander, M.S. (1992). *The republic in danger: General Maurice Gamelin and the politics of French defence, 1933–1940*. Cambridge: Cambridge University Press.

Alic, J.A. (2007). *Trillions for military technology: How the Pentagon innovates and why it costs so much*. New York: Springer.

Altman, D. (2020). The evolution of territorial conquest after 1945 and the limits of the territorial integrity norm. *International Organization*, 74(3), 490–522.

Asoni, A., Gilli, A., Gilli, M., and Sanandaji, T. (2020). A mercenary army of the poor? Technological change and the demographic composition of the post-9/11 US military. *Journal of Strategic Studies*, 1–47.

Auslin, M. (2016). Japan's new realism: Abe gets tough. *Foreign Affairs*, 95(2), 125–134.

Bardach, J. (1970). L'union de Lublin: Ses origines et son rôle historique. *Acta Poloniae Historica*, 21, 69–92.

Barnett, M.N., and Levy, J.S. (1991). Domestic sources of alliances and alignments: The case of Egypt, 1962–73. *International Organization*, 45(3), 369–395.

Becker, J. (2017). The correlates of transatlantic burden sharing: Revising the agenda for theoretical and policy analysis. *Defense & Security Analysis*, 33(2), 131–157.

Becker, J., and Malesky, E. (2017). The continent or the

"grand large"? Strategic culture and operational burden-sharing in NATO. *International Studies Quarterly*, 61(1), 163–180.

Beckley, M. (2015). The myth of entangling alliances: Reassessing the security risks of US defense pacts. *International Security*, 39(4), 7–48.

Beckley, M. (2018). *Unrivaled: Why America will remain the world's sole superpower.* Ithaca, NY: Cornell University Press.

Beissinger, M.R. (2002). *Nationalist mobilization and the collapse of the Soviet State.* Cambridge: Cambridge University Press.

Belkin, P., Mix, D.E., and Woehrel, S. (2014). NATO: Response to the crisis in Ukraine and security concerns in Central and Eastern Europe. *Congressional Research Service* R43478.

Bensahel, N. (2007). International alliances and military effectiveness: Fighting alongside allies and partners. In R.A. Brooks and E.A. Stanley (eds.), *Creating military power: The sources of military effectiveness*, pp. 187–206. Stanford, CA: Stanford University Press.

Benson, B.V. (2012). *Constructing international security: Alliances, deterrence, and moral hazard.* Cambridge: Cambridge University Press.

Berger, T.U. (1998). *Cultures of antimilitarism: National security in Germany and Japan.* Baltimore, MD: Johns Hopkins University Press.

Berkemeier, M., and Fuhrmann, M. (2018). Reassessing the fulfillment of alliance commitments in war. *Research & Politics*, 5(2), 1–5.

Biddle, S.D. (2004). *Military power: Explaining victory and defeat in modern battle.* Princeton, NJ: Princeton University Press.

Biden, J.R. (2020). Why America must lead again: Rescuing US foreign policy after Trump. *Foreign Affairs*, 99(2), 64–76.

Bluth, C. (1995). *Britain, Germany and Western nuclear strategy.* Oxford: Clarendon Press.

Bow, B. (2009). Defence dilemmas: Continental defence

cooperation, from Bomarc to BMD, *Canadian Foreign Policy Journal*, 15(1), 40–59.

Bowers, I., and Hiim, H.S. (2020/21). Conventional counterforce dilemmas: South Korea's deterrence strategy and stability on the Korean peninsula. *International Security*, 45(3), 7–39.

Brands, H. (2017). US grand strategy in an age of nationalism: Fortress America and its alternatives. *The Washington Quarterly*, 40(1), 73–94.

Braumoeller, B.F. (2019). *Only the dead: The persistence of war in the modern age.* New York: Oxford University Press.

Brawley, M.R. (2004). The political economy of balance of power theory. In T.V. Paul, J.J. Wirtz, and M. Fortmann (eds.), *Balance of Power: Theory and Practice in the 21st Century*, pp. 76–101. Stanford, CA: Stanford University Press.

Brigham Young University Library. (2020). *The World War I Documentary Archive.* https://wwi.lib.byu.edu/index.php/Main_Page.

Brooks, R.A. (2007). Introduction: The impact of culture, society, institutions, and international forces on military effectiveness. In R.A. Brooks and E.A. Stanley (eds.), *Creating military power: The sources of military effectiveness*, pp. 1–26. Stanford, CA: Stanford University Press.

Brooks, S.G., and Wohlforth, W.C. (2008). *World out of balance: International relations and the challenge of American primacy.* Princeton, NJ: Princeton University Press.

Brooks, S.G., and Wohlforth, W.C. (2016). *America abroad: The United States' global role in the 21st century.* New York: Oxford University Press.

Bunce, V. (1985). The empire strikes back: The evolution of the Eastern Bloc from a Soviet asset to a Soviet liability. *International Organization*, 39(1), 1–46.

Bury, P. (2017). Recruitment and retention in British Army reserve logistics units. *Armed Forces & Society*, 43(4), 608–631.

Buszynski, L. (1981). SEATO: Why it survived until 1977 and why it was abolished. *Journal of Southeast Asian Studies*, 12(2), 287–296.

Butt, A.I. (2019). Why did the United States invade Iraq in 2003? *Security Studies*, 28(2), 250–285.

Butterworth, S.B. (1974). Daladier and the Munich crisis: A reappraisal. *Journal of Contemporary History*, 9(3), 191–216.

Cannadine, D. (2017). *Victorious century: The United Kingdom, 1800–1906*. London, UK: Penguin.

Carley, M.J. (1976). The origins of the French intervention in the Russian Civil War, January–May 1918: A reappraisal. *The Journal of Modern History*, 48(3), 413–439.

Cha, V.D. (2000). Abandonment, entrapment, and neoclassical realism in Asia: The United States, Japan, and Korea. *International Studies Quarterly*, 44(2), 261–291.

Cha, V.D. (2016). *Powerplay: The origins of the American alliance system in Asia*. Princeton, NJ: Princeton University Press.

Chalmers, M. (2001). The Atlantic burden-sharing debate: Widening or fragmenting? *International Affairs*, 77(3), 569–585.

Chalmers, M., and Unterseher, L. (1988). Is there a tank gap? Comparing NATO and Warsaw Pact tank fleets. *International Security*, 13(1), 5–49.

Chongkittavorn, V. (2020). Thai–US alliance comes with new twists. *Bangkok Post*, July 14. https://www.bangkokpost.com/opinion/opinion/1950976/thai–us–alliance–comes–with–new–twists.

Christensen, T.J. (2001). Posing problems without catching up: China's rise and challenges for US security policy. *International Security*, 25(4), 5–40.

Christensen, T.J. (2011). *Worse than a monolith: Alliance politics and problems in coercive diplomacy in Asia*. Princeton, NJ: Princeton University Press.

Christensen, T.J., and Snyder, J. (1990). Chain gangs and passed bucks: Predicting alliance patterns in multipolarity. *International Organization*, 44(2), 137–168.

Christie, E.H. (2019). The demand for military expenditure

in Europe: The role of fiscal space in the context of a resurgent Russia. *Defence and Peace Economics*, 30(1), 72–84.

Chung, J.H., and Choi, M.H. (2013). Uncertain allies or uncomfortable neighbors? Making sense of China–North Korea relations, 1949–2010. *The Pacific Review*, 26(3), 243–264.

Ciorciari, J.D. (2010). *The limits of alignment: Southeast Asia and the great powers since 1975*. Washington, DC: Georgetown University Press, 2010.

Clark, C. (2012). *The sleepwalkers: How Europe went to war in 1914*. London: Penguin.

Coe, A.J., and Vaynman, J. (2015). Collusion and the nuclear nonproliferation regime. *The Journal of Politics*, 77(4), 983–997.

Cohen, J.B., and Lanoszka, A. (n.d.). The reliability of alliance reliability. Working paper.

Coker, C. (1982). The Western Alliance and Africa 1949–81. *African Affairs*, 81(324), 319–335.

Cooley, A. (2008). *Base politics: Democratic change and the US military overseas*. Ithaca, NY: Cornell University Press.

Cooley, A., and Spruyt, H. (2009). *Contracting states: Sovereign transfers in international relations*. Princeton, NJ: Princeton University Press.

Cooley, A., and Nexon, D.H. (2016). Interpersonal networks and international security: US–Georgia relations during the Bush administration. In D.D. Avant and O. Westerwinter (eds.), *The new power politics: Networks and transnational security governance*, pp. 74–102. Oxford: Oxford University Press.

Copeland, D.C. (2001). *The origins of major war*. Ithaca, NY: Cornell University Press.

Cosmas, G.A. (2009). *The Joint Chiefs of Staff and the war in Vietnam: 1960–1968 (pt. 2)*. Office of Joint History, Office of the Chairman of the Joint Chiefs of Staff.

Costa Buranelli, F. (2018). Spheres of influence as negotiated hegemony: The case of Central Asia. *Geopolitics*, 23(2), 378–403.

Coticchia, F. (2011). The "enemy" at the gates? Assessing the European military contribution to the Libyan War. *Perspectives on Federalism*, 3(3), 48–70.

Crawford, T.W. (2008). Wedge strategy, balancing, and the deviant case of Spain, 1940–41. *Security Studies*, 17(1), 1–38.

Crawford, T.W. (2011). Preventing enemy coalitions: How wedge strategies shape power politics. *International Security*, 35(4), 155–189.

Crawford, T.W. (2014). The alliance politics of concerted accommodation: Entente bargaining and Italian and Ottoman interventions in the First World War. *Security Studies*, 23(1), 113–147.

Cropsey, S. (2020). Strengthening the US–Taiwan alliance. *Hudson Institute*, January 9. https://www.hudson.org/research/15623–strengthening–the–u–s–taiwan–alliance.

Crump, L. (2015). *The Warsaw Pact reconsidered: International relations in Eastern Europe, 1955–1969*. London: Routledge.

Cruz De Castro, R. (2020). Abstract of crisis in Philippine–US security relations: From an alliance to security partnership? *The Pacific Review*, 10.1080/09512748.2020.1845227.

Dafoe, A., Renshon, J., and Huth, P. (2014). Reputation and status as motives for war. *Annual Review of Political Science*, 17, 371–393.

Dafoe, A., and Caughey, D. (2016). Honor and war: Southern US presidents and the effects of concern for reputation. *World Politics*, 68(2), 341–381.

David, S.R. (1991). Explaining third world alignment. *World Politics*, 43(2), 233–256.

Davidson, J. (2011). *America's allies and war: Kosovo, Afghanistan, and Iraq*. New York: Palgrave Macmillan.

Davis, C.L. (2009). Linkage diplomacy: Economic and security bargaining in the Anglo-Japanese alliance, 1902–23. *International Security*, 33(3), 143–179.

Dawisha, K. (1990). *Eastern Europe, Gorbachev, and reform: The great challenge*, 2nd ed. Cambridge: Cambridge University Press.

Debs, A., and Monteiro, N.P. (2014). Known unknowns:

Power shifts, uncertainty, and war. *International Organization*, 68(1), 1–31.

Debs, A., and Monteiro, N.P. (2018). Cascading chaos in nuclear Northeast Asia. *The Washington Quarterly*, 41(1), 97–113.

Delcour, L., and Wolczuk, K. (2015). Spoiler or facilitator of democratization? Russia's role in Georgia and Ukraine. *Democratization*, 22(3), 459–478.

Deni, J.R. (2017). *Rotational deployments vs. forward stationing: How can the Army achieve assurance and deterrence efficiently and effectively.* Carlisle, PA: US Army War College.

Driscoll, J., and Maliniak, D. (2016). With friends like these: Brinkmanship and chain-ganging in Russia's near abroad. *Security Studies*, 25(4), 585–607.

Duchin, B.R. (1992). The "agonizing reappraisal": Eisenhower, Dulles, and the European defense community. *Diplomatic History*, 16(2), 201–221.

Duffield, J.S. (1995). *Power rules: The evolution of NATO's conventional force posture.* Stanford, CA: Stanford University Press.

Edelstein, D.M., and Shifrinson, J.R.I. (2018). It's a trap! Security commitments and the risks of entrapment. In A.T. Thrall and B.H. Friedman (eds.), *US Grand Strategy in the 21st Century*, pp. 19–41. Abingdon, UK: Routledge.

Elleman, B. (1996). Sino–Soviet Relations and the February 1979 Sino–Vietnamese conflict. Lubbock: Texas Tech University.

Epstein, R.A. (2005). NATO enlargement and the spread of democracy: Evidence and expectations. *Security Studies*, 14(1), 63–105.

Evans, L., Wasielewski, P., and Von Buseck, C.R. (1982). Compulsory seat belt usage and driver risk-taking behavior. *Human Factors*, 24(1), 41–48.

Fazal, T.M. (2007). *State death: The politics and geography of conquest, occupation, and annexation.* Princeton, NJ: Princeton University Press.

Fazal, T.M. (2014). Dead wrong? Battle deaths, military

medicine, and exaggerated reports of war's demise. *International Security*, 39(1), 95–125.

Fazal, T.M. (2018). *Wars of law: Unintended consequences in the regulation of armed conflict*. Ithaca, NY: Cornell University Press.

Fearon, J.D. (1994). Domestic political audiences and the escalation of international disputes. *American Political Science Review*, 88(3), 577–592.

Fearon, J.D. (1995). Rationalist explanations for war. *International Organization*, 49(3), 379–414.

Fearon, J.D. (1997). Signaling foreign policy interests: Tying hands versus sinking costs. *Journal of Conflict Resolution*, 41(1), 68–90.

Fettweis, C.J. (2013). *The pathologies of power: Fear, honor, glory, and hubris in US foreign policy*. Cambridge: Cambridge University Press.

Fierke, K.M., and Wiener, A. (1999). Constructing institutional interests: EU and NATO enlargement. *Journal of European Public Policy*, 6(5), 721–742.

Fischer, F. (1974). *World power or decline: The controversy over Germany's aims in the first world war*. New York: W.W. Norton.

Foley, R.T. (2005). *German strategy and the path to Verdun: Erich von Falkenhayn and the development of attrition, 1870–1916*. Cambridge: Cambridge University Press.

Ford, M. (2017). *Weapon of choice: Small arms and the culture of military innovation*. Oxford: Oxford University Press.

*Foreign Relations of the United States, 1952–1954*, vol. V. Washington, DC: US Government Printing Office.

*Foreign Relations of the United States, 1958–1960*, vol. VII. Washington, DC: US Government Printing Office.

*Foreign Relations of the United States, 1961–1963*, vol. XIII. Washington, DC: US Government Printing Office.

Friedman, J.A. (2019). *War and chance: Assessing uncertainty in international politics*. New York: Oxford University Press.

Fuhrmann, M. (2020). When do leaders free-ride? Business

experience and contributions to collective defense. *American Journal of Political Science*, 64(2), 416–431.

Gannon, J.A., and Kent, D. (2021). Keeping your friends close, but acquaintances closer: Why weakly allied states make committed coalition partners. *Journal of Conflict Resolution*, 65(5), 889–918.

Gartzke, E., and Gleditsch, K.S. (2004). Why democracies may actually be less reliable allies. *American Journal of Political Science*, 48(4), 775–795.

Gaubatz, K.T. (1996). Democratic states and commitment in international relations. *International Organization*, 50(1), 109–139.

Gavin, F.J. (2001). The myth of flexible response: United States strategy in Europe during the 1960s. *International History Review*, 23(4), 847–865.

Gavin, F.J. (2004). *Gold, dollars, and power: The politics of international monetary relations, 1958–1971*. Chapel Hill, NC: UNC Press.

Gavin, F.J. (2015). Strategies of inhibition: US grand strategy, the nuclear revolution, and nonproliferation. *International Security*, 40(1), 9–46.

German Bundestag. (2020). *Annual Report 2019 (61st Report) by the Parliamentary Commissioner for the Armed Forces*. Berlin, Germany, January 28.

Gerzhoy, G. (2015). Alliance coercion and nuclear restraint: How the United States thwarted West Germany's nuclear ambitions. *International Security*, 39(4), 91–129.

Gholz, E., Press, D.G., and Sapolsky, H.M. (1997). Come home, America: The strategy of restraint in the face of temptation. *International Security*, 21(4), 5–48.

Gilboa, E. (2013). Obama in Israel: Fixing American–Israeli relations. *Israel Journal of Foreign Affairs*, 7(2), 19–28.

Gill, T.D., and Ducheine, P.A.L. (2013). Anticipatory self-defense in the cyber context. *International Law Studies*, 89(438), 438–471.

Gilli, A., and Gilli, M. (2016). The diffusion of drone warfare? Industrial, organizational, and infrastructural constraints. *Security Studies*, 25(1), 50–84.

Gilli, A., and Gilli, M. (2019). Why China has not caught

up yet: Military-technological superiority and the limits of imitation, reverse engineering, and cyber espionage. *International Security*, 43(3), 141–189.

Glaser, B.S., Green, M.J., and Bush, R.C. (2020). *Toward a stronger US–Taiwan relationship*. Washington, DC: Center for Strategic and International Studies.

Goldberg, J. (2016). The Obama doctrine. *The Atlantic*, April. https://www.theatlantic.com/magazine/archive/2016/04/the-obama-doctrine/471525/.

Gordon, J., Johnson, S., Larrabee, F.S., and Wilson, P.A. (2012). NATO and the challenge of austerity. *Survival*, 54(4), 121–142.

Gould–Davies, N. (2020). Belarus and Russian policy: Patterns of the past, dilemmas of the present. *Survival*, 62(6), 179–198

Goulter, C. (2015). The British experience: Operation Ellamy. In K.P. Mueller (ed.), *Precision and purpose: Airpower in the Libyan Civil War*, pp. 153–182. Washington, DC: RAND.

Government Printing Office, *Public Papers of the Presidents of the United States: Richard Nixon, 1969* (Washington, DC: Government Printing Office, 1971).

Gowa, J. (1995). *Allies, adversaries, and international trade*. Princeton, NJ: Princeton University Press.

Granatstein, J.L. (2020). Mackenzie King and Canada at Ogdensberg, August 1940. In J.L. Granatstein (ed.), *Canada at War: Conscription, Diplomacy, and Politics*, pp. 137–154. Toronto, ON: University of Toronto Press.

Gray, J. (2018). Life, death, or zombie? The vitality of international organizations. *International Studies Quarterly*, 62(1), 1–13.

Green, B.R. (2020). *The revolution that failed: Nuclear competition, arms control, and the Cold War*. Cambridge: Cambridge University Press.

Greenhalgh, E. (2005). *Victory through coalition: Britain and France during the First World War*. Cambridge: Cambridge University Press.

Grynaviski, E. (2015). Brokering cooperation: Intermediaries and US cooperation with non-state allies, 1776–1945. *European Journal of International Relations*, 21(3), 691–717.

Haesebrouck, T. (2021). Belgium: The reliable free rider. *International Politics*, 58(1), 37–48.

Haftendorn, H. (1996). *NATO and the nuclear revolution: A crisis of credibility, 1966–1967*. Oxford: Oxford University Press.

Haftendorn, H., Keohane, R.O., and Wallander, C.A. (1999). *Imperfect unions: Security institutions over time and space*. New York: Oxford University Press.

Haglund, D. (1997). The NATO of its dreams? Canada and the co-operative security alliance. *International Journal*, 52(3), 463–382.

Han, Z., and Papa, M. (2020). Alliances in Chinese international relations: Are they ending or rejuvenating? *Asian Security*, 1–20.

Harrison, G.A. (1951). *Cross-channel attack*. Washington, DC: US Army Center of Military History.

Helwig, N. (2020). Out of order? The US alliance in Germany's foreign and security policy. *Contemporary Politics*, 26(4), 439–457.

Hemmer, C., and Katzenstein, P.J. (2002). Why is there no NATO in Asia? Collective identity, regionalism, and the origins of multilateralism. *International Organization*, 56(3), 575–607.

Henke, M.E. (2019). *Constructing allied cooperation: Diplomacy, payments, and power in multilateral military coalitions*. Ithaca, NY: Cornell University Press.

Henry, I.D. (2020). What allies want: Reconsidering loyalty, reliability, and alliance interdependence. *International Security*, 44(4), 45–83.

Hensley, G. (2013). *Friendly fire: Nuclear politics and the politics of ANZUS, 1984–1987*. Auckland, NZ: Auckland University Press.

Herzog, S. (2011). Revisiting the Estonian cyber attacks: Digital threats and multinational responses. *Journal of Strategic Security*, 4(2), 49–60.

Heuser, B. (1998). Victory in a nuclear war? A comparison of

NATO and WTO war aims and strategies. *Contemporary European History*, 7(3), 311–327.

Hodges, B., Lawrence, T., and Wojcik, R. (2020). *Until something moves: Reinforcing the Baltic region in crisis and war.* Tallinn, Estonia: International Centre for Defence and Security.

Hoffman, F. (2009). *Hybrid warfare and challenges.* Washington, DC: Institute for National Strategic Studies.

Horowitz, M.C., Pasandideh, S., Gilli, A., and Gilli, M. (2019). Correspondence: Military-technological imitation and rising powers. *International Security*, 44(2), 185–192.

Horowitz, M.C., Poast, P., and Stam, A.C. (2017). Domestic signaling of commitment credibility: Military recruitment and alliance formation. *Journal of Conflict Resolution*, 61(8), 1682–1710.

Hunzeker, M.A. (2021). *Dying to learn: Wartime lessons from the Western Front.* Ithaca, NY: Cornell University Press.

Hunzeker, M.A., and Lanoszka, A. (2016). Landpower and American credibility. *Parameters*, 45(4), 17–26.

Hura, M. et al. (2000). *Interoperability: A continuing challenge in coalition air operations.* Santa Monica, CA: RAND Corporation.

Ikenberry, G.J. (2001). *After victory: Institutions, strategic restraint, and the rebuilding of order after major wars.* Princeton, NJ: Princeton University Press.

Ikenberry, G.J. (2005). Power and liberal order: America's postwar world order in transition. *International Relations of the Asia-Pacific*, 5(2), 133–152.

Ikenberry, G.J. (2017). The plot against American foreign policy: Can the liberal order survive? *Foreign Affairs*, 96(3), 2–9.

Ikenberry, G.J. (2020). *A world safe for democracy: Liberal internationalism and the crises of global order.* New Haven, CT: Yale University Press.

İpek, P. (2007). The role of oil and gas in Kazakhstan's foreign policy: Looking east or west? *Europe-Asia Studies*, 59(7), 1179–1199.

Izumikawa, Y. (2020). Network connections and the

emergence of the hub-and-spokes alliance system in East Asia. *International Security*, 45(2), 7–50.

Jackson, V. (2018a). Buffers, not bridges: Rethinking multilateralism and the resilience of Japan–South Korea friction. *International Studies Review*, 20(1), 127–151.

Jackson, V. (2018b). *On the brink: Trump, Kim, and the threat of nuclear war*. Cambridge: Cambridge University Press.

Jakobsen, J. (2018). Is European NATO *really* free-riding? Patterns of material and non-material burden-sharing after the Cold War. *European Security*, 27(4), 490–514.

Jakobsen, J., and Jakobsen, T.G. (2019). Tripwires and free-riders: Do forward-deployed US troops reduce the willingness of host-country citizens to fight for their country? *Contemporary Security Policy*, 40(2), 135–164.

Jervis, R. (1978). Cooperation under the security dilemma. *World Politics*, 30(2), 167–214.

Jervis, R. (1979). Deterrence theory revisited. *World Politics*, 31(2), 289–324.

Jervis, R. (1982). Security regimes. *International Organization*, 36(2), 357–378.

Jervis, R. (1989). *The meaning of the nuclear revolution*. Ithaca, NY: Cornell University Press.

Jervis, R. (2001). Was the Cold War a security dilemma? *Journal of Cold War Studies*, 3(1), 36–60.

Jervis, R. (2020). Liberalism, the Blob, and American foreign policy: Evidence and methodology. *Security Studies*, 29(3), 434–456.

Jinks, J., and Hennessy, P. (2015). *The silent deep: The Royal Navy Submarine Service since 1945*. London, UK: Penguin.

Jockel, J.T., and Sokolsky, J.J. (2009). Canada and NATO: Keeping Ottawa in, expenses down, criticism out … and the country secure. *International Journal*, 64(2), 315–336.

Johannes, C. (2018). *Achieving multinational tactical radio interoperability*. Canadian Forces College, JSCP 44 Service Paper.

Johnson, D.D., and Toft, M.D. (2013/14). Grounds for war:

The evolution of territorial conflict. *International Security*, 38(3), 7–38.

Johnson, J.C. (2015). The cost of security: Foreign policy concessions and military alliances. *Journal of Peace Research*, 52(5), 665–679.

Jones, M. (2010). *After Hiroshima: The United States, race and nuclear weapons in Asia, 1945–1965*. Cambridge: Cambridge University Press.

Jones, M. (2016). The alliance that wasn't: Germany and Austria-Hungary in World War I. In P.R. Mansoor and W. Murray (eds.), *Grand strategy and military alliances*, pp. 284–312. Cambridge: Cambridge University Press.

Kaldor, M. (2012). *New and old wars: Organized violence in a global era*, 3rd ed. Cambridge: Polity.

Kallis, A.A. (2000). *Fascist ideology: Territory and expansionism in Italy and Germany, 1922–1945*. London: Routledge.

Kann, R. (1976). Alliances vs. ententes. *World Politics*, 28(4), 611–621.

Kaufmann, W.W. 1954. *The requirements of deterrence, memorandum #7*. Princeton, NJ: Center for International Studies.

Kenwick, M.R., Vasquez, J.A., and Powers, M.A. (2015). Do alliances really deter? *The Journal of Politics*, 77(4), 943–954.

Keohane, R.O. (1988). Alliances, threats, and the uses of neorealism. *International Security*, 13(1), 169–176.

Khanna, P. (2008). *The second world: Empires and influence in the new global order*. New York: Random House.

Kim, T. (2011). Why alliances entangle but seldom entrap states. *Security Studies*, 20(3), 350–377.

Kim, Y. (2019). North Korea's relations with China and Russia in the security realm. In J. Choo, Y. Kim, A. Lukin, and E. Wishnick (eds.), *The China–Russia Entente and the Korean Peninsula* (NBR Special Report #78), pp. 13–19. Washington, DC: The National Bureau of Asia Research.

Kitchen, V.M. (2009). Argument and identity change in the Atlantic security community. *Security Dialogue*, 40(1), 95–114.

Knopf, J.W. (2011). Varieties of assurance. *Journal of Strategic Studies*, 35(3), 375–399.

Koremenos, B., Lipson, C., and Snidal, D. (2001). The rational design of international institutions. *International Organization*, 55(4), 761–799.

Korolev, A. (2019). On the verge of an alliance: Contemporary China–Russia military cooperation. *Asian Security*, 15(3), 233–252.

Krasner, S.D. (1999). *Sovereignty: Organized hypocrisy*. Princeton, NJ: Princeton University Press.

Kraus, C. (2017). "The danger is two-fold": Decolonisation and cold war in anti-communist Asia, 1955–7. *The International History Review*, 39(2), 256–273.

Krebs, R.R., and Spindel, J. (2018). Divided priorities: Why and when allies differ over military intervention. *Security Studies*, 27(4), 575–606.

Kreps, S. (2010). Elite consensus as a determinant of alliance cohesion: Why public opinion hardly matters for NATO-led operations in Afghanistan. *Foreign Policy Analysis*, 6(3), 191–215.

Kroenig, M. (2011). *Exporting the bomb: Technology transfer and the spread of nuclear weapons*. Ithaca, NY: Cornell University Press, 2011.

Kroenig, M. (2013). Nuclear superiority and the balance of resolve: Explaining nuclear crisis outcomes. *International Organization*, 67(1), 141–171.

Kroenig, M. (2018). *The logic of American nuclear strategy: Why strategic superiority matters*. New York: Oxford University Press.

Kroenig, M. (2020). *The return of great power rivalry: Democracy versus autocracy from the ancient world to the US and China*. New York: Oxford University Press.

Kunda, Z. (1990). The case for motivated reasoning. *Psychological Bulletin*, 108(3), 480–498.

Kunz, D.B. (1991). *The economic diplomacy of the Suez crisis*. Chapel Hill: University of North Carolina Press.

Kuo, R. (2021). *Following the leader: International order, alliance strategies, and emulation*. Stanford, CA: Stanford University Press.

Kwon, E. (2018). South Korea's deterrence strategy against North Korea's WMD. *East Asia*, 35(1), 1–21.

Kyle, J. (2019). Perspectives roadblocks: Georgia's long road to NATO membership. *Demokratizatsiya*, 27(2), 237–247.

Lai, B., and Reiter, D. (2000). Democracy, political similarity, and international alliances, 1816–1992. *Journal of Conflict Resolution*, 44(2), 203–227.

Lake, D.A. (2011). *Hierarchy in international relations.* Ithaca, NY: Cornell University Press.

Lambeth, B.S. (2001). *NATO's air war for Kosovo: A strategic and operational assessment.* Santa Monica, CA: RAND.

Lanoszka, A. (2015). Do allies really free ride? *Survival*, 57(3), 133–152.

Lanoszka, A. (2016). Russian hybrid warfare and extended deterrence in eastern Europe. *International Affairs*, 92(1), 175–195.

Lanoszka, A. (2018a). Alliances and nuclear proliferation in the Trump era. *The Washington Quarterly*, 41(4), 85–101.

Lanoszka, A. (2018b). *Atomic assurance: The alliance politics of nuclear proliferation.* Ithaca, NY: Cornell University Press.

Lanoszka, A. (2018c). Nuclear proliferation and nonproliferation among Soviet allies. *Journal of Global Security Studies*, 3(2), 217–233.

Lanoszka, A. (2018d). Tangled up in rose? Theories of alliance entrapment and the 2008 Russo–Georgian war. *Contemporary Security Policy*, 39(2), 234–257.

Lanoszka, A. (2020a). Poland in a time of geopolitical flux. *Contemporary Politics*, 26(4), 458–474.

Lanoszka, A. (2020b). Thank goodness for NATO enlargement. *International Politics*, 57(3), 451–470.

Lanoszka, A., and Hunzeker, M.A. (2019). *Conventional deterrence and landpower in Northeastern Europe.* Carlisle, PA: US Army War College.

Lanoszka, A., and Simón, L. (2021). A military drawdown from Europe? US force posture from Trump to Biden. *The Washington Quarterly*, 44(1), 199–218.

Lanoszka, A., Leuprecht, C., and Moens, A. (2020). *Lessons from the Enhanced Forward Presence, 2017–2020.* Rome: NATO Defence College.

Layne, C. (2006). *The peace of illusions: American grand strategy from 1940 to the present.* Ithaca, NY: Cornell University Press.

Lebow, R.N., and Stein, J.G. (1995). Deterrence and the Cold War. *Political Science Quarterly,* 110(2), 157–81.

Leeds, B.A. (2003). Alliance reliability in times of war: Explaining state decisions to violate treaties. *International Organization,* 57(4), 801–827.

Leeds, B.A., and Savun, B. (2007). Terminating alliances: Why do states abrogate agreements? *The Journal of Politics,* 69(4), 1118–1132.

Leeds, B.A., Long, A.G., and Mitchell, S.M. (2000). Reevaluating alliance reliability: Specific threats, specific promises. *Journal of Conflict Resolution,* 44(5), 686–699.

Leeds, B.A., Mattes, M., and Vogel, J.S. (2009). Interests, institutions, and the reliability of international commitments. *American Journal of Political Science,* 53(2), 461–476.

Leeds, B.A., Ritter, J.M., Mitchell, S.M., and Long. A.G. (2002). Alliance treaty obligations and provisions, 1815–1944. *International Interactions,* 28, 237–260.

Levy, J.S. (1981). Alliance formation and war behavior: An analysis of the great powers, 1495–1975. *Journal of Conflict Resolution,* 25(4), 581–613.

Levy, J.S. (2004). What do great powers balance against and when? In T.V. Paul, J.J. Wirtz, and M. Fortmann (eds.), *Balance of power: Theory and practice in the 21st century,* pp. 29–51. Stanford, CA: Stanford University Press.

Liberman, P. (1998). *Does conquest pay? The exploitation of occupied industrial societies.* Princeton, NJ: Princeton University Press.

Lieber, K.A. (2005). *War and the engineers: The primacy of politics over technology.* Ithaca, NY: Cornell University Press.

Lieber, K.A., and Press, D.G. (2020). *The myth of the nuclear revolution: Power politics in the atomic age.* Ithaca, NY: Cornell University Press.

Liff, A.P. (2016). Whither the balancers? The case for a methodological reset. *Security Studies*, 25(3), 420–459.

Lind, J.M. (2004). Pacifism or passing the buck? Testing theories of Japanese security policy. *International Security*, 29(1), 92–121.

Lindsay, J.M. (1992/3). Congress and foreign policy: Why the Hill matters. *Political Science Quarterly*, 107(4), 607–628.

Lindsay, J.R. (2015). The impact of China on cybersecurity: Fiction and friction. *International Security*, 39(3), 7–47.

Lipson, C. (2005). *Reliable partners: How democracies have made a separate peace.* Princeton, NJ: Princeton University Press.

Liska, G. (1962). *Nations in alliance: The limits of interdependence.* Baltimore, MD: Johns Hopkins University Press.

Logevall, F. (2001). *Choosing war: The lost chance for peace and the escalation of war in Vietnam.* Berkeley: University of California Press.

Lüthi, L.M. (2010). *The Sino–Soviet split: Cold War in the communist world.* Princeton, NJ: Princeton University Press.

MacDonald, P.K., and Parent, J.M. (2018). *Twilight of the titans: Great power decline and retrenchment.* Ithaca, NY: Cornell University Press.

Macinnes, A.I. (2007). *Union and empire: The making of the United Kingdom in 1707.* Cambridge: Cambridge University Press.

Macmillan, M. (2014). *The war that ended peace: The road to 1914.* New York: Random House.

Mahnken, T.G. (2011). Weapons: The growth and spread of the precision-strike regime. *Daedalus*, 140(3), 45–57.

Mann, M. (2018). Have wars and violence declined? *Theory and Society*, 47(1), 37–60.

Marin, A. (2020). *The Union State of Belarus and Russia: Myths and realities of political-military integration.* Vilnius: Vilnius Institute for Policy Analysis.

Martin, D. (2018). NATO hits back at President Trump's Montenegro World War III remarks. *Deutsche Welle*, July 18. https://www.dw.com/en/nato–hits–back–at–president–trumps–montenegro–world–war–iii–remarks/a–44734118.

Massie, J. (2016). Why democratic allies defect prematurely: Canadian and Dutch unilateral pullouts from the war in Afghanistan. *Democracy and Security*, 12(2), 85–115.

Matějka, Z. (1997). How the Warsaw Pact was dissolved. *Perspectives*, (8), 55–65.

Mattes, M. (2012). Democratic reliability, precommitment of successor governments, and the choice of alliance commitment. *International Organization*, 66(1), 153–172.

Mattes, M., and Vonnahme, G. (2010). Contracting for peace: Do nonaggression pacts reduce conflict? *The Journal of Politics*, 72(4), 925–938.

Mattis, J. (2018). *Summary of the National Defense Strategy: Sharpening the American military's competitive edge.* Arlington, VA: US Department of Defense.

Mazarr, M.J. (2012). The risks of ignoring strategic insolvency. *The Washington Quarterly*, 35(4), 7–22.

McKoy, M.K., and Miller, M.K. (2012). The patron's dilemma: The dynamics of foreign–supported democratization. *Journal of Conflict Resolution*, 56(5), 904–932.

Mearsheimer, J.J. (1990). Back to the future: Instability in Europe after the Cold War. *International Security*, 15(1), 5–56.

Mearsheimer, J.J. (2018). *The great delusion: Liberal dreams and international realities.* New Haven, CT: Yale University Press.

Mello, P.A. (2019). National restrictions in multinational military operations: A conceptual framework. *Contemporary Security Policy*, 40(1), 38–55.

Mello, P.A. (2020). Paths towards coalition defection: Democracies and withdrawal from the Iraq War. *European Journal of International Security*, 5(1), 45–76.

Menon, R. (2003). The end of alliances. *World Policy Journal*, 20(2), 1–20.

Menon, A. (2011). European defence policy from Lisbon to Libya. *Survival*, 53(3), 75–90.

Mëhilli, E. (2017). *From Stalin to Mao: Albania and the socialist world*. Ithaca, NY: Cornell University Press.

Miller, C. (2016). *The struggle to save the Soviet economy: Mikhail Gorbachev and the collapse of the USSR*. Chapel Hill, NC: UNC Press.

Miller, G.D. (2003). Hypotheses on reputation: Alliance choices and the shadow of the past. *Security Studies*, 12(3), 40–78.

Ministry of Foreign Affairs of Japan. (n.d.). *Japan–US Security Treaty*. https://www.mofa.go.jp/region/n–america/us/q&a/ref/1.html.

Moller, S.B. (2016). *Fighting friends: Institutional cooperation and military effectiveness in multinational war*. Doctoral dissertation, Columbia University.

Moller, S.B., and Rynning, S. (2021). Revitalizing transatlantic relations: NATO 2030 and beyond. *The Washington Quarterly*, 44(1), 177–197.

Monson, R.A. (1986). Star Wars and AirLand Battle: Technology, strategy, and politics in German–American relations. *German Studies Review*, 9(3), 599–624.

Moody, S.J. (2017). Enhancing political cohesion in NATO during the 1950s or: How it learned to stop worrying and love the (tactical) bomb. *Journal of Strategic Studies*, 40(6), 817–838.

Morrow, J.D. (1991). Alliances and asymmetry: An alternative to the capability aggregation model of alliances. *American Journal of Political Science*, 35(4), 904–933.

Morrow, J.D. (1993). Arms versus allies: Trade-offs in the search for security. *International Organization*, 47(2), 207–233.

Morrow, J.D. (2000). Alliances: Why write them down? *Annual Review of Political Science*, 3(1), 63–83.

Mueller, J. (1988). The essential irrelevance of nuclear weapons: Stability in the postwar world. *International Security*, 13(2), 55–79.

Mueller, J. (1989). *Retreat from doomsday: The obsolescence of major power war*. New York: Basic Books.

NATO. (1949 [2019]). The North Atlantic Treaty. April 10. https://www.nato.int/cps/en/natolive/official_texts_17120.htm.

NATO. (1997 [2009]. Founding Act. May 27. https://www.nato.int/cps/en/natohq/official_texts_25468.htm?.

NATO. (2006). Backgrounder: Interoperability for Joint Operations. July. https://www.nato.int/nato_static_fl2014/assets/pdf/pdf_publications/20120116_interoperability-en.pdf.

NATO. (2008 [2014]). Bucharest Summit Declaration. April 3. https://www.nato.int/cps/en/natolive/official_texts_8443.htm.

NATO. (2019). Defence expenditure of NATO countries (2013–2019). *NATO Public Diplomacy Division Press Release*, November 29.

NATO. (n.d.). France and NATO. https://www.nato.int/cps/en/natohq/declassified_160672.htm.

Nedal, D.K., and Nexon, D.H. (2019). Anarchy and authority: International structure, the balance of power, and hierarchy. *Journal of Global Security Studies*, 4(2), 169–189.

Nichol, J. (2020). *Lancaster: The forging of a very British legend*. London: Simon and Schuster.

Nixon, R.M. (1969 [n.d.]). Informal remarks in Guam with newsmen online by Gerhard Peters and John T. Woolley, *The American Presidency Project*. https://www.presidency.ucsb.edu/node/239667.

North, D.C. (1991). *Institutions, institutional change and economic performance*. Cambridge: Cambridge University Press.

Nossal, K.R. (2016). *Charlie foxtrot: Fixing defence procurement in Canada*. Toronto, ON: Dundurn.

Nye, J.S. Jr. (2011). A shift in perceptions of power. *The Los Angeles Times*, April 6, p. 17.

Oberdorfer, D. (1999). *The two Koreas: A contemporary history*. New York: Basic Books.

Olson, M. (1971). *The logic of collective action: Public goods and the theory of groups*. Cambridge, MA: Harvard University Press.

Owen, R.C. (2017). US Air Force airlift and the Army's relevance. *Parameters*, 47(2), 103–112.

Oye, K.A. (1985). Explaining cooperation under anarchy: Hypotheses and strategies. *World Politics*, 38(1), 1–24.

Pannier, A. (2020). *Rivals in arms: The rise of UK–France defence relations in the twenty–first century.* Kingston, ON: McGill-Queen's University Press.

Paquette, G. (2020). Anglo-Portuguese relations in the mid-nineteenth century: Informal Empire, arbitration, and the durability of an asymmetrical alliance. *The English Historical Review,* 135(575), 836–859.

Park, H., and Park, J.J. (2017). How not to be abandoned by China: North Korea's nuclear brinkmanship revisited. *Korean Journal of Defense Analysis,* 29(3), 371–387.

Philpott, W.J. (1996). *Anglo-French relations and strategy on the Western Front, 1914–18.* Houndsmills, UK: Palgrave Macmillan.

Pinker, S. (2012). *The better angels of our nature: Why violence has declined.* New York: Penguin.

Poast, P. (2013). Can issue linkage improve treaty credibility? Buffer state alliances as a "hard case." *Journal of Conflict Resolution,* 57(5), 739–764.

Poast, P. (2019). *Arguing about alliances: The art of agreement in military-pact negotiations.* Ithaca, NY: Cornell University Press.

Pollack, J. (2003). Anti-Americanism in contemporary Saudi Arabia. *Middle East Review of International Affairs,* 7(4), 30–43.

Pollack, J.D. (2011). *No exit: North Korea, nuclear weapons, and international security.* London, UK: Routledge.

Popescu, N. (2020). A captive ally: Why Russia isn't rushing to Armenia's aid. *European Council on Foreign Relations,* October 8. https://ecfr.eu/article/a_captive_ally_why_russia_isnt_rushing_to_armenias_aid/.

Posen, B.R. (2014). *Restraint: A new foundation for US grand strategy.* Ithaca, NY: Cornell University Press.

Poznansky, M. (2020). *In the shadow of international law: Secrecy and regime change in the postwar world.* New York: Oxford University Press.

Prince, T. (2021). Biden's top diplomat pick says US seeks "stronger" Iran nuclear deal, condemns Russia over Navalny arrest. *Radio Free Europe/Radio Liberty,* January

20. https://www.rferl.org/a/blinken-iran-nuclear-russia-navalny-/31053093.html.

Rabinowitz, O., and Miller, N.L. (2015). Keeping the bombs in the basement: US nonproliferation policy toward Israel, South Africa, and Pakistan. *International Security*, 40(1), 47–86.

Ramsay, K.W. (2008). Settling it on the field: Battlefield events and war termination. *Journal of Conflict Resolution*, 52(6), 850–879.

Rapp-Hooper M. (2014). Ambivalent Albion, ambitious ally: Britain's decision for no separate peace in 1914, *Security Studies*, 23(4), 814–844.

Rapp-Hooper, M. (2015). *Absolute alliances: Extended deterrence in international politics.* Doctoral dissertation, Columbia University.

Rapp-Hooper, M. (2020). *Shields of the republic: The triumph and peril of America's alliances.* Cambridge, MA: Harvard University Press.

Rathbun, B.C. (2007). Uncertain about uncertainty: Understanding the multiple meanings of a crucial concept in international relations theory. *International Studies Quarterly*, 51(3), 533–557.

Ravenal, E.C. (1982). Counterforce and alliance: The ultimate connection. *International Security*, 6(4), 26–43.

Ravenal, E.C. (1988). Coupling and decoupling: The prospects for extended deterrence. In P.T. Hopmann and F. Barnaby (eds.), *Rethinking the nuclear weapons dilemma in Europe*, pp. 59–70. London: Palgrave Macmillan.

Reiter, D. (1995). Exploding the powder keg myth: Preemptive wars almost never happen. *International Security*, 20(2), 5–34.

Resnick, E.N. (2010/11). Strange bedfellows: US bargaining behavior with allies of convenience. *International Security*, 35(3), 144–184.

Rice, A.J. (1997). Command and control: The essence of coalition warfare. *Parameters*, 27(1), 152–167.

Rice, C. (1984). *The Soviet Union and the Czechoslovak army, 1948–1983: Uncertain allegiance.* Princeton, NJ: Princeton University Press.

Ringsmose, J. (2010). NATO burden-sharing redux: Continuity and change after the Cold War. *Contemporary Security Policy*, 31(2), 319–338.

Robb, T.K., and Gill, D.J. (2019). *Divided allies: Strategic cooperation against the communist threat in the Asia-Pacific during the early Cold War*. Ithaca, NY: Cornell University Press.

Rogin, J. (2021). *Chaos under heaven: Trump, Xi, and the battle for the twenty-first century*. New York: Houghton Mifflin Harcourt.

Romberg, A.D. (2003). *Rein in at the brink of the precipice: American policy toward Taiwan and US–PRC relations*. Washington, DC: The Henry L. Stimson Center.

Rosendorff, B.P., and Milner, H.V. (2001). The optimal design of international trade institutions: Uncertainty and escape. *International Organization*, 55(4), 829–857.

Sabrosky, A. (1980). Interstate alliances: Their reliability and the expansion of war. In J.D. Singer (ed.), *The Correlates of War II, Testing some realpolitik models*, pp. 161–198. Glencoe, IL: Free Press.

Sagan, S.D. (1986). 1914 revisited: Allies, offense, and instability. *International Security*, 11(2), 151–175.

Sagan, S.D. (1990). *Moving targets: Nuclear strategy and national security*. Princeton, NJ: Princeton University Press.

Saideman, S.M., and Auerswald, D.P. (2012). Comparing caveats: Understanding the sources of national restrictions upon NATO's mission in Afghanistan. *International Studies Quarterly*, 56(1), 67–84.

Sartre, J.-P. (1948 [1984]). *Being and nothingness: A phenomenological essay on ontology*. New York: Washington Square Press.

Sayle, T.A. (2019). *Enduring alliance: A history of NATO and the postwar global order*. Ithaca, NY: Cornell University Press.

Sayle, T.A. (2020). A nuclear education: The origins of NATO's Nuclear Planning Group. *Journal of Strategic Studies*, 43(6–7), 920–956.

Schelling, T.C. (1966 [2009]). *Arms and influence*. New Haven, CT: Yale University Press.

Schmitt, O. (2018). *Allies that count: Junior coalition partners in wartime*. Washington, DC: Georgetown University Press.

Schroeder, P.W. (2004). Alliances, 1815–1945: Weapons of power and tools of management. In P.W. Schroeder (ed.), *Systems, stability, and statecraft: Essays on the international history of modern Europe*, pp. 195–222. New York: Palgrave Macmillan.

Schweller, R.L. (1994). Bandwagoning for profit: Bringing the revisionist state back in. *International Security*, 19(1), 72–107.

Schweller, R.L. (1996). Neorealism's status-quo bias: What security dilemma? *Security Studies*, 5(3), 90–121.

Shapiro, A.J. (2012). A new era for US security assistance. *The Washington Quarterly*, 35(4), 23–35.

Shen, J.C.H. (1983). *The US and free China: How the U.S. sold out its ally*. Washington, DC: Acropolis Books.

Shlapak, D.A., and Johnson, M.W. (2016). *Reinforcing deterrence on NATO's eastern flank: Wargaming the defense of the Baltics*. Santa Monica, CA: RAND Corporation.

Silaev, N. (2021). Russia and its allies in three strategic environments. *Europe-Asia Studies*, 1–12. https://doi.org/10.1080/09668136.2021.1887087.

Simon, M.W., and Gartzke, E. (1996). Political system similarity and the choice of allies: Do democracies flock together, or do opposites attract? *Journal of Conflict Resolution*, 40(4), 617–635.

Simón, L., and Fiott, D. (2014). Europe after the US Pivot. *Orbis*, 58(3), 413–428.

Simón, L., Lanoszka, A., and Meijer, H. (2021). Nodal defence: The changing structure of US alliance systems in Europe and East Asia. *Journal of Strategic Studies*, 44(3), 360–388.

Slantchev, B.L. (2005). Territory and commitment: The Concert of Europe as self-enforcing equilibrium. *Security Studies*, 14(4), 565–606.

Snyder, G.H. (1965). The balance of power and the balance of terror. In P. Seabury (ed.), *The Balance of Power*, pp. 184–201. San Francisco, CA: Chandler.

Snyder, G.H. (1997). *Alliance politics*. Ithaca, NY: Cornell University Press.

Sperling, J., and Webber, M. (2019). Trump's foreign policy and NATO: Exit and voice. *Review of International Studies*, 45(3), 511–526.

Steinberg, J., and Cooper, C. (1990). Political and economic issues within the alliance: The future of burden-sharing and the southern region. Santa Monica, CA: RAND.

Stoicescu, K., and Lebrun, M. (2019). *Estonian-French defence cooperation: Where Estonian pragmatism meets French vision*. Tallinn, Estonia: International Centre for Defence and Security.

Stoltenberg, J. (2019). NATO will defend itself. *Prospect*, October 4.

Strachan, H. (2004). *The outbreak of the First World War*. Oxford: Oxford University Press.

Sukin, L. (2020). Credible nuclear security commitments can backfire: Explaining domestic support for nuclear weapons acquisition in South Korea. *Journal of Conflict Resolution*, 64(6), 1011–1042.

Swenson-Wright, J. (2005). *Unequal allies? United States security and alliance policy toward Japan, 1945–1960*. Stanford, CA: Stanford University Press.

Szalontai, B., and Radchenko, S.S. (2006). North Korea's efforts to acquire nuclear technology and nuclear weapons: Evidence from Russian and Hungarian archives (No. 53). Washington, DC: Woodrow Wilson International Center for Scholars.

Taliaferro, J.W. (2004). *Balancing risks: Great power intervention in the periphery*. Ithaca, NY: Cornell University Press.

Taliaferro, J.W. (2019). *Defending frenemies: Alliances, politics, and nuclear nonproliferation in US foreign policy*. Oxford: Oxford University Press.

Talmadge, C. (2015). *The dictator's army: Battlefield effectiveness in authoritarian regimes*. Ithaca, NY: Cornell University Press.

Tamm, H. (2016). The origins of transnational alliances:

Rulers, rebels, and political survival in the Congo Wars. *International Security*, 41(1), 147–181.

Tannenwald, N. (2007). *The nuclear taboo: The United States and the non-use of nuclear weapons since 1945.* Cambridge: Cambridge University Press.

Tertrais, B. (2004). The changing nature of military alliances. *The Washington Quarterly*, 27(2), 133–150.

*The Economist.* (2019). Emmanuel Macron in his own words (French). November 9. https://www.economist.com/europe/2019/11/07/emmanuel–macron–in–his–own–words–french.

Thies, W.J. (2003.) *Friendly rivals: Bargaining and burden-shifting in NATO.* London: Routledge.

Thrall, A.T., Cohen, J., and Dorminey, C. (2020). Power, profit, or prudence? US arms sales since 9/11, *Strategic Studies Quarterly*, 14(2), 100–126.

Thucydides. (2008). *The landmark Thucydides: A comprehensive guide to the Peloponnesian War*, ed. R.B. Strassler. New York: Simon and Schuster.

Tierney, D. (2011). Does chain-ganging cause the outbreak of war? *International Studies Quarterly*, 55(2), 285–304.

Trachtenberg, M. (1999). *A constructed peace: The making of the European settlement, 1945–1963.* Princeton, NJ: Princeton University Press.

Trachtenberg, M. (2011). The French factor in US foreign policy during the Nixon–Pompidou period, 1969–1974. *Journal of Cold War Studies*, 13(1), 4–59.

Tracy, C.L., and Wright, D. (2020). Modeling the performance of hypersonic boost-glide missiles. *Science & Global Security*, 1–27.

Trubowitz, P. (1998). *Defining the national interest: Conflict and change in American foreign policy.* Chicago, IL: University of Chicago Press.

Tsygankov, A.P., and Tarver-Wahlquist, M. (2009). Duelling honors: power, identity and the Russia–Georgia divide. *Foreign Policy Analysis*, 5(4), 307–326.

Tucker, N.B. (2005). Taiwan expendable? Nixon and Kissinger go to China. *The Journal of American History*, 92(1), 109–135.

Tuminez, A.S. (2003). Nationalism, ethnic pressures, and the breakup of the Soviet Union. *Journal of Cold War Studies*, 5(4), 81–136.

United Nations. (1955). Treaty of Friendship, Co-operation and Mutual Assistance. Signed at Warsaw, on May 14, 1955. *United Nations Treaty Collection*, 219(2962).

United States Forces Korea. (n.d.). Mission of the ROK/US Combined Forces Command. https://www.usfk.mil/About/Combined–Forces–Command/.

US Department of Defense. (2004). *JP 1-02: Department of Defense Dictionary of Military and Associated Terms*. Arlington, VA.

US Department of Defense. (2011). Remarks by Secretary Gates at the Security and Defense Agenda, Brussels, Belgium, June 10. https://archive.defense.gov/Transcripts/Transcript.aspx?TranscriptID=4839.

Van Evera, S. (1984). The cult of the offensive and the origins of the First World War. *International Security*, 9(1), 58–107.

Vasilyan, S. (2017). "Swinging on a pendulum": Armenia in the Eurasian Economic Union and with the European Union. *Problems of Post-communism*, 64(1), 32–46.

Vermeiren, J. (2016). *The First World War and German national identity*. Cambridge: Cambridge University Press.

von Borzyskowski, I., and Vabulas, F. (2019). Hello, goodbye: When do states withdraw from international organizations? *Review of International Organizations*, 14(2), 335–366.

von Hlatky, S. (2013). *American allies in time of war: The great asymmetry*. New York: Oxford University Press.

Vysotskaya Guedes Vieira, A. (2014). The politico-military alliance of Russia and Belarus: Re-examining the role of NATO and the EU in light of the intra-alliance security dilemma. *Europe-Asia Studies*, 66(4), 557–577.

Wallander, C.A. (2000). Institutional assets and adaptability: NATO after the Cold War. *International Organization*, 54(4), 705–735.

Walt, S.M. (1987). *The origins of alliances*. Ithaca, NY: Cornell University Press.

Walt, S.M. (1996). *Revolution and war.* Ithaca, NY: Cornell University Press.

Walt, S.M. (1997). Why alliances endure or collapse. *Survival,* 39(1), 156–179.

Walt, S.M. (2009). Alliances in a unipolar world. *World Politics,* 61(1), 86–120.

Waltz, K.N. (1979 [2010]). *Theory of international politics.* Long Grove, IL: Waveland Press.

Waltz, K.N. (1981). *The spread of nuclear weapons: More may be better. The Adelphi Papers,* 21(171).

Wandycz, P.S. (1962). *France and her eastern allies, 1919–1925: French–Czechoslovak–Polish relations from the Paris Peace Conference to Locarno.* Minneapolis, MN: University of Minnesota Press.

Wandycz, P.S. (1988). *The twilight of French eastern alliances, 1926–1936: French–Czechoslovak–Polish relations from Locarno to the remilitarization of the Rhineland.* Princeton, NJ: Princeton University Press.

Washington, G. (1892). *The writings of George Washington 1794–1798,* vol. XIII, ed. W.C. Ford. New York: G.G. Putnam's Sons.

Wągrowska, M. (2004). *Polish participation in the armed intervention and stabilization mission in Iraq.* Warsaw, Poland: Center for International Relations.

Weisiger, A., and Yarhi-Milo, K. (2015). Revisiting reputation: How past actions matter in international politics. *International Organization* 69(2), 473–495.

Weitsman, P.A. (1997). Intimate enemies: The politics of peacetime alliances. *Security Studies,* 7(1), 156–193.

Wenger, A. (2004). Crisis and opportunity: NATO's transformation and the multilateralization of détente, 1966–1968. *Journal of Cold War Studies,* 6(1), 22–74.

Wheeler, D.L. (1986). The price of neutrality: Portugal, the wolfram question, and World War II. *Luso-Brazilian Review,* 23(1), 107–127.

White House. (2021). Remarks by President Biden in press conference, June 14. https://www.whitehouse. gov/briefing-room/speeches-remarks/2021/06/14/ remarks-by-president-biden-in-press-conference-3/.

Wigell, M. (2019). Hybrid interference as a wedge strategy: A theory of external interference in liberal democracy. *International Affairs*, 95(2), 255–275.

Wilkins, T.S. (2012). "Alignment," not "alliance" – the shifting paradigm of international security cooperation: Toward a conceptual taxonomy of alignment. *Review of International Studies*, 38(1), 53–76.

Williams, B. (2020). US covert action in Cold War Japan: The politics of cultivating conservative elites and its consequences. *Journal of Contemporary Asia*, 50(4), 593–617.

Williams, C. (2013). Accepting austerity: The right way to cut defense. *Foreign Affairs*, 92(6), 54–64.

Williams, P. (1976). Whatever happened to the Mansfield amendment? *Survival*, 18(4), 146–153.

Wohlforth, W.C., Little, R., Kaufman, S.J., Kang, D., Jones, C.A., Tin-Bor Hui, V., Eckstein, A., Deudney, D., and Brenner, W.L. (2007). Testing balance-of-power theory in world history. *European Journal of International Relations*, 13(2), 55–185.

Yale Law School. (2008a). The Dual Alliance between Austria-Hungary and Germany; October 7, 1879. *The Avalon Project: Documents in Law, History, and Diplomacy.* https://avalon.law.yale.edu/19th_century/dualalli.asp.

Yale Law School. (2008b). Mutual Defense Treaty Between the United States and the Republic of Korea; October 1, 1953. *The Avalon Project: Documents in Law, History, and Diplomacy.* https://avalon.law.yale.edu/20th_century/kor001.asp.

Yale Law School. (2008c). Mutual Defense Treaty Between the United States and the Republic of the Philippines; August 30, 1951. *The Avalon Project: Documents in Law, History, and Diplomacy.* https://avalon.law.yale.edu/20th_century/phil001.asp.

Yale Law School. (2008d). Thomas Jefferson First Inaugural Address. *The Avalon Project: Documents in Law, History, and Diplomacy.* https://avalon.law.yale.edu/19th_century/jefinau1.asp.

Yarhi-Milo, K. (2018). *Who fights for reputation: The*

*psychology of leaders in international conflict.* Princeton, NJ: Princeton University Press.

Yarhi-Milo, K., Lanoszka, A., and Cooper, Z. (2016). To arm or to ally? The patron's dilemma and the strategic logic of arms transfers and alliances. *International Security*, 41(2), 90–139.

Young, R.J. (1978). *In command of France: French foreign policy and military planning, 1933–1940.* Cambridge, MA: Harvard University Press.

Young, T. (2001/2). NATO command and control for the 21st century. *Joint Forces Quarterly*, 29, 40–45.

Zaborowski, M. (2004). *From America's protégé to constructive European: Polish security policy in the twenty-first century* (Occasional paper no. 56). Brussels, Belgium: European Union Institute for Security Studies.

Zaborowski, M., and Longhurst, K. (2007). *The new Atlanticist: Poland's foreign and security policy priorities.* Oxford: Blackwell.

Zimmermann, H. (2002). *Money and security: Troops, monetary policy, and West Germany's relations with the United States and Britain, 1950–1971.* Cambridge: Cambridge University Press.

# Index